SUPERSTARS

★ ★ ★ ★ OF THE ★ ★ ★ ★

WORLD
CUP

SUPERSTARS

★ ★ ★ ★ OF THE ★ ★ ★ ★

WORLD
CUP

THE ULTIMATE GUIDE
TO THE STARS OF THE
2006 WORLD CUP

p

This is a Parragon Book
First Published in 2006

Parragon
Queen Street House
4 Queen Street
Bath BA1 1HE, UK

ISBN 1-40546-331-7

Writers: Julian Flanders and Adrian Besley
Project Editor: Julian Flanders
Designer: Craig Stevens

Photographs: Empics

Printed in China

CONTENTS

Introduction

At last the wait is almost over, all eyes are on Germany as the 32 finalists assemble to take part in what for many is the world's most exciting sporting tournament – the World Cup. Germany 2006, the 18th football world championship, promises to be the biggest and best tournament ever. With revenues expected to be in hundreds of billions of pounds and a TV audience of some 60 billion, the world's greatest players will perform at twelve state-of-the-art venues around the country.

The draw for the group stage took place in Leipzig on 9 December. Eight groups of four were drawn, each featuring one seed, and one team from each of three other pots. Surprisingly, this time, apart from the eight seeds, the pots were themed geographically. In effect this system has proved that the football world has its own hierarchy of power as the geographical division almost mirrored the quality of football in each country. There is no 'group of death' – a group featuring at least three top teams which would result in the elimination of one championship contender at the group stage – and it seems likely that all eight seeds will take their places in the quarter-finals. This is a poor prospect for those that love cup upsets but will ultimately mean that the best team will win the tournament.

In all 17 tournaments played so far the winners have come from South America (nine times) and Europe (eight times), and it seems likely that the same thing will happen this time with Brazil, England and Argentina already emerging as the bookies' favourites. The likely winners will come from the eight seeds: Argentina, Brazil, England, France, Germany, Italy, Mexico and Spain – and who would bet against Brazil? But there's sure to be some thrills, spills and tremendous excitement along the way.

Star-spangled start

The event starts with the opening ceremony, on 7 June in Berlin, when a star-spangled cast from the world of show business and the music industry will give a 90-minute multi-media gala of music and dance. An opening anthem has been written by Brian Eno, Peter Gabriel has written a full score, Jessye Norman will sing, hip-hop/rap artists the Black Eyes Peas will perform and a cast of 132 former World Cup winners will be in attendance to witness the event along with an audience paying anywhere between 100 and 750 Euros for the privilege of being there. 'It's like having Maradona, Pelé, Cruyff and Di Stefano all in the same team,' says Franz Beckenbauer one of the tournament's main organisers. It'll be the first time that the opening ceremony has not been immediately followed by the opening match. That will take place two days later

Supermodel Heidi Klum and Franz Beckenbauer Chairman of the Organising Committee at the World Cup draw in Leipzig.

at the FIFA World Cup stadium in Munich when host nation Germany takes on Costa Rica.

From then on the games come thick and fast. The draw has thrown up a number of interesting groups. Group C has put Argentina, Holland and the dangerous Serbia & Montenegro together, while Group E includes USA, Italy, Czech Republic and Ghana, the most dangerous African representative. Perennial moaners Italy have already complained bitterly about it and the US coach Bruce Arena has expressed his disappointment that the group is so strong. Group F too looks interesting, as Brazil will meet strong resistance from Croatia, Japan and new boys Australia.

England's prospects

Once the knockout rounds begin, the draw is in two parts, which means teams from the top half will not meet teams from the bottom half until the Final. This means that should England qualify, and they certainly should, then they will avoid the Czech Republic, Italy, Brazil, France and Spain. On the other hand if they win their group, Group B – which includes Paraguay, Trinidad & Tobago and Sweden – then they might meet Holland or Argentina in the quarter-finals. If they come runners-up then things might get serious in the second round in a match up with Germany.

Of course, by that time it doesn't matter because to win the tournament you have to beat whoever you are drawn against. Of the other contenders, Czech Republic, Holland and Portugal look strong. The Asian teams, led by Japan and South Korea will be looking to build on their success at the last tournament, and though Iran are confident Asian teams traditionally don't travel well. The African teams are mostly first timers and will win over the neutrals with their style and verve but it seems unlikely that they will progress from the group games. Of the North and Central American teams the USA are depressed about their draw, Mexico will play their part and hope that they can spring an upset along the lines of their 1-0 win over Brazil in the 2005 Confederations Cup victory, and Costa Rica will play attractive football but probably be eliminated at the group stage.

Nothing but the best

The tournament will undoubtedly be organised superbly well and the German security services are confident that they will be able to deal with any violence that might occur around the host cities. That aside the most likely area of

Right World Cup mascots Goleo and his chum Pille (the ball).

Above right Known as the World Cup Globe, this glass sculpture has been chosen as the symbol of Germany 2006.

concern to the teams taking part will be the refereeing. The last few tournaments have been dogged with refereeing controversies, particularly around the issues of dangerous tackles, diving or dissent. Although the final list will not be announced until the early part of 2006, FIFA has been running a referees project since early 2005 for 46 referees likely to be selected for the tournament – Graham Poll is the only English representative. The candidates have been observed during various FIFA competitions during the last year and will be assessed on their performances at domestic and international level before the selection process is undertaken. The purpose of this exercise is to try and standardise refereeing decisions, eliminate obvious discrepancies and ensure the highest standards of refereeing possible. 'Top quality is the goal,' says FIFA president Sepp Blatter, '… [the purpose of the programme] is to help us identify, train and prepare match officials for the 2006 World Cup so that we have nothing but the best referees on the pitch.' It's a great shame that Pierluigi Collina has retired but it is time to find some new dependable referees for the future. Only time will tell if this project has worked.

Superstars of World Cup History

Ever since Frenchman Jules Rimet and Henri Delauney's idea for a global tournament was first set in motion the World Cup has captured the imagination of fans around the world for its excitement and shocks and as a showcase for the greatest players on the planet.

The World Cup has many themes, but it is the clash of Europe and South America that has always pervaded the finals. Throughout the 20th century, the two dominant footballing continents hosted alternate tournaments – the flamboyant, but often physical, style of the South Americans clashing with the pragmatic European game. The Brazilians with five wins have dominated, with Argentina providing a major force in the last quarter of the century, but Germany, Italy, Holland and England have all done their bit for the Europeans. With the rise of the African and the Far East nations and FIFA's policy of hosting the tournament around the world, some of this rivalry has disappeared, but it was these games that produced the superstars of past competitions.

1958 Pelé
Brazil

In 1958, the World Cup unveiled a 17-year-old sensation – Pelé. The precociously talented youngster had everything: power, pace, balance, mesmerising skills and a deadly finish. In the semi-final, against a strong French team, the young star hit a blistering 21-minute hat-trick and in the Final, against the hosts Sweden, he hit a post in the first half, but wasn't to be denied the goal he deserved. On 55 minutes he chested down a ball, flicked it over a defender with his thigh and volleyed it home (below). Then, in the last minute, he headed his second, having set his winger up with a back heel. In the end Brazil won 5-2. A true star, Pelé would grace another three tournaments with his superb skills and for many he still remains the greatest footballer in the world, but no one would ever forget his first appearance in the World Cup finals.

WORLD CUP FINALS

YEAR	HOST				
1930	Uruguay	URUGUAY	4	2	ARGENTINA
1934	Italy	ITALY	2	1	CZECHOSLOVAKIA
1938	France	ITALY	4	2	HUNGARY
1950	Brazil	URUGUAY	2	1	BRAZIL
1954	Switzerland	WEST GERMANY	3	2	HUNGARY
1958	Sweden	BRAZIL	5	2	SWEDEN
1962	Chile	BRAZIL	3	1	CZECHOSLOVAKIA
1966	England	ENGLAND	4	2	WEST GERMANY
1970	Mexico	BRAZIL	4	1	ITALY
1974	West Germany	WEST GERMANY	2	1	HOLLAND
1978	Argentina	ARGENTINA	3	1	HOLLAND
1982	Spain	ITALY	3	1	WEST GERMANY
1986	Mexico	ARGENTINA	3	2	WEST GERMANY
1990	Italy	WEST GERMANY	1	0	ARGENTINA
1994	USA	BRAZIL	0	0	ITALY (Brazil won 3-2 on pens)
1998	France	BRAZIL	0	3	FRANCE
2002	Japan/South Korea	BRAZIL	2	0	GERMANY

1974 Johann Cruyff
Holland

The architects of Total Football, the Dutch played a fluid game bereft of tactics and systems and lit up the tournament in Germany. At the heart of their exhilarating play was Johan Cruyff. In all their goals on the way to the Final, Cruyff was the originator or the finisher – sometimes both. His balance and ball control made him both elegant and deadly with the famous 'Cruyff turn' – turning Swedish right back Gunnar Olsson inside out – a lasting reminder of his greatness. When he won a penalty in the second minute of the Final it seemed he would win the cup for Holland, but the West Germans – especially Bertie Vogts who kept Cruyff quiet in the match – were made of sterner stuff.

1966 Bobby Moore
England

The 1966 tournament saw the centre back mature into the greatest defender in the world. In the white-hot quarter-final against Argentina he had kept his calm to marshal his team-mates, and in the semi-final he had held the defence back to quell the threat of Portugal's Eusebio. In the Final, he was superb, not only for his masterly organisation of the defence but for his perfectly clipped free-kick for England's first and for his cool ball out of defence for the final goal. In the 1970 finals, he would show his mettle again – particularly against Brazil – but no England captain ever deserved his moment of glory more than Bobby Moore.

1986 Diego Maradona
Argentina

Has one man ever played such a huge part in a team's success? From Argentina's first match when he created each of their three goals against South Korea to the Final when he threaded the ball through the German defence for Burruchaga's 85th-minute winner, Maradona was head and shoulders above every other player on the pitch. In between, he had scored the famous 'Hand of God' goal and another of individual brilliance against England in their quarter-final and, in case anyone had missed it, scored an almost identical one – his second against Belgium in the semi-finals. As one-man shows go; Maradona's was breathtaking.

1990 Paul Gascoigne
England

After calling him 'daft as a brush', manager Bobby Robson soon realised the value of 'Gazza'. His driving runs, penetrating through balls and magnificent free-kicks inspired England's run to the World Cup semi-final in Italy. The free-kick cross against Egypt that found Wright's head, the great drive and upfield ball that led to Platt's winner against Belgium and the precise through ball for Lineker to strike against Cameroon all came as England looked like floundering. His tears after the semi-final against Germany confirmed his star status, but left out of the squad by Glenn Hoddle in 1998, he never graced another finals tournament.

2002 Ronaldo
Brazil

The supposed 'best player in the world' had finished the 1998 Final in tears after a humiliating 3-0 defeat to France. It seemed that serious injury would rob Ronaldo of another chance in 2002, but the striker almost miraculously recovered. He soon gave warning he was back to his best, but his goal in the semi-final – a great run and an audacious toe-poke – put him back in a class of his own. Two more in the Final – the second a sweetly placed shot into the corner – took his total in the tournament to eight. Once again he ended the finals crying but this time they were tears of joy.

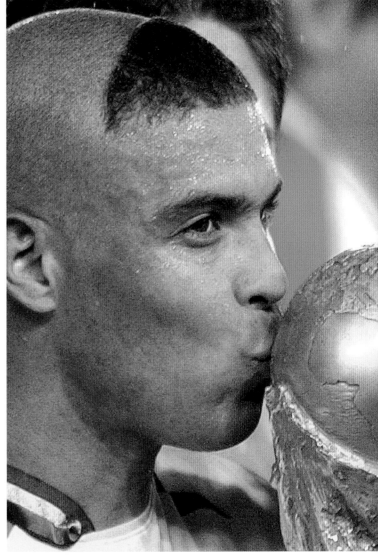

1998 Zinedine Zidane
France

The World Cup Final was billed as a showdown between the two greatest players in the world, Brazil's Ronaldo and Zidane. Ronaldo's goals had dominated the tournament, but Zidane had been sent-off in his second match and banned until the quarter-final. Gradually the playmaker's superb skills began to emerge but in the semi-final against Croatia, *Zizou* the architect really shone. Perhaps spurred by Ronaldo's mystery illness, he took the Final by storm even scoring two rare headed goals. Zidane had performed on the greatest stage – and the Brazilians would have to wait another four years to win the coveted trophy.

The Venues

The 64 matches that comprise the 2006 World Cup will be played in 12 host cities across Germany: Berlin, Cologne, Dortmund, Frankfurt am Main, Gelsenkirchen, Hamburg, Hanover, Kaiserslautern, Leipzig, Munich, Nuremberg and Stuttgart. Leipzig is the only host city in what was the old East Germany. The stadiums are either completely new or have undergone extensive refurbishment in advance of the competition.

 As FIFA prohibit the use of sponsors in stadium names, many of the stadiums will be officially known by a different name for the duration of the tournament. The tournament names are used below.

BERLIN, OLYMPIASTADION
Host club: Hertha Berlin
Capacity: 66,021
Originally built for the 1936 Olympics, the stadium has undergone extensive reconstruction. The most notable feature is the vast new oval roof which is interrupted only by the Marathon Gate, a feature retained from the original stadium. The Olympiastadion will host several group games, a quarter-final and the Final.

COLOGNE, FIFA WORLD CUP STADIUM
Host club: 1.FC Koln
Capacity: 40,590
A modification of the old Mungersdorfer stadium, the new arena has had the running track removed and has been designed to produce a much more intense atmosphere than before with the pitch very close to the stands. The stadium will host several group games and one second round match.

DORTMUND, WESTFALENSTADION
Host club: Borussia Dortmund
Capacity: 67,000
Known to Bundesliga fans as the 'opera house', this is the most popular stadium in Germany and nearly always full to capacity on matchday. Features the 25,000 capacity South Stand from where the locals support their team. Will play host to several group games, a second round match and a semi-final.

FRANKFURT AM MAIN, WALDSTADION
Host club: Eintracht Frankfurt
Capacity: 48,000
This brand new, rather futuristic arena, features a translucent roof that provides what is described as a 'cathedral-like' atmosphere. Hosted the Final of the 2005 Confederations Cup. The Waldstadion will host several group games and a quarter-final.

GELSENKIRCHEN, THE VELTINS ARENA
Host club: FC Schalke 04
Capacity: 51,000
Another new stadium which features some of the most modern technology in the world, including a moveable pitch, a giant video cube, a retractable roof and electronic admission controls. The 'six star' stadium will host several group games and a quarter-final.

HAMBURG, FIFA WORLD CUP STADIUM

Host club: Hamburger SV

Capacity: 50,000

A fine new stadium built on the site of the old Volksparkstadion. The old pitch has been rotated and all four stands completely rebuilt. Awarded a maximum five stars by the UEFA inspection committee. Will play host to several group games and a quarter-final.

HANOVER, FIFA WORLD CUP STADIUM

Host club: Hannover 96

Capacity: 45,000

A reconstruction of the old Niedersachsenstadion, the new arena features a free-standing roof. The sections of roof that overhang the pitch are made from ultra-violet permeable foil ensuring the grass gets the light it needs to remain in perfect condition. Will host group games and a second round match.

KAISERSLAUTERN, FRITZ-WALTER-STADION

Host club: 1.FC Kaiserslautern

Capacity: 48,500

Purpose-built to host football matches in 1920, the stadium was renamed in 1985 in honour of the 1954 German World Cup captain. Built on the Betzenberg, a hill in the centre of the city, the arena has been extended on several occasions. Will host four group games and a quarter-final.

LEIPZIG, ZENTRALSTADION

Host club: FC Sachsen Leipzig

Capacity: 42,655

Built within the old Zentralstadion walls, spectators get to their seats via newly constructed bridges. A spectacular roof with integrated floodlights provides a visual highlight of the new arena. The Zentralstadion, the only venue in the old East Germany, will play host to four group games and a second round match.

MUNICH, FIFA WORLD CUP STADIUM

Host clubs: Bayern Munich, TSV 1860

Capacity: 66,000

Known as the Allianz Arena, this brand-new stadium has already become the symbol of the 2006 World Cup. Its façade, made of translucent foil panels, is floodlit in a variety of colours which make for a spectacular backdrop for night matches. Germany will kick off the tournament at this stadium on 9 June, and it will host other group games, a second round match and a semi-final.

NUREMBERG, FRANKEN-STADION

Host club: 1.FC Nurnberg

Capacity: 45,500

One of only three World Cup stadiums with a running track around the pitch, the Franken-Stadion nevertheless generates an exciting atmosphere. An extensive reconstruction has seen the pitch lowered and the capacity increased by 5,500. The arena will host four group games and a second round match.

STUTTGART, GOTTLIEB-DAIMLER-STADION

Host club: VfB Stuttgart

Capacity: 54,500

Based on the original Neckar-Stadion built in 1933, the arena has been extensively modernised. Its outstanding feature is a textile roof with a fine and intricate lattice supporting structure. The stadium will host several group games, a second round match and the Third Place play-off.

Hamburg

Berlin

Hanover

Dortmund

Leipzig

Gelsenkirchen

Cologne

Frankfurt

Kaiserslautern

Nuremburg

Stuttgart

Munich

Match Schedule

The 32 teams have been divided into eight groups of four. In Stage 1 each team will play each other once in a league system and the top two from each group will proceed to Stage 2 (the Round of 16), from when the competition will be decided on a knockout basis.

STAGE 1

GROUP A

GERMANY | COSTA RICA | POLAND | ECUADOR

MATCH	DATE	VENUE	
1	9 June	Munich	GERMANY v COSTA RICA
2	9 June	Gelsenkirchen	POLAND v ECUADOR
17	14 June	Dortmund	GERMANY v POLAND
18	15 June	Hamburg	ECUADOR v COSTA RICA
33	20 June	Berlin	ECUADOR v GERMANY
34	20 June	Hanover	COSTA RICA v POLAND

GROUP B

ENGLAND | PARAGUAY | TRINIDAD & TOBAGO | SWEDEN

MATCH	DATE	VENUE	
3	10 June	Frankfurt	ENGLAND v PARAGUAY
4	10 June	Dortmund	TRINIDAD & TOBAGO v SWEDEN
19	15 June	Nuremberg	ENGLAND v TRINIDAD & TOBAGO
20	15 June	Berlin	SWEDEN v PARAGUAY
35	20 June	Cologne	SWEDEN v ENGLAND
36	20 June	Kaiserslautern	PARAGUAY v TRINIDAD & TOBAGO

GROUP C

ARGENTINA | IVORY COAST | SERBIA & MONTENEGRO | HOLLAND

MATCH	DATE	VENUE	
5	10 June	Hamburg	ARGENTINA v IVORY COAST
6	11 June	Leipzig	SERBIA & MONTENEGRO v HOLLAND
21	16 June	Gelsenkirchen	ARGENTINA v SERBIA & MONTENEGRO
22	16 June	Stuttgart	HOLLAND v IVORY COAST
37	21 June	Frankfurt	HOLLAND v ARGENTINA
38	21 June	Munich	IVORY COAST v SERBIA & MONTENEGRO

GROUP D

MEXICO | IRAN | ANGOLA | PORTUGAL

MATCH	DATE	VENUE	
7	11 June	Nuremberg	MEXICO v IRAN
8	11 June	Cologne	ANGOLA v PORTUGAL
23	16 June	Hanover	MEXICO v ANGOLA
24	17 June	Frankfurt	PORTUGAL v IRAN
39	21 June	Gelsenkirchen	PORTUGAL v MEXICO
40	21 June	Leipzig	IRAN v ANGOLA

GROUP E

ITALY | GHANA | USA | CZECH REPUBLIC

MATCH	DATE	VENUE	
9	12 June	Hanover	ITALY v GHANA
10	12 June	Gelsenkirchen	USA v CZECH REPUBLIC
25	17 June	Kaiserslautern	ITALY v USA
26	17 June	Cologne	CZECH REPUBLIC v GHANA
41	22 June	Hamburg	CZECH REPUBLIC v ITALY
42	22 June	Nuremberg	GHANA v USA

GROUP F

BRAZIL | CROATIA | AUSTRALIA | JAPAN

MATCH	DATE	VENUE	
11	13 June	Berlin	BRAZIL v CROATIA
12	12 June	Kaiserslautern	AUSTRALIA v JAPAN
27	18 June	Munich	BRAZIL v AUSTRALIA
28	18 June	Nuremberg	JAPAN v CROATIA
43	22 June	Dortmund	JAPAN v BRAZIL
44	22 June	Stuttgart	CROATIA v AUSTRALIA

GROUP G

FRANCE | SWITZERLAND | SOUTH KOREA | TOGO

MATCH	DATE	VENUE	
13	13 June	Stuttgart	FRANCE v SWITZERLAND
14	13 June	Frankfurt	SOUTH KOREA v TOGO
29	18 June	Leipzig	FRANCE v SOUTH KOREA
30	19 June	Dortmund	TOGO v SWITZERLAND
45	23 June	Cologne	TOGO v FRANCE
46	23 June	Hanover	SOUTH KOREA v SWITZERLAND

GROUP H

SPAIN | UKRAINE | TUNISIA | SAUDI ARABIA

MATCH	DATE	VENUE	
15	14 June	Leipzig	SPAIN v UKRAINE
16	14 June	Munich	TUNISIA v SAUDI ARABIA
31	19 June	Stuttgart	SPAIN v TUNISIA
32	19 June	Hamburg	SAUDI ARABIA v UKRAINE
47	23 June	Kaiserslautern	SAUDI ARABIA v SPAIN
48	23 June	Berlin	UKRAINE v TUNISIA

If two or more teams finish the group stage with the same number of points then the following criteria will be used to determine the final ranking: **1** Points won head-to-head. **2** Goal difference head-to-head. **3** Number of goals scored head-to-head. **4** Goal difference in all group games. **5** Goals scored in all group games. **6** Drawing lots.

In the knockout rounds, if a match is level after 90 minutes, a further 30 minutes extra time will be played. If the score is level after extra time, there will be a penalty shootout.

STAGE 2/ROUND OF 16

MATCH	DATE	VENUE	
49	24 June	Munich	WINNERS GROUP A v RUNNERS-UP GROUP B
50	24 June	Leipzig	WINNERS GROUP C v RUNNERS-UP GROUP D
51	25 June	Stuttgart	WINNERS GROUP B v RUNNERS-UP GROUP A
52	25 June	Nuremberg	WINNERS GROUP D v RUNNERS-UP GROUP C
53	26 June	Kaiserslautern	WINNERS GROUP E v RUNNERS-UP GROUP F
54	26 June	Cologne	WINNERS GROUP G v RUNNERS-UP GROUP H
55	27 June	Dortmund	WINNERS GROUP F v RUNNERS-UP GROUP E
56	27 June	Hanover	WINNERS GROUP H v RUNNERS-UP GROUP G

QUARTER-FINALS

MATCH	DATE	VENUE	
57	30 June	Berlin	WINNERS MATCH 49 v WINNERS MATCH 50
58	30 June	Hamburg	WINNERS MATCH 53 v WINNERS MATCH 54
59	1 July	Gelsenkirchen	WINNERS MATCH 51 v WINNERS MATCH 52
60	1 July	Frankfurt	WINNERS MATCH 55 v WINNERS MATCH 56

SEMI-FINALS

MATCH	DATE	VENUE	
61	4 July	Dortmund	WINNERS MATCH 57 v WINNERS MATCH 58
62	5 July	Munich	WINNERS MATCH 59 v WINNERS MATCH 60

THIRD PLACE PLAY-OFF

MATCH	DATE	VENUE	
63	8 July	Stuttgart	LOSERS MATCH 61 v LOSERS MATCH 62

FINAL

MATCH	DATE	VENUE	
64	9 July	Berlin	WINNERS MATCH 61 v WINNERS MATCH 62

GERMANY

YOUTH, HOPE AND A PRAYER

A nation holds its breath as coach Jurgen Klinsmann tries to turn a struggling team into World Cup winners using a blend of youth, attacking football and optimism.

Three times winners, three times runners-up, Germany host the 2006 finals with the nation's hearts, if not their heads, believing they can win. New coach Jurgen Klinsmann promised an influx of talented youngsters combined with an attacking strategy, but results have been mixed. Michael Ballack, Bastian Schweinsteiger and Lukas Podolski have emerged as true stars and the team now scores freely, but the players' inexperience and a shaky defence have let them down more than once. The German public fear an early exit, but their team could prove one of the most exciting to watch and might yet prove people wrong.

FIRST TEST PASSED

After the pretty dismal performances of Euro 2004, few believed Germany would be able to make a mark on their World Cup.

Above Robert Huth (right) is one of the options for coach Klinsmann in a slightly suspect defence.

Too many players at the end of their careers, a dearth of quality up-and-coming talent, and a real lack of self belief made them grateful they didn't have to qualify for the finals.But, Klinsmann has brought an attacking philosophy, given a chance to some youngsters and some hope to the fans.

As hosts Germany faced no competitive qualifiers, so the 2005 Confederations Cup was their first real test. They passed. Scoring 11 goals in four games, and reaching the semi finals – a respectable 2-3 defeat to Brazil – the team finally ignited the nation's World Cup fever. Subsequent disappointing result, however, have brought them back to earth. The defence seems patchy, Oliver Kahn and Jens Lehmann are involved in an unseemly row and the goals have dried up. A long list of friendlies leading up to the finals gives them time to sort some of these problems, but there are still more questions than answers.

Opposite Striker Lukas Podolski of Cologne has to come of age for Germany in the summer of 2006.

Kevin Kuranyi (left) scores against Australia – his goals will be at a premium for Germany in 2006.

HOW THEY'LL LINE UP

While some of the squad – especially Schweinsteiger, Torsten Frings and Ballack – can feel pretty confident about their places in the team, there are some interesting issues to be resolved before June. Has Lehmann done enough to displace Kahn in goal and will including both of them be disruptive to the squad? The centre of defence is still a weakness; can Per Mertesacker or Robert Huth prove their worth or will the coach resort to including the 34-year-old veteran Christian Woerns?

The midfield is quite settled and has width and class. Frings does the fetching

1954 WEST GERMANY 3-2 HUNGARY

WORLD CUP FINAL
Wankdorf Stadium, Berne, Switzerland

GREAT MATCH

In Germany they still refer to it as the 'Miracle of Berne'. The result meant so much more than a football match should. It gave a beaten people back their pride and led to an upswelling of joy only the fall of the Berlin Wall has since matched. It would also be the springboard for the German domination of European football for the next 50 years.

Having only just been allowed back to the World Cup by FIFA, few gave the Germans a chance against the 'Magnificent Magyars' who had gone 32 games unbeaten, boasted the likes of Puskas and Hidegkuti and had already beaten them 8-3 in the group stage. But the Germans had regrouped around a core of Kaiserslauten players and had slowly improved as they progressed through the tournament. With the news that Puskas was to play even though only half-fit, all they needed now was a minor miracle.

Hungary led 2-0 after only eight minutes, the match seemed to be following the script, but the Germans dug in and their flair player Helmut Rahn came into his own, crossing for Max Morlock to get a goal back and slamming home an angled volley for the equaliser on 35 minutes. For the rest of the game, they were pinned back, relying on the heroics of keeper Toni Turek. Then, with just five minutes remaining, a cross somehow landed at the feet of Rahn who calmly slotted it home. West Germany were back on the football map – and they had no plans to leave.

Two down in eight minutes, then, after 10 minutes, striker Max Morlock slid in to score West Germany's first goal and start their miraculous comeback.

Back row (left to right): Kevin Kuranyi, Robert Huth, Per Mertesacker, Arne Friedrich, Thomas Hitzlsperger, Michael Ballack. Front row: Bastian Schweinsteiger, Torsten Frings, Oliver Kahn, Bernd Schneider and Lukas Podolski.

and carrying, Ballack will push forward and Schweinsteiger has freedom to roam. The talented Sebastian Diesler and Fabian Ernst are also in the reckoning and Tim Borowski should be included as stand-in playmaker if the unthinkable befalls Ballack.

POSSIBLE SQUAD

Goalkeepers: Oliver Kahn (Bayern Munich), **Timo Hildebrand** (Stuttgart), **Jens Lehmann** (Arsenal)

Defenders: Arne Friedrich (Hertha Berlin), **Phillipp Lahm** (Bayern Munich), **Robert Huth** (Chelsea), **Marcell Jansen** (Borussia Monchengladbach), **Per Mertesacker** (Hannover), **Christoph Metzelder** (Borussia Dortmund), **Patrick Owomoyela** (Werder Bremen), **Lukas Sinkiewicz** (Cologne)

Midfielders: Michael Ballack (Bayern Munich), **Tim Borowski** (Werder Bremen), **Sebastian Deisler** (Bayern Munich), **Fabian Ernst** (Schalke), **Torsten Frings** (Werder Bremen), **Thomas Hitzlsperger** (Stuttgart), **Bernd Schneider** (Bayer Leverkusen), **Bastian Schweinsteiger** (Bayern Munich)

Forwards: Miroslav Klose (Werder Bremen), **Kevin Kuranyi** (Schalke), **Oliver Neuville** (Borussia Monchengladbach), **Lukas Podolski** (Cologne)

VITAL STATISTICS

WORLD RANKING 16th   **KEEPER AND DEFENCE** 6/10   **MIDFIELD** 8/10   **ATTACK** 6/10

STRENGTHS AND WEAKNESSES

A midfield that can hold its own with any in the tournament – especially in the multi-talented Ballack – is unfortunately sandwiched by a defence and forward line that are still to impress.

HOW FAR WILL THEY GO?

Sheer host-nation momentum should carry them to the quarter-finals, but at that point their talent might begin to be stretched.

Up front, however, it really is up for grabs as goals from strikers have been few and far between for Klinsmann's side. Fans will hope the exciting Lukas Podolski gets a run and Brazilian-born Kevin Kuranyi impressed in 2005, but the bulky Gerald Asamoah offers something different while veterans Miroslav Klose and Oliver Neuville have nothing more to prove.

ONE TO WATCH
Per Mertesacker

As Germany's great defensive mainstays Woerns and Jens Nowotny reached the twilight of their careers, a massive gap appeared in the centre of the German defence. Who better to fill it than the 6-foot-4-inch figure of Hannover's Per Mertesacker?

Per was called up to the national side after just 20 Bundesliga matches, making his debut in front of 110,000 fans in Tehran in late 2004. By the time the Confederations Cup had come around in June 2005, Mertesacker had gone a fair way towards establishing his place in the starting line-up.

Klinsmann seemed as impressed with the 21-year-old's calmness on the ball as with his imposing physical presence. After a 2-2 draw against Argentina, the coach remarked: 'It's fantastic the way he goes about things. He doesn't just kick the ball out of defence but he hits the ideal pass to a team-mate.'

Unlike the other youngsters Schweinsteiger and Podolski, he seems more of a 'mild one' than a wild one. Per still lives with his parents, plays for his home town club and even turned down a big money move to Werder Bremen to stay close to his roots. If he impresses in the finals, you can bet there will be bigger clubs joining the queue to drag him away.

COACH
Jurgen Klinsmann
(born 30 July 1964)
Record: P22 W12 D6 L4
Many were gobsmacked when 'Klinsi' was appointed coach of the national team. He had no coaching experience, no intention of living in

Germany and a reputation for creating enemies. From the start, Klinsmann insisted on doing things his way – introducing a new coaching structure, employing the latest training techniques from the US and continuing to live in California. He brought in a new group of young players and, contrary to German tradition, put the tactical emphasis on attack.

The Confederations Cup successes won over many doubters but as soon as the results began to go against them, the critics – including Franz Beckenbauer himself – emerged. They questioned the commitment of an overseas-based coach, doubted the quality of many of his new players and were critical of the bitter goalkeeper feud. Klinsi

would have expected this. He knew he had a tough job and he'll be judged soon enough when the talking stops and the finals begin.

World Cup fever: Germany's football-mad fans will be quick to condemn the team if things go badly in the group stage.

'Drive and motivation are our keys to success. We don't have the extra touch of class enjoyed by others. We all know that. That's why Klinsmann's route is the right one.'

Michael Ballack

As coach of the host nation, Jurgen Klinsmann will feel the pressure as the tournament draws nearer.

QUALIFIED AS HOSTS			
FINALS GROUP A			
GERMANY		Date	Venue
Costa Rica		9 June	Munich
Poland		14 June	Dortmund
Ecuador		20 June	Berlin

Torsten FRINGS

FOR A PLAYER WHO SUFFERED HEARTBREAK IN THE 2002 WORLD CUP FINAL, FRINGS CAN ONLY GET BETTER ...

For many German fans, Torsten Frings is the unsung hero of the national team. He is a player who seems to raise his game in the international arena, tirelessly supporting the playmakers like Ballack and Schweinsteiger, yet given the chance has a fabulous creative ability himself.

It did, however, take Frings some time to find his true position. Valued for his versatility, he was first signed by Werder Bremen from Alemannia Aachen in 1997. They played him first as a striker and then in a right back role, but it was only when he was moved into the centre of midfield that he began to attract attention, making his debut for the national team in 2001.

'He is an incredibly important player, the kind who changes a game, allowing us to take charge. He always fires on all cylinders and is a perfect professional.'

Jurgen Klinsmann

Despite playing for quite a number of different clubs, Torsten Frings has been a regular member of the national squad since his debut in 2001.

After such a great season, it came as no surprise to find Frings as a mainstay of Germany's 2002 World Cup campaign, but Frings found the defeat to Brazil a particularly bitter pill to swallow. However, an understanding with Ballack had developed astonishingly quickly, despite Frings playing 'out of position' in the right berth. With many of Europe's leading clubs now showing interest, Frings opted for a

22

FACT FILE | MIDFIELDER | 48 CAPS | 6 GOALS | WERDER BREMEN

Date of birth: **22.11.1976**
Height: **182 cm**
Weight: **80 kg**
Previous clubs: **Bayern Munich, Borussia Dortmund, Alemannia Aachen**
International debut: **27.02.2001 v France**
Previous World Cups: **2002**

move to Borussia Dortmund for a fee of around £7 million.

A serious cruciate ligament injury kept him out of the first half of the 2003–04 Bundesliga season but his return prompted an upturn in fortunes for Dortmund. Now operating as a playmaker, he scored four times in 16 games and fought his way back into the national side in time for Euro 2004 where he scored against Holland.

The chance to join Bayern Munich and link up with Ballack was too great an opportunity to resist, so a big money move found him moving south. A league and cup double and a great Champions League run followed, but Frings wasn't enjoying his football. He felt he was being played out of position and fell out with coach Felix Magath, and in 2005, he moved back to Werder Bremen.

Through all his domestic moves, Frings' place in the national team has remained secure, his consistency allowing Klinsmann to give his younger stars an opportunity to shine. Frings has made the No. 8 shirt his own in the pre-World Cup matches and, barring injury, will be shoring up the midfield, releasing Ballack and maybe even hitting a well-aimed free-kick or two in the finals.

STYLE GUIDE

⚽ Admired for his boundless stamina and remarkably consistent performances, Frings might appear to be an unexciting player. But his pace and close control switches defence to attack in an instant. With a powerful shot and deadly accurate free-kicks and penalties, he could also find his name appearing on the scoresheet.

FOR EIGHT YEARS HE WAS THE GREATEST GOALKEEPER IN THE WORLD. NOW, OLLI FINDS HE HAS TO PROVE HIMSELF AGAIN

At the 2002 finals, Oliver Kahn was named player of the tournament, the first time such an accolade had gone to a goalkeeper. But, with hindsight, his howler that allowed Ronaldo to score in the Final seemed to mark the beginning of his decline. We might well have seen the end of him, but Olli isn't the type to walk quietly off into the sunset.

Since joining Bayern Munich from Karlsruhe in 1994, Kahn has reaped accolades and honours: Bundesliga titles, a UEFA Cup and the UEFA Champions League (his three saves in the 2001 Champions League Final penalty shoot-out proved decisive). In 1999 and 2001 he was voted the world's best goalkeeper and, of course, in the 2002 World Cup, he almost single-handedly dragged Germany into the Final.

'The best strikers in the world rate him highly, Kahn intimidates them when they play against him.'

Sepp Maier, German goalkeeping hero

He built a reputation as a dominating presence – not only for his keeping heroics, but in the way he would bully his own players as well as opposition strikers. His nicknames: 'King Kahn', 'Titan' or 'The Gorilla', all contain an element of mocking caricature as well as respect. Often in the headlines for the wrong reasons, the temperamental keeper was perhaps terminally exacerbated when, in 2005,

FACT FILE | GOALKEEPER | 83 CAPS | 0 GOALS | BAYERN MUNICH

Date of birth: **15.06.1969**
Height: **188 cm**
Weight: **91 kg**
Previous clubs: **Karlsruhe**
International debut: **23.06.1995 v Switzerland**
Previous World Cups: **1998, 2002**

he left his heavily-pregnant wife for a 24-year-old barmaid.

After that clanger in Yokohama, Kahn's glow really began to fade. Other high-profile mistakes in Champions League games against Real Madrid and Juventus and in the Bundesliga put his keeping under the media spotlight and, for the first time in years, some questioned his right to the national team's goalkeeping jersey.

Chief among his critics was – surprise, surprise – his deputy, Arsenal's Jens Lehmann. Kahn reacted with characteristic rancour and Lehmann threatened to quit. Coach Klinsmann, eager to promote competition for the place, played them in alternate games, but such was the ferocious animosity between the two keepers only one of them was included in the squad at a time.

Despite having his captaincy of the national team taken away, a series of good performances for club and country has made Olli favourite to gain the World Cup place. Oliver Kahn is a legend and there will certainly be precious few of the world's strikers looking forward to seeing this formidable figure take his place between the sticks again.

A big man in every way, Kahn's is a reassuring presence in the German goal, but has he had his day?

STYLE GUIDE

A great shot-stopper with instinctive reflexes, Kahn is a charismatic presence who dominates his defence and intimidates the opposition. With a great positional awareness, he excels in penalty shoot-outs and one-on-ones. His only flaw is his volatile temperament, which has often led to confrontations with opponents and team-mates.

CAPTAIN AND TALISMAN, MICHAEL BALLACK'S IMPORTANCE TO THE GERMAN NATIONAL TEAM CANNOT BE OVERSTATED

'Balla' has never been short of self-confidence. Having just broken into the Kaiserslautern team at the age of 20, he fell out with coach Otto Rehhagel and moved to Bayer Leverkusen in 1999. There he had the audacity to choose the No. 13 shirt, once worn by club hero Rudi Voller.

Travelling with the national side to Euro 2000 he made just one substitute appearance, but on his return, a move from defensive midfield to a more attacking role seemed to unleash his talents. The 2001–02 season saw Ballack take his side to the Champions League Final and earned him the German player of the year award.

Few were surprised when he took the 2002 World Cup by storm – scoring three and making the FIFA tournament team as Germany marched into the Final. In the semi-final against Korea, he hit the winning goal despite receiving a booking four minutes earlier that meant he would miss the Final, an act viewed by a now adoring German public as the ultimate self-sacrifice.

The inevitable move to Bayern Munich came shortly after as Ballack continued to improve as a player. He was Germany's

Good with both feet, a regular goalscorer and captain of the side, Michael Ballack is arguably Germany's only truly world-class player.

'Michael Ballack comes close to having a Brazilian's class. He has a marvellous mixture of wonderful skills on the ball and strength in man against man situations.'

Carlos Alberto Parreira, Brazil coach

FACT FILE | MIDFIELDER | 61 CAPS | 29 GOALS | BAYERN MUNICH

Date of birth: **26.09.1976**
Height: **189 cm**
Weight: **80 kg**
Previous clubs: **Bayer Leverkusen, Kaiserslautern, Karl Marx Stadt**
International debut: **28.04.1999 v Scotland**
Previous World Cups: **2002**

player of the year again in 2003 and 2005, and in the Euro 2004 finals, he shined despite being played out of position. Klinsmann made Ballack captain as soon as he took over and has fashioned the side around him. Balla responded by inspiring the team in the 2005 Confederations Cup with four goals and three man of the match awards in four games.

It is testament to his quality that three of the biggest clubs in the world – Bayern, Real and Manchester United – are currently in a desperate struggle to secure his services. The saga threatens to disrupt his

World Cup campaign but Germany need him to keep his mind on the task ahead – he's the man who could make their dreams come true.

STYLE GUIDE

Perhaps the most complete footballer in the world today, Ballack has a delicate touch, delivers crunching tackles and is equally masterful with either foot. His eye for goal is fabulous with a repertoire of powerful shots, clipped free-kicks and lethal headers. As a captain he inspires and organises in equal measures.

FOR A NATION LOOKING FOR A HERO, IT SEEMS THAT THE IRREPRESSIBLE 'POLDI' HAS EMERGED IN THE NICK OF TIME

Gerd Muller believes he will be world-class at 21, Bayern Munich have waved their cheque book in his direction and to the expectant German supporters he is 'Der Prinz'. And yet, last year, Lukas Podolski was plying his trade in the country's second division.

'I believe that in Germany 2006, Podolski can make the same impact as Wayne Rooney at Euro 2004 ... To watch him play, you wouldn't say he was only 20, the boy has the temperament of a veteran.'

Felix Magath, Bayern Munich coach

Born in Poland, but brought up in Germany with a footballing father, Lukas Podolski joined FC Cologne at the age of ten. Bursting onto the Bundesliga scene in 2003, the mercurial 18-year-old netted ten goals in his first 19 games, but couldn't prevent his adopted club being relegated. As he joined the national squad in Portugal for Euro 2004 (making his debut as a substitute against Hungary), many wondered which colours he would be wearing in the new season.

Loaded with star quality, Lukas Podolski will carry a great weight of expectation as the hopes of the nation rest on his young shoulders.

FACT FILE | STRIKER | 20 CAPS | 10 GOALS | COLOGNE

Date of birth: **04.06.1985**
Height: **180 cm**
Weight: **81 kg**
Previous clubs: **None**
International debut: **06.06.2004 v Hungary**
Previous World Cups: **None**

STYLE GUIDE

⚽ For a striker of lightning pace and great balance, Podolski has tremendous upper-body strength. He has quickly developed a reputation as a great finisher – tap-ins as well as thunderbolt shots. Backed by a cool temperament and immense self-confidence, he immediately looked the part on the international scene.

Buoyed by national coach Rudi Voller's advice that the Zweite Liga would be a great training ground for a young striker, Lukas stayed with Cologne. As he completed the season with 24 goals, Voller seemed vindicated: Poldi was a better player in almost all departments. And with Cologne winning the league, the young charge was back in the Bundesliga.

On the international scene, Podolski was also beginning to make headlines, culminating with his performances in the 2005 Confederations Cup. Three goals, including one cracking 18-yarder against Mexico, set Poldi-fever raging across the country. By September, as he hit a hat-trick in Germany's 4-2 friendly win over South Africa,

it was a national epidemic. Seven goals in his first 13 games confirmed the rumours: Germany had a new star and Klinsmann was fighting to contain the excitement.

In 2005, as Cologne struggled in their new Bundesliga campaign, Lukas' form dipped. While the inevitable backlash began, some argued he was just not receiving adequate supply in a mediocre team. It certainly didn't stop the overtures from Bayern or rumours of a move to Barcelona. Whether he joins a super-club or remains with his beloved Cologne, one thing is sure: the nation will all be Poldi fans come June 2006.

HE'S THE NEW HEDGEHOG-HAIRED PRODIGY OF GERMAN FOOTBALL AND THEY'RE EXPECTING THE WORLD OF HIM

In the soul-searching that followed Germany's ignominious exit from Euro 2004, the name of Bastian Schweinsteiger was exempt from criticism. The young midfielder had given fans a glimpse of the flair and creativity that could set their World Cup alight. Two years later, 'Basti' is in the vanguard of Klinsmann's new attack-minded Germany and is still seen as the man who could ignite the host nation in the finals.

Schweinsteiger's talent was immediately obvious. From the age of 19, he was playing in Bayern's first team and making waves in the Bundesliga. His vision and distribution perfectly complemented Bayern's key man Ballack, and when Rudi Voller called him up to the national team, he found the same man at his side.

Many worried that Basti would squander his natural talent as he became involved in a series of off-the-field escapades. He was caught speeding; was cautioned by his club for late-night disco visits; and was caught using the whirlpool at Bayern's practice ground at night with a female he later said was his 'cousin'.

'He just goes out there and gets on with it. He's already a lot like Mehmet Scholl. He's not put off if he tries something but loses the ball.'

Michael Ballack, Germany skipper

Bastian Schweinsteiger's performances were the one positive that Germany took from a disappointing campaign at Euro 2004.

FACT FILE | MIDFIELDER | 23 CAPS | 4 GOALS | BAYERN MUNICH

Date of birth: **01.08.1984**
Height: **181 cm**
Weight: **77 kg**
Previous clubs: **TVS 1860 Rosenheim, Oberaudorf**
International debut: **06.06.2004 v Hungary**
Previous World Cups: **None**

All that was forgotten as he turned in some eye-catching performances in Euro 2004.

He did, however, return from Portugal to a shock. For the 2004–05 season, new Bayern manager Felix Magath had sent him back to play in Bayern's reserves. It was a test of character for Germany's new found star and he emerged with great credit, knuckling down and returning to play a role in the double-winning campaign as well as scoring in Bayern's Champions League quarter-final first-leg defeat at Chelsea.

Schweinsteiger's standing was further improved by the 2005 Confederations Cup where his impressive performances included well-taken goals against Tunisia and Mexico. A blossoming friendship with Lukas Podolski seemed to be reflected on the pitch; the two prodigies making chances for each other as Germany reached the semi-finals.

Basti's ability to do the unexpected and bring his team-mates into the game promises to lift a team that may be low on inspiration. Cheeky, confident and seemingly carefree, Basti has brought a badly-needed freshness to the German squad. If he can bring them success as well, he'll be a star for life.

STYLE GUIDE

Often compared to Steffen Effenberg, Basti shares his ability to create chances through slide-rule passes or fabulous runs. Cited as the fittest player in the Bundesliga, Schweinsteiger never stops running and his willingness to try the unexpected – back heels, lobs, flicks – makes him a defender's nightmare.

COSTA RICA

FOOTBALL-CRAZY 'TICOS' DREAMING OF GLORY

In danger of elimination at several points during the qualifying campaign, a change of manager brought three wins in the last four matches to guarantee World Cup tickets for Costa Rica.

Hopes were high after a good showing at the World Cup in 2002 when Costa Rica were unlucky not to emerge from an opening group that also included eventual winners Brazil and third-placed Turkey. With four points from three games, a win over China, a 1-1 draw with Turkey and a 5-2 defeat by Brazil in one of the most entertaining games of the tournament, they finished on the same points total as Turkey who went through with more goals scored.

Far left Striker Paulo Wanchope (right) in action.

Left Coach Alexandre Guimaraes – a national hero in football-mad Costa Rica.

Qualifiying for Germany 2006 started badly, Costa Rica only getting through the first stage on away goals. Things then got worse with a 0-0 draw against local rivals Honduras, crowd trouble during a 2-1 home defeat by Mexico and a fatal car crash in which striker Whayne Wilson was killed. Only last-minute goals against Panama and Guatemala kept the Ticos in the competition.

However, the return of coach Alexandre Guimaraes in March 2005 was the catalyst for a revival in the team's fortunes. Guimaraes played for Costa Rica in the 1990 World Cup, the nation's first, in which they reached the last 16. He coached the team to the 2002 World Cup – their second – and the successful campaign this time has cemented his place as a national hero. Qualification was finally achieved after a 3-0 defeat of the USA in San Jose in October 2005, which was

VITAL STATISTICS

WORLD RANKING 21st   **KEEPER AND DEFENCE** 5/10
MIDFIELD 7/10   **ATTACK** 6/10
STRENGTHS AND WEAKNESSES
Conceded more goals than they scored in the qualifying stages and this will let them down on the world stage. However, their 3-0 win against the USA shows that they are no mugs.
HOW FAR WILL THEY GO?
Costa Rica will play attractive football in Germany and will win fans along the way. Their finals group draw gives them a chance of progressing to the second round.

greeted with a standing ovation from 18,000 football-mad supporters in the stadium.

Three teams dominate domestic football in Costa Rica – Deportivo Saprissa, CD Herediano and LD Alajuelense – and provide most of the players for the national squad. That and the fact that the squad for 2006 is likely to be very similar to that of 2002 gives Guimaraes the basis of a settled team full of experienced players like veteran midfielder Ronald Gomez, with over a hundred caps to his name, and striker Paulo Wanchope, whose record of 43 goals in 67 internationals – including eight in the World Cup 2006 qualifying competition – is an impressive one. Wanchope announced that he is going to retire from international football at the end of the World Cup. Add to the mix some

young talent, such as midfielders Carlos Hernandez and Alvaro Saborio, and you have quite an effective brew.

Costa Rica's supporters are dreaming of glory, the kind of glory that they achieved at Italia 90 when they reached the second round, and a favourable draw, in Group A with hosts Germany, Ecuador and Poland gives them a good chance of achieving just that.

POSSIBLE SQUAD

Goalkeepers: **Alvaro Mesen** (Herediano), **Donny Grant** (Perez Zeledon), **Jose Francisco Porras** (Saprissa)

Defenders: **Gilberto Martinez** (Brescia), **Michael Umana** (Los Angeles Galaxy), **Danny Fonseca** (Cartago), **Mauricio Wright** (Herediano), **Leo Gonzalez** (Herediano), **Roy Miller** (Bodo Glimt), **Gabriel Badilla** (Saprissa), **Jervis Drummond** (Saprissa), **Harold Wallace** (Alajuelense)

Midfielders: **Steven Bryce** (Anorthosis Famagusta), **Carlos Hernandez** (Alajuelense), **Cristian Bolanos** (Saprissa), **Walter Centeno** (Saprissa), **Mauricio Solis** (Comunicaciones), **Douglas Sequeira** (Chivas USA), **Alvaro Saborio** (Saprissa)

Forwards: **Paulo Wanchope** (Al Gharafa), **Ronald Gomez** (Saprissa), **Oscar Rojas** (Dorados de Sinaloa), **Winston Parks** (Saturn Moskovskaya Oblast)

CONCACAF FINAL STAGE – FINAL TABLE							
TEAM	P	W	D	L	F	A	Pts
USA	10	7	1	2	16	6	22
MEXICO	10	7	1	2	22	9	22
COSTA RICA	10	5	1	4	14	16	16
TRINIDAD & TOBAGO	10	4	1	5	10	15	13
GUATEMALA	10	3	2	5	16	18	11
PANAMA	10	0	2	8	4	21	2

Back row (left to right): Jose Francisco Porras, Mauricio Solis, Alvaro Saborio, Carlos Hernandez, Paulo Wanchope, Ronald Gomez, Walter Centeno. Front row: Gilberto Martinez, Luis Marin, Harold Wallace and Jervis Drummond.

FINALS GROUP A			
	COSTA RICA	Date	Venue
	Germany	9 June	Munich
	Ecuador	15 June	Hamburg
	Poland	20 June	Hanover

POLAND

WELL PLACED FOR REVIVAL

The coach of the Polish national football team, Pavel Janas, knows what it takes to win World Cup matches. In 1982 he played for Poland at the World Cup in Spain where they lost 2-0 in the semi-final to eventual winners Italy, but beat France in a play-off for third spot.

That was just about the last time that Poland has ever registered football glory on the international stage. Since then things haven't gone well. In 2002 the team promised much in the qualifiers, but played poorly in Japan and Korea and exited in the first round. Pavel Janas, who had a great deal of success as a club coach and the national Olympic coach in Poland, took over the hot-seat in early 2004. It was too late for him to rescue their attempts to qualify for Euro 2004, when the team had been coached by the Polish footballing legend Zbigniew Boniek, but his first aim was to qualify for Germany 2006.

That they qualified for the finals was no great surprise as, England apart, Poland looked to be one of the strongest teams in a weak group. But what was so good for the Poles was the way in which they did it. Eight wins, including away wins in Ireland and Austria, an 8-0 demolition of Azerbaijan, 27 goals scored in 10 games and all done with an attractive attacking style. In fact, going in to the last game

Below Tomasz Frankowski and strike partner Maciej Zurawski scored 14 of Poland's 27 goals during qualifying.

Below right Stern-faced coach Paval Janas.

VITAL STATISTICS

WORLD RANKING 22nd **KEEPER AND DEFENCE** 5/10
MIDFIELD 6/10 **ATTACK** 6/10
STRENGTHS AND WEAKNESSES
The fact that they will be underrated may well be to their advantage but they will need to keep up their scoring rate.
HOW FAR WILL THEY GO?
Will do well to proceed to the knockout rounds.

Back row (left to right) Kamil Kosowski, Jacek Bak, Artur Boruc, Radoslaw Sobolewski, Grzegorz Rasiak. Front row: Tomasz Rzasa, Mariusz Jop, Marcin Baszczynski, Maciej Zurawski, Miroslaw Szymkowiak and Euzebiusz Smolarek.

against England at Old Trafford, Poland were in top spot.

Janas has assembled a strong squad of players, with several from domestic champions Wisla Krakow as well as players playing in other European leagues, and he has been consistent in his team selection during the qualifiers. The team seems much more organised, stronger and has a will to win that has been missing from the Polish teams at the last few international tournaments.

With Champions League winner Jerzy Dudek in goal and rock-solid captain Tomasz Hajto organising things at the back, he has a solid base on which to work. Strikers Tomasz Frankowski and Maciej Zurawski bagged 14 goals between them in qualifying; so much will depend on the effectiveness of the midfield.

POSSIBLE SQUAD

Goalkeepers: Jerzy Dudek (Liverpool), **Artur Boruc** (Celtic), **Wojciech Kowalewski** (Spartak Moscow)

Defenders: Marcin Baszczynski (Wisla Krakow), **Jacek Bak** (RC Lens), **Arkadiusz Glowacki** (Wisla Krakow), **Tomasz Hajto** (Nurnberg), **Radoslaw Kaluzny** (Bayer Leverkusen), **Tomasz Klos** (Wisla Krakow), **Tomasz Rzasa** (Heerenveen), **Michal Zewlakow** (Anderlecht)

Midfielders: Damian Gorawski (Wisla Krakow), **Kamil Kosowski** (Southampton), **Jacek Krzynowek** (Bayer Leverkusen), **Mariusz Kukielka** (Wisla Krakow), **Sebastian Mila** (Groclin Dyskobolia Grodzisk), **Miroslaw Szymkowiak** (Wisla Krakow), **Marek Zienczuk** (Wisla Krakow)

Forwards: Tomasz Frankowski (Elche CF), **Ireneusz Jelen** (Wisla Plock), **Pavel Kryszalowicz** (Wisla Krakow), **Grzegorz Rasiak** (Tottenham Hotspur), **Maciej Zurawski** (Celtic)

EUROPE QUALIFYING GROUP 6 – FINAL TABLE							
TEAM	P	W	D	L	F	A	Pts
ENGLAND	10	8	1	1	17	5	25
POLAND	10	8	0	2	27	9	24
AUSTRIA	10	4	3	3	15	12	15
NORTHERN IRELAND	10	2	3	5	10	18	9
WALES	10	2	2	6	10	15	8
AZERBAIJAN	10	0	3	7	1	21	3

FINALS GROUP A			
	POLAND	Date	Venue
	Ecuador	9 June	Gelsenkirchen
	Germany	14 June	Dortmund
	Costa Rica	20 June	Hanover

ECUADOR

LOOKING FOR A TOUCH OF THE HIGH LIFE

Any other team who had beaten Brazil and Argentina on the way to Germany would be one of the tournament's favourites, but Ecuador's victories always come at altitude. Can this potentially exciting outfit reproduce their home form on the lowlands of Europe?

When Ecuador returned from Japan and Korea in 2002, they received a hero's welcome. Despite being knocked out at the group stage, they had beaten Croatia – their first ever World Cup victory. Now, with a rejuvenated team, captain Ivan Hurtado and star striker Augustin Delgado are going back for more.

After a disastrous Copa America campaign in 2004, the Colombian Luis Fernandez Suarez took charge of the Ecuador national team. 'The Professor' made few changes, but transformed the fortunes of the team. Critics often focus on their advantage of playing at altitude – they secured 23 of their 28 points in

qualifying at home – and while they obviously have a fragile centre, they also have the skill and craft to spring some surprises.

Suarez's preparation has been far from ideal. Striker Otilino Tenorio tragically died in a car crash; midfielder Ivan Kaviedes has fallen out with him; keeper Edwin Villafuerte and striker Delgado were sacked by Barcelona (the Ecuadorian version) and new star Franklin Salas has suffered a recurrent knee injury.

The coach still feels he has a team that can compete in the finals. In defence centre back Giovanni Espinoza has been a star in the qualifiers and veteran skipper Ivan Hurtado still provides some exquisite touches.

Despite the retirement of legend Alex Aguinaga in 2005, Suarez has a powerful midfield. The No. 10 shirt went to 25-year-old Christian Lara whose stature, change of pace, and running style has invited comparisons with Robinho. But it was Edison Mendez who emerged as Ecuador's hero in the qualifiers scoring five invaluable goals. If the coach is able to make peace with Kaviedes he will have a midfield who could trouble any of the teams in their group.

Above *Ecuador's veteran captain Ivan Hurtado.*

Above right *Giovanni Espinoza (right) congratulates Edison Mendez on his goal against Bolivia, one of five he scored during the qualifiers.*

Back row (left to right): Agustin Delgado, Damian Lanza, Jorge Guagua, Luis Saritama, Richard Calderon. Front row: Felix Borja, Otilino Tenorio, Ulises de la Cruz, Antonio Valencia, Edwin Tenorio and Marlon Ayovi.

VITAL STATISTICS

WORLD RANKING 37th **KEEPER AND DEFENCE** 5/10
MIDFIELD 7/10 **ATTACK** 6/10
STRENGTHS AND WEAKNESSES
The defence looks a little flimsy, but a talented midfield could produce some sparks.
HOW FAR WILL THEY GO?
The second round looks unlikely, but they could collect another memorable World Cup win.

In attack, Ecuador have the 20-year-old talent Felix Borja and, fitness permitting, El Mago ('The Wizard') Franklin Salas. The nation's diminutive golden boy has speed, skill and a fine eye for goal. So far Suarez has used him mainly as a sub, but he is one who could make his name in Germany.

To cause a shock, Ecuador will have to get their stars back on board and hope their youngsters come good. But if they made heroes of the 2002 one-match winning team, imagine the reception Ecuador will receive if they can qualify from Group A!

POSSIBLE SQUAD

Goalkeepers: Cristian Mora (LDU), **Damian Lanza** (Deportivo Cuenca), **Edwin Villafuerte** (Unattached)

Defenders: Ivan Hurtado (El Arabi), **Jorge Guagua** (El Nacional), **Giovanni Espinoza** (LDU), **Jose Cortez** (Aucas), **Ulises de la Cruz** (Aston Villa), **Erick de Jesus** (El Nacional), **Neicer Reasco** (LDU), **Paul Ambrossi** (LDU)

Midfielders: Edwin Tenorio (Barcelona), **Segundo Castillo** (El Nacional), **Luis Saritama** (Deportivo Quito), **Luis Caicedo** (Olmedo), **Antonio Valencia** (Villareal), **Marlon Ayovi** (Deportivo Quito), **Edison Mendez** (LDU), **Christian Lara** (El Nacional)

Forwards: Roberto Mina (Dallas), **Franklin Salas** (LDU), **Felix Borja** (El Nacional), **Augustin Delgado** (Unattached)

SOUTH AMERICA QUALIFYING GROUP – FINAL TABLE							
TEAM	P	W	D	L	F	A	Pts
BRAZIL	18	9	7	2	35	17	**34**
ARGENTINA	18	10	4	4	29	17	**34**
ECUADOR	18	8	4	6	23	19	**28**
PARAGUAY	18	8	4	6	23	23	**28**
URUGUAY	18	6	7	5	23	28	**25**
COLOMBIA	18	6	6	6	24	16	**24**
CHILE	18	5	7	6	18	22	**22**
VENEZUELA	18	5	3	10	20	28	**18**
PERU	18	4	6	8	20	28	**18**
BOLIVIA	18	4	2	12	20	37	**14**

FINALS GROUP A			
	ECUADOR	Date	Venue
	Poland	9 June	Gelsenkirchen
	Costa Rica	15 June	Hamburg
	Germany	20 June	Berlin

ENGLAND

HEROES OR VILLAINS?

Some see England as certain finalists, others as potential failures. There's talent galore, but will that be enough to win football's most important competition?

Whether it was misfortune – Rooney's injury and Ronaldinho's 'freak' goal – or tactical error, England will not want to repeat the disappointments of Japan and Korea or Euro 2004. If anything, the team has improved, with the emergence of John Terry and Ashley Cole as world-class defenders, the amazing progress of Lampard and the maturity – at least as a footballer – of Rooney. But the questions remain. How does Sven accommodate Gerrard, Beckham and Lampard in the midfield? Is Joe Cole the man to answer the long-standing left-side problem? And do England have the flexibility to change styles and formations to suit the match? If they can answer these questions, they could well come home as heroes.

***Above** For England to succeed in Germany much depends on the link-up play between Frank Lampard and captain David Beckham.*

***Opposite** The time has come for the fast-maturing Joe Cole to prove that he can make it on the world stage.*

MORE QUESTIONS THAN ANSWERS

England's qualifying group looked pretty easy on paper, but somehow they managed to give the impression of struggling through. Sven kept faith with the team who had largely disappointed in Portugal, only really giving a chance to Paul Robinson (who took it) and Jermain Defoe (who didn't). England got off to a flyer – winning in Poland and in a tricky match against Wales – but defeat to Northern Ireland was a setback.

Added to a 1-4 friendly defeat against a mediocre Denmark, the result created tremors. England now had two must-win matches and sections of the press were already calling for Sven's head. They doubted his tactical sense, accused him of letting his captain, Beckham, run the team and claimed he played out-of-form players out of position. When Beckham was sent off in the penultimate match against Austria – the game looked up. But England held on for a 1-0 victory and as other results went their

In keeper Paul Robinson England have found the perfect replacement for David Seaman who retired from international football after the 2002 World Cup.

way, qualified with a game to spare. In the final match they enjoyed an impressive 2-1 victory over Poland. Everyone was heartened, but somehow the result merely underlined the existing questions.

HOW THEY'LL LINE UP

Sven has been very loyal to his players and it seems unlikely he'll change his spots now. The spine of the team is settled and contains England's world beaters in Robinson, Lampard, Gerrard, Rooney and Michael Owen. Around them only the left-sided midfield postion looks up for grabs as Joe Cole still fails to look completely at home.

2002	ENGLAND 1-0 ARGENTINA	WORLD CUP, GROUP STAGE
		Sapporo Dome, Sapporo, Japan

GREAT MATCH

England finally laid to rest the Indian sign Argentina had held over them for 15 years with a determined and fantastically organized victory. Man-of-the match Nicky Butt put his Manchester United team-mate Veron in the shade, and Michael Owen provided a constant threat.

It was an early injury to Hargreaves that helped England gel. Sinclair replaced him and made inroads down the left and Scholes moved into the centre, where he drove the team forward. The goal came with just two minutes to go to half-time, Owen slipped around Pochettino, fell over his outstretched leg and referee Collina pointed to the spot. David Beckham, whose life had been made a misery after being sent-off in the 1998 match, took a deep breath, before hammering the ball past Cavallero.

Argentina camped themselves in England's half for the last 30 minutes of the game, but were frustrated by the midfield line and a brilliant Seaman save to deny Pochettino. Revenge was sweet – the blue-and-whites were all but boarding the plane home.

Injury or tactical manoeuvres could, however, lead to some interesting changes. England could utilise their strengths and play three at the back. A holding midfielder might provide a better mainspring for attack. And Sven might even consider switching to the

POSSIBLE SQUAD

Goalkeepers: **Paul Robinson** (Tottenham Hotspur), **David James** (Manchester City), **Robert Green** (Norwich City)

Defenders: **Ashley Cole** (Arsenal), **Sol Campbell** (Arsenal), **Gary Neville** (Manchester United), **Rio Ferdinand** (Manchester United), **John Terry** (Chelsea), **Wayne Bridge** (Chelsea), **Luke Young** (Charlton Athletic), **Jamie Carragher** (Liverpool), **Ledley King** (Tottenham Hotspur)

Midfielders: **Steven Gerrard** (Liverpool), **David Beckham** (Real Madrid), **Joe Cole** (Chelsea), **Frank Lampard** (Chelsea), **Shaun Wright-Phillips** (Chelsea), **Jermaine Jenas** (Tottenham Hotspur), **Michael Carrick** (Tottenham Hotspur)

Forwards: **Wayne Rooney** (Manchester United), **Michael Owen** (Newcastle United), **Jermain Defoe** (Tottenham Hotspur), **Peter Crouch** (Liverpool)

Back row (left to right): Ashley Cole, Rio Ferdinand, Jamie Carragher, Frank Lampard, Paul Robinson.
Front row: Wayne Rooney, Joe Cole, David Beckham, Steven Gerrard, Luke Young and Shaun Wright-Phillips.

4-5-1 formation that Chelsea, Manchester United and others have used to great effect.

If such changes are employed there are a number of players waiting for their chance: Luke Young as a foraging full back; Ledley King, Michael Carrick or Jermaine Jenas in the midfield role and Shaun Wright-Phillips as a quick, skilful winger. Up front the tall Peter Crouch has shown he can offer something different, while Jermain Defoe could unleash his talent if he is given a run in the team.

ONE TO WATCH
Shaun Wright-Phillips

'I don't think he's the finished article yet, he can only get better.' Stuart Pearce's parting words on his young star implied Chelsea might have got the 21-year-old for a 'bargain' £21 million. In his few England appearances, Shaun has added to the argument, exhibiting a blistering turn of pace (he's the quickest at the club, claim Chelsea), great control and a

wicked shot. Bearing the tag of 'Ian Wright's adopted son' couldn't have been easy, particularly when Nottingham Forest let him go at 15 for being 'too small'. Switching to Manchester City, he soon impressed – on either flank and as a wing-back. Making his debut at 18, Shaun helped City into the Premier League and set about making his mark.

Premiership defenders soon discovered his twisting, turning runs to their cost. The 2003–04 campaign saw him bag 11 goals and make many more, forcing his price beyond the wallets of the chasing Liverpool and Arsenal: only Chelsea could afford him.

Shortly after arriving at Stamford Bridge in July 2005, Shaun marked his England debut with a superb solo goal. Suddenly, England had a new option: a lightning winger with the ability to beat defenders. It excited the fans and the media – but to accommodate Shaun would mean the unthinkable: dropping the captain. Barring a tactical rethink, Shaun

VITAL STATISTICS

WORLD RANKING 9th
KEEPER AND DEFENCE 8/10
MIDFIELD 8/10
ATTACK 7/10
STRENGTHS AND WEAKNESSES
The nucleus of Eriksson's team has been together for two previous tournaments and know what is needed and what to expect. The defence will be tight and if Rooney comes alight, he could take the team a long way, if not they could struggle to score and go out with all too familiar limp performances.
HOW FAR WILL THEY GO?
If they can get over that elusive quarter-final hurdle, the doubts will disappear and they'll make the Final.

Shaun Wright-Phillips exhibits the sort of skills that make him such an exciting prospect for club and country.

goes to Germany as Beckham's understudy, but if he gets a chance, remember Psycho's words and don't be surprised to see a lot more of this youngster's stunning talent.

Sven-Goran Eriksson knows that Germany 2006 represents his last chance for glory with England.

COACH

Sven Goran-Eriksson

(born 5 February 1948)

Record: P59 W34 D15 L10

The exact opposite of his predecessor Kevin Keegan, the Swede was a proven winner, a tactician rather than a motivator, unemotional and – for some, most controversially – a foreigner. Any initial outrage, though, was soon forgotten as Sven's tenure began well. Sven, and his assistant Tord Grip, brought their partnership – forged at Benfica and Lazio – to England and imposed their blueprint to great effect. Faithful to a 4-4-2 formation and reliant on pacy counter-attack, they built a reputation on loyalty to players and a calm response to victory or defeat.

After the defeat to Northern Ireland, criticism of Sven's management style gathered momentum. True to character, he rode the flak and calmly led his team to the World Cup – but for the first time, the press seemed to have bruised him. The ice cold Swede now knows for sure, it's do or die in Germany.

ROUTE TO THE FINALS			
DATE			
04.09.04	AUSTRIA **2**	**2** ENGLAND	
08.09.04	POLAND **1**	**2** ENGLAND	
09.10.04	ENGLAND **2**	**0** WALES	
13.10.04	AZERBAIJAN **0**	**1** ENGLAND	
26.03.05	ENGLAND **4**	**0** NORTHERN IRELAND	
30.03.05	ENGLAND **2**	**0** AZERBAIJAN	
03.09.05	WALES **0**	**1** ENGLAND	
07.09.05	NORTHERN IRELAND **1**	**0** ENGLAND	
08.10.05	ENGLAND **1**	**0** AUSTRIA	
12.10.05	ENGLAND **2**	**1** POLAND	

EUROPE QUALIFYING GROUP 6 – FINAL TABLE							
TEAM	P	W	D	L	F	A	Pts
ENGLAND	10	8	1	1	17	5	**25**
POLAND	10	8	0	2	27	9	**24**
AUSTRIA	10	4	3	3	15	12	**15**
NORTHERN IRELAND	10	2	3	5	10	18	**9**
WALES	10	2	2	6	10	15	**8**
AZERBAIJAN	10	0	3	7	1	21	**3**

FINALS GROUP B			
	ENGLAND	Date	Venue
	Paraguay	10 June	Frankfurt
	Trinidad & Tobago	15 June	Nuremberg
	Sweden	20 June	Cologne

DON'T THINK WE'VE SEEN THE LAST OF 'GOLDEN-BALLS' YET – BECKHAM IS STILL ONE OF THE FEW MATCH-WINNING PLAYERS IN THE FINALS

He is the world's most recognisable sportsman, his image a carefully managed mix of family man, fashion model and smiling celebrity. But every now and then, a trademark stunning free-kick, a viciously curling cross or a pitch-length chase back to tackle will cut through all the fluff and remind us that the England captain is also one of the best footballers on the planet.

Now in his 30s, 'Becks' approaches the twilight of his career with a lorry load of memories already packed away. Back in 1996 his sensational goal from the halfway line against Wimbledon brought him to the nation's attention. By 1998, he finally forced his way into Glenn Hoddle's World Cup team, scoring against Colombia with a free-kick, only to be sent-off against Argentina for petulantly kicking-out.

By the 2002 World Cup qualifiers he was the captain, and with a captain's performance against Greece – including another fantastic free-kick – he single-handedly dragged England

'I think David Beckham is still one of the best players in the world. He's the best passer in the world and also one of the greatest players in his position on the pitch. I would love him to be Brazilian.'

Roberto Carlos

FACT FILE | MIDFIELD | 86 CAPS | 16 GOALS | REAL MADRID

Date of birth: **02.05.1975**
Height: **183 cm**
Weight: **74 kg**
Previous clubs: **Manchester United**
International debut: **01.09.1996 v Moldova**
Previous World Cups: **1998, 2002**

to the finals. Making it to the tournament despite a serious injury, he gained revenge on Argentina by scoring the penalty that beat them, but otherwise seemed out-of-sorts as England crashed out.

David Beckham has grown-up in public: winning the treble at Manchester United, his alleged bust-up with Alex Ferguson in the case of the flying boot and his high-profile transfer to Real Madrid. Trophies might have been elusive since he left for Spain, but the esteem in which he is held by the club and its fans leaves no doubt as to his contribution. Last season at Madrid, Beckham returned to the kind of form he showed at Manchester United. In contrast, although he continued to lead England with passion and exuberance, being moved from wing to centre to holding role seemed to dent his talents. He even handed his penalty-taking responsibility to Frank Lampard.

With his captaincy and even his place in the team under threat don't be surprised to see the usual Beckham reaction to adversity. He rolls up his sleeves, works even harder and pulls out a performance that leaves fans open-mouthed. This could well be his last World Cup, don't expect him to go out with a whimper.

David Beckham has over 80 caps for England, the friendly against Argentina was his 50th match as captain.

STYLE GUIDE

⚽ 'Becks' is still England's talisman: at his best, his sheer energy is inspiring: a magnificent team player, he tracks back, launches himself into tackles and wants to take every free-kick or throw-in. England, if anything, take for granted his match-winning play from the right wing berth, complete with crossfield passes, curling pin-point crosses, buzz-bomb corners and, of course, awesome free-kicks.

HAVE ENGLAND FINALLY FOUND THAT SPECIAL TALENT THAT CAN TAKE THEM ALL THE WAY TO THE WORLD CUP FINAL?

Never before have England placed so much expectation on such a young talent. And yet, such is the power, dynamism and skill exhibited by the 20-year-old, that he too will face the world's finest, knowing that he could be the difference between his country's glory and failure.

> 'He can shoot from distance, get on the end of crosses, hit free-kicks – anything. He is someone who plays with absolutely no fear and when you have a striker like that then there are no limits.'
>
> Thierry Henry

Powerful and direct, Rooney has all the weapons to trouble the world's greatest defences.

Wayne Rooney is no David Beckham. He lacks the good looks, the well-groomed image and film-star lifestyle, but he has the chance to be an even greater talisman for the national side. Ever since Everton's 17-year-old prodigy's scintillating shot passed the outstretched arms of Arsenal's David Seaman, England have believed they have found a Pelé or Maradona – a superstar who could take them right to the top.

Rooney quickly became England's youngest-ever player and goalscorer and at Euro 2004, he made a global impact not witnessed since Pelé in 1958. Having been man-of-the-match in all of England's group

FACT FILE | FORWARD | 28 CAPS | 11 GOALS | MANCHESTER UNITED

Date of birth: **24.10.1985**
Height: **178 cm**
Weight: **78 kg**
Previous clubs: **Everton**
International debut: **12.02.2003 v Australia**
Previous World Cups: **None**

games, he scared the living daylights out of the host nation, Portugal until, after 15 minutes, he limped off having broken a bone in his foot. England's tournament hopes soon followed.

Meanwhile, at home, 'Rooneymania' had taken root and the boy-turned-man found himself on his way from Goodison Park to Old Trafford. On his Champions League debut against Ferencvaros, Rooney scored a magnificent hat-trick, instantly justifying his £28 million fee. Superlatives kept coming as his performances electrified the Theatre of Dreams and gave England a cutting edge that seemed a million miles away when he was injured – or suspended.

Indeed, the wonderkid had an Achilles heel after all – his volatile temper. For club and country he would react to frustration with uncontrolled aggression. As some questioned his suitability, Rooney returned from international suspension to face Poland. He produced another thrilling man-of-the match performance, revitalising a moribund England and sending them to the top of their qualifying group. Suspect temper? Unsavoury private life? Perhaps: but without him England are champagne without the fizz – and who wants that?

STYLE GUIDE

⚽ When Rooney first hit the headlines, it was his powerful shooting, his incredible surging runs and boundless energy that won him accolades. Amazingly, the teenage prodigy added to his game – a superb positional sense, great vision and passing and an ability to animate his team-mates. Only his childlike reaction to frustrations belies his growing maturity.

John **TERRY**

ALREADY A CHELSEA LEGEND, THE IMMACULATE STOPPER HAS COME OF AGE FOR ENGLAND IN THE NICK OF TIME

9 July 2006 – England skipper John Terry wipes a still sweating brow, pauses, and lifts high the World Cup. A far-fetched dream? Not any more. In England's final qualification match, a substituted Michael Owen handed the captain's armband to the Chelsea skipper. Terry's journey from England outcast to national leadership material was complete.

A series of inspirational performances for his club Chelsea during their championship winning season in 2004–05 have seen John Terry take his place as England's first-choice central defender.

Among Chelsea's treasure trove of talent, John Terry stands alone as never having cost a penny. Yet, their home-grown hero can hold his own against any of the multi-million pound imports. Terry has been the spearhead of the Abramovich revolution: the mainstay of an impenetrable defence, the scorer of valuable goals and, most of all, an inspirational leader – Chelsea through and through.

Following a loan period at Gillingham, Terry got his break in the Chelsea side after an injury to Frank Leboeuf. As his replacement went from strength to strength, the World Cup winner never regained his place. When he was made club captain at the age of 23, Marcel Desailly dubbed Terry a 'Chelsea legend in the making', and Jose Mourinho was moved to call him the 'perfect player'. By the end of the 2004–05 season his fellow professionals seemed to agree, voting him the PFA Footballer of the Year.

Terry's England career was not keeping pace. An altercation with a night club bouncer left him with a court case pending. The FA, nervy after previous bad publicity, deferred his national call-up until the end of the case. Finally cleared of all offences, Terry made his belated debut against Serbia & Montenegro in 2003 – but there was still

FACT FILE | CENTRE-HALF | 21 CAPS | 0 GOALS | CHELSEA

Date of birth: **07.12.1980**
Height: **185 cm**
Weight: **88 kg**
Previous clubs: **None**
International debut: **03.06.2003 v Serbia & Montenegro**
Previous World Cups: **None**

STYLE GUIDE

⚽ Often compared to Tony Adams, the Chelsea stopper exerts his influence physically, verbally and by superb example. An immovable rock at the centre of the defence, Terry reads the game impeccably; he's powerful in the tackle, dominant in the air, and an ever-present attacking threat at free-kicks and corners.

'He is young but he has grown up. I hope I've taught him that off the pitch he has to be a leader.'

Marcel Desailly

the problem of Rio Ferdinand and Sol Campbell, a partnership that continued to live off the players' acclaimed performances in Japan and Korea.

Ferdinand's notorious suspension gave Terry his chance in time for Euro 2004, but playing with a hamstring injury, he failed to put in a permanent claim to the shirt. However, as Chelsea's championship season progressed, Terry's faultless performances, week after week, could not be ignored. By the autumn of 2005, Terry had become England's first-choice central defender, while Sol and Rio fought to partner him. Then came the armband and a snowballing press campaign to make him the full-time skipper.

Frank **LAMPARD**

HIS MANAGER THINKS HE'S THE BEST PLAYER IN EUROPE, AND IF HE PLAYS TO HIS POTENTIAL, LAMPS COULD LIGHT UP GERMANY

Heartbroken after narrowly missing the 2002 World Cup squad, the Chelsea midfielder was determined to make the plane next time round. In those four years, he's done more than that – he's become a Premiership winner, Footballer of the Year and an irreplaceable part of the England team.

Frank Lampard was never an ordinary player, but few believed he would make the progression to being a world-class midfielder. Now, through self-belief, great coaching and sheer hard work, he stands on the threshold of global recognition.

As the son of a Hammer hero, Frank began his career at West Ham – seemingly forever burdened with the suffix 'Junior'. There, alongside the likes of Rio Ferdinand, Joe Cole, and Michael Carrick, he impressed enough to make England Under-21 captain and

'The guy is simply a phenomenon. He never misses a game but doesn't look like he gets tired. Not just that, he was leading scorer for Chelsea in the Premiership last season. He inspires everyone around him.'

Sam Allardyce,
Bolton Wanderers manager

FACT FILE | MIDFIELD | 38 CAPS | 10 GOALS | CHELSEA

Date of birth: **20.06.1978**
Height: **183 cm**
Weight: **88 kg**
Previous clubs: **West Ham United**
International debut: **10.10.1999 v Belgium**
Previous World Cup: **None**

his debut in the senior side. But only when he left Upton Park and became *the* Frank Lampard did he really blossom.

In the early days at Stamford Bridge, Frank looked overweight and under-confident – his fee of £11 million rather extravagant. But under, first Ranieri, and then Mourinho, an altogether sharper player emerged. As more and more distinguished players joined the new 'Chelski', so Frank raised his game, daring his manager to leave him out. In the 2004–05 season he started in 58 games – and won the Footballer of the Year award.

Eriksson liked the look of the new slimline Frank, but he lost out in the final cut for Japan and Korea. By Euro 2004, however, he had established a settled place alongside Steven Gerrard, and emerged as one of England's stars of the tournament.

The qualifiers saw him impress further as a goalscoring midfielder, a natural successor to Paul Scholes. The only doubt was whether the presence of the similar forward-looking Gerrard limited Frank's game. While experts debated the point, Frank took over as penalty taker from Beckham, and carried on scoring.

STYLE GUIDE

⚽ 'Lamps' is the epitome of the modern midfielder: he'll cover box to box all day long, his vision is stunning, his passing accurate and his tackling clinical. What takes him to another level is his incredible stamina and a stunning strike rate whether from his razor-sharp shooting, deadly free-kicks or penetrating runs from deep.

Frank Lampard is regarded as one of the best midfielders in England. Next stop – the World Cup.

THE NATION MAY HAVE A NEW TEENAGE HERO, BUT THE MATURE QUICKSILVER FORWARD IS STILL ENGLAND'S BABY-FACED ASSASSIN

If there is one team in the tournament who understand the true danger of Michael Owen it is Argentina. As a teenage prodigy, he took them on single-handedly; as an established international, he helped knock them out of the World Cup finals; and as a battle-worn forward, he nodded home two late goals to defeat them in the tense match in Geneva in November 2005.

Yet just a few months before that, unceremoniously dumped by Real Madrid, in poor form and overshadowed by the performances of new England idol Wayne Rooney, the No. 10 shirt he had owned for seven years looked under threat.

Owen had left Liverpool in August 2004 with nothing to prove. Consistently among the Premier League's top scorers, he helped Liverpool to the League Cup, FA Cup and UEFA Cup in 2001 and became the first British player for 20 years to win the European Footballer of the Year award. However, Liverpool's inability to make headway in the Champions League finally led to his move to Real Madrid for £8 million.

From being England's youngest ever scorer (a record now held by Rooney), Owen has grown up in the England team. After scoring as a substitute against Romania and netting the goal of the tournament against Argentina in the World Cup in 1998, he was an automatic selection. He became the only player to score in four major tournaments (the 1998 and 2002 World Cups and the 2000 and 2004 European Championships) for England and hit a hat-trick in the 5-1 victory over Germany in 2001. Established as Beckham's deputy captain, he became the youngest skipper

FACT FILE | FORWARD | 75 CAPS | 35 GOALS | NEWCASTLE UNITED

Date of birth: **14.12.1979**
Height: **175 cm**
Weight: **65 kg**
Previous clubs: **Real Madrid, Liverpool**
International debut: **11.02.1998 v Chile**
Previous World Cups: **1998, 2002**

since Bobby Moore in 2002 and regularly steps in if Beckham is absent.

Far from a disaster in Spain (he scored 13 goals with limited opportunities), Owen's return to the Premiership in 2005 – joining Newcastle United for £17 million – nevertheless rejuvenated the striker, though a broken toe in early 2006 might be a major setback.

No wonder England are smiling, once again, his pace, positional sense and lust for goals are clear to see. No defenders will be keen to see his name on England's teamsheet – least of all Argentina's.

STYLE GUIDE

⚽ The combination of raw pace, great positional sense and a clinical finish make Owen the complete forward. His international experience has seen his touch improve markedly and for such a short man he is lethal in the air. Some doubt his ablilty to form a partnership with Rooney, but Owen is a natural goalscorer who can thrive on the creativity of his young team-mate.

'He's a great goalscorer, one of the best in the world. In the big games, he's always there and he's shown that for many years.'

Sven-Goran Eriksson

Goals, goals, goals: Michael Owen is a typical striker, a predator who can appear uninterested in the game, then suddenly get on the end of a half-chance and score.

PARAGUAY

ATTACK IS THE BEST FORM OF DEFENCE

For the *Albirroja* ('white and reds') an ageing but experienced defence has teamed up with a young and hungry strike force in an effort to sustain what is an enviable World Cup record in Germany 2006.

Veteran Uruguayan coach Anibal Ruiz took over the national team after Cesare Maldini (Paulo's father) had led them in the 2002 World Cup finals. It was always going to be a difficult job. Paraguay had also qualified for the finals in 1998 but Japan and Korea represented the last chance for the 'golden generation' of Paraguayan players to bring home the bacon. Legendary stars like Jose Luis Chilavert, Celso Ayala and Francisco Arce retired after the tournament in which the team reached the second round only to be beaten 1-0 by Germany.

When any great team is dismantled there has to be a period of readjustment and results often suffer, but rather than make wholesale changes Ruiz has phased out some of the old guard and brought in some new talent. It is a formula that worked for the notoriously difficult South American World Cup qualifying tournament. Preferring experience in defence, he has chosen Justo Villar to replace Chilavert in goal, while

VITAL STATISTICS

WORLD RANKING 30th   KEEPER AND DEFENCE 4/10
MIDFIELD 5/10   ATTACK 6/10
STRENGTHS AND WEAKNESSES
Paraguay will need to tighten up at the back where their defence was a little leaky during the qualifiers, this will allow their natural attacking tendencies to shine through.
HOW FAR WILL THEY GO?
If Santa Cruz is fit, his goals might take them through to the second round.

Back row (left to right): Roque Santa Cruz, Julio Manzur, Jose De Vaca, Edgar Balbuena, Carlos Bonet, Derlis Gomez. Front row: Angel Ortiz, Cesar Ramirez, Juan Cardoza, Cristian Riveros and Aureliano Torres.

record appearance maker Carlos Gamarra (104 caps) and Julio Cesar Caceres pair up in the centre. It is up front that Ruiz has discovered his new talent. Both main strikers ply their trade in the Bundesliga: Roque Santa Cruz at Bayern Munich and Nelson Haedo Valdez at Werder Bremen. Santa Cruz is a legend among Paraguayan fans for scoring the winner in the 1-0 win over Argentina during the qualifiers, but he has recently sustained a major ligament injury and faces a race to be fit in time for the finals.

Paraguay's berth in the finals was secured with a 1-0 win in Venezuela with a goal from Valdez on the 'Night of Maracaibo' and the team seem to be justified in claiming their place as the 'third' force in South American football behind rivals Brazil and Argentina. England, Trinidad & Tobago and Sweden will soon find out if this claim is valid.

Above left National hero Roque Santa Cruz celebrates the winner against Argentina.

Below left Coach Anibal Riuz in pensive mood.

POSSIBLE SQUAD

Goalkeepers: Justo Villar (Newell's Old Boys), **Derlis Gomez** (Sportivo Luqueno), **Miguel Cardenas** (Nacional)

Defenders: Carlos Gamarra (Palmeiras), **Denis Caniza** (Cruz Azul), **Julio Cesar Caceres** (Atletico Mineiro), **Juan Daniel Caceres** (Estudiantes), **Jorge Nunez** (Racing Club), **Paulo Da Silva** (Toluca)

Midfielders: Carlos Paredes (Reggina), **Edgar Barreto** (NEC Nijmegen), **Cristian Riveros** (Libertad), **Julio Dos Santos** (Cerro Porteno), **Roberto Acuna** (Deportivo La Coruna), **Domingo Salcedo** (Cerro Porteno), **Diego Galivan** (Internacional), **Cristian Riveros** (Libertad)

Forwards: Roque Santa Cruz (Bayern Munich), **Jose Cardozo** (San Lorenzo), **Nelson Haedo Valdez** (Werder Bremen), **Salvador Cabanas** (Chiapas), **Cesar Ramirez** (Cerro Porteno), **Nelson Cuevas** (Pachuca)

SOUTH AMERICA QUALIFYING GROUP – FINAL TABLE							
TEAM	P	W	D	L	F	A	Pts
BRAZIL	18	9	7	2	35	17	**34**
ARGENTINA	18	10	4	4	29	17	**34**
ECUADOR	18	8	4	6	23	19	**28**
PARAGUAY	18	8	4	6	23	23	**28**
URUGUAY	18	6	7	5	23	28	**25**
COLOMBIA	18	6	6	6	24	16	**24**
CHILE	18	5	7	6	18	22	**22**
VENEZUELA	18	5	3	10	20	28	**18**
PERU	18	4	6	8	20	28	**18**
BOLIVIA	18	4	2	12	20	37	**14**

FINALS GROUP B			
	PARAGUAY	Date	Venue
	England	10 June	Frankfurt
	Sweden	15 June	Berlin
	Trinidad & Tobago	20 June	Kaiserslautern

TRINIDAD & TOBAGO

WIN OR LOSE, THE SOCA WARRIORS AIM TO MAKE A MARK IN GERMANY

One of the lowest ranked teams in the competition certain to be among the bookies' absolute outsiders, yet Trinidad & Tobago vow to play with a smile and promise to bring the most colourful and noisy fans to Germany.

When the Soca Warriors triumphed in the last of their 20-match qualification marathon – the longest route of any of the finalists – the nation of just over one million people went bananas. Not so long before, the finals had been beyond their dreams, but three men – all long in the tooth – engineered an incredible turnaround.

VITAL STATISTICS

WORLD RANKING 50th= **KEEPER AND DEFENCE** 5/10
MIDFIELD 5/10 **ATTACK** 4/10
STRENGTHS AND WEAKNESSES
They'll be organised and look for a break, but their stars are veterans and the squad is weak.
HOW FAR WILL THEY GO?
Just one victory will be enough to send the island partying in the streets again.

Three games into their final qualification stage, Trinidad and Tobago were lying bottom of their group. Then newly appointed coach 63-year-old Dutchman Leo Beenhakker, former Manchester United hero, Dwight Yorke, and veteran Russell Latapy, the inspirational figure of Trinidadian football, came together. T & T went on to win four of their last five qualifiers and a play-off with Bahrain where, despite a 1-1 draw in the Caribbean, a headed goal from Dennis Lawrence in the Gulf state saw them win 1-0 and sent the islanders into ecstasy.

Beenhakker, who has taken Ajax and Real Madrid to league titles and coached Holland in the 1990 World Cup, has brought discipline and organisation to his limited resources.

Left Veteran coach Leo Beenhakker has been a calm presence on the bench throughout the qualifiers.

Far left Ian Cox (left) and Chris Birchall leap on Russell Latapy after their play-off victory over Bahrain.

Players from the British leagues dominate the team. Shaka Hislop takes the goalkeeping duties, with Rangers' Marvin Andrews and Wrexham's Dennis Lawrence in front of him. In midfield Chris Birchall – the first white man to play for T & T – looks after Dwight Yorke, now the team's captain and playmaker. Small, slight and incredibly skilful, Russell Lapaty had been the team's star for over a decade, but had retired from international football in 2001. At 37, now player-coach at Falkirk, Beenhakker brought him back to the fold as a player and assistant coach and his experience and guile have proved invaluable. Alongside him, Derby's Stern John provides the striker's touch and he'll be the man most likely to score their first World Cup goal.

T & T are desperate to do their country proud and a prize draw against England has made them more excited. They may not win a game but people are going to remember when the Soca Warriors came to the finals.

Back row (left to right): Marvin Andrews, John Avery, Kelvin Jack, Chris Birchall, Dwight Yorke, Dennis Lawrence. Front row: Carlos Edwards, Silvio Spann, Aurtis Whitley, Russell Latapy and Stern John.

POSSIBLE SQUAD

Goalkeepers: Kelvin Jack (Dundee), **Shaka Hislop** (West Ham United), **Tony Warner** (Fulham)

Defenders: Dennis Lawrence (Wrexham), **Marvin Andrews** (Rangers), **Cyd Gray** (San Juan Jabloteh), **John Avery** (New England Revolution), **Brent Sancho** (Gillingham), **Ian Cox** (Gillingham), **David Atiba Charles** (W Connection)

Midfielders: Silvio Spann (Yokohama), **Densill Theobald** (Caledonia AIA Fire), **Christopher Birchall** (Port Vale), **Carlos Edwards** (Luton Town), **Anthony Wolfe** (North East Stars), **Aurtis Whitley** (San Juan Jabloteh), **Dwight Yorke** (Sydney FC)

Forwards: Jason Scotland (St Johnstone), **Scott Sealy** (Kansas City Wizards), **Stern John** (Derby County), **Cornell Glen** (Columbus Crew), **Russell Latapy** (Falkirk), **Kenwyne Jones** (Southampton)

PLAY-OFFS

DATE		
12.11.05	TRINIDAD & TOBAGO 1	1 BAHRAIN
16.11.05	BAHRAIN 0	1 TRINIDAD & TOBAGO

Trinidad & Tobago won 2-1 on aggregate

CONCACAF FINAL STAGE – FINAL TABLE

TEAM	P	W	D	L	F	A	Pts
USA	10	7	1	2	16	6	22
MEXICO	10	7	1	2	22	9	22
COSTA RICA	10	5	1	4	14	16	16
TRINIDAD & TOBAGO	10	4	1	5	10	15	13
GUATEMALA	10	3	2	5	16	18	11
PANAMA	10	0	2	8	4	21	2

FINALS GROUP B

		Date	Venue
	TRINIDAD & TOBAGO		
	Sweden	10 June	Dortmund
	England	15 June	Nuremberg
	Paraguay	20 June	Kaiserslautern

SWEDEN

EXPOSING THE SECRET SWEDES

Quietly, Sweden have been building a side capable of taking on the best in the world. But you can't keep a world-class attack secret forever ...

Excitement is mounting in a Scandinavian country not known for heady emotion. Throughout the World Cup qualifiers their yellow-and-blue heroes have been getting better and better – some supporters are beginning to believe they have one of their best teams ever.

Considered unlucky in both the 2002 World Cup (defeat to Senegal in extra-time) and the 2004 Euro Finals (beaten on penalties by Holland in the quarter-finals), Sweden look an even better prospect this time round. Co-coaches Lars Lagerback and Roland Andersson have maintained the solidity of the team, but with the blossoming talent of Zlatan Ibrahimovic, have been able to add a sharper cutting edge.

Apart from reaching the 1958 Final on home soil, Sweden's best World Cup was in the USA in 1994 when they came third inspired by Tomas Brolin, Martin Dahlin and Kennet Andersson. Ten years on and comparisons are being made with Freddie Ljungberg, Henrik Larsson and Ibrahimovic – a quality trio who between them carry Sweden's hopes into this year's competition.

HEADS DOWN, NO-NONSENSE

From a 7-0 hammering of Malta to a 3-1 dismissal of Iceland, Sweden's road to the finals was paved with goals. Only Croatia stood in the way of the men in yellow-and-blue, everyone else was swept aside in a series of impressive performances. Averaging over three goals a game, Sweden forced their way into the FIFA World top ten rankings for the first time. Clearly, a team on the up, the big question remains whether they can perform against the top nations. Their two defeats – however close – to Croatia have left many wondering ...

Henrik Larsson (centre) has had a superb club career with Celtic and Barcelona, now it's time for him to find success on the world stage.

Markus Rosenberg of Ajax may well get a chance to impress up front if given a run-out from the bench.

Freddie Ljungberg will need to be at his best if Sweden are to progress against top quality opposition.

VITAL STATISTICS

Fotboll
SVENSKA FÖRBUNDET

WORLD RANKING 14th

KEEPER AND DEFENCE 7/10

MIDFIELD 6/10

ATTACK 8/10

STRENGTHS AND WEAKNESSES

Solid at the back, dangerous up front, but will they create enough chances against tough opposition?

HOW FAR WILL THEY GO?

A lucky draw has seen them confident of a quarter-final place and a shot at real glory.

HOW THEY'LL LINE-UP

Despite some disappointments the coaches have kept faith with their players and have been rewarded with some burgeoning talent. Rugged and well-organised at the back, they are a hard nut to crack; but it is in their attacking wing-play and red-hot strikeforce that they really pack a punch.

Still only 25, excellent stopper Andreas Isaksson has occupied the No. 1 spot for four years now and grows in confidence and reputation. He is supported by a defence that has played together since the World Cup. Led by the captain, Aston Villa centre half Olof Mellberg and featuring former Spurs' full back Erik Edman, the experienced Teddy Lucic and Feyenoord's Alexander Ostlund, the tight unit conceded only four goals in the qualifiers.

Marshalled by the tough, but forward-looking, Anders Svensson in the holding position, the midfield contains a potent attacking force in the thundering left-foot shot of Kim Kallstrom, the familiar threat of Freddie Ljungberg on the left and young star Christian Wilhelmsson.

Strikers Larsson and Ibrahimovic will strike fear into any defence – both have proved in the Champions League and at Euro 2004 that they can perform at the highest level. But keep an eye on Ajax's impressive goalscorer Markus Rosenberg if he gets a run from the bench.

POSSIBLE SQUAD

Goalkeepers: Andreas Isaksson (Stade Rennes), **Eddie Gustafsson** (Ham-Kam), **John Alvbage** (Viborg)

Defenders: Christoffer Andersson (Lillestrom), **Mikael Nilsson** (Panathinaikos), **Erik Edman** (Stade Rennes), **Petter Hansson** (Heerenveen), **Teddy Lucic** (BK Hacken), **Olof Mellberg** (Aston Villa), **Alexander Ostlund** (Feyenoord)

Midfielders: Niclas Alexandersson (IFK Gothenburg), **Daniel Andersson** (Malmo), **Kim Kallstrom** (Stade Rennes), **Tobias Linderoth** (FC Copenhagen), **Fredrik Ljungberg** (Arsenal), **Anders Svensson** (Elfsborg), **Christian Wilhelmsson** (Anderlecht)

Forwards: Marcus Allback (FC Copenhagen), **Johan Elmander** (Brondby), **Zlatan Ibrahimovic** (Juventus), **Mattias Jonson** (Djurgardens), **Henrik Larsson** (Barcelona), **Markus Rosenberg** (Ajax)

Back row (left to right): Teddy Lukic, Olof Mellberg, Zlatan Ibrahimoviic, Alexander Ostlund, Henrik Larsson. Front row: Erik Edman, Christian Wilhelmsson, Tobias Linderoth, Andreas Isaksson, Anders Svensson and Freddie Ljungberg.

ONE TO WATCH
Christian Wilhelmsson

Anderlect's dynamic wide man has been attracting scouts from the big-money clubs. At 26, he's something of a late developer, but over the past two seasons he has emerged as a genuinely dangerous attacking midfielder on either flank. With a style compared to his compatriot Ljungberg,

Although he made his international debut in 2001 Wilhelmsson only established himself in the run up to Euro 2004. He is now a regular member of the squad.

he has great control, likes to get forward and brings crowds to their feet with his dangerous mazy runs at defenders.

COACH
Lars Lagerback
(born 16 July 1948)
Record: P86 W38 D30 L18

After a modest playing career Lars Lagerback began international coaching in 1980, slowly working his way up the ranks from junior level to national team assistant coach until in 1999, national first-team coach Tommy Soderberg asked him to become his partner. Conventional wisdom suggests that two men cannot be in charge of a football team, but it seemed to work for them and together they took Sweden to Euro 2000, the World Cup in 2002 and Euro 2004. When Soderberg stepped down after Portugal, former player Roland Andersson

soon stepped up as assistant coach, and the new partnership have taken the yellow-and-blues to Germany conceding only four goals in the process. In the new team Lagerback is said to be the thinker who looks after tactics, while Andersson has a more hands-on role with the players.

In leading Sweden to Germany 2006, Lagerback has helped his country qualify for four consecutive finals.

ROUTE TO THE FINALS		
DATE		
04.09.04	MALTA **0**	**7** SWEDEN
08.09.04	SWEDEN **0**	**1** CROATIA
09.10.04	SWEDEN **3**	**0** HUNGARY
13.10.04	ICELAND **1**	**4** SWEDEN
26.03.05	BULGARIA **0**	**3** SWEDEN
04.06.05	SWEDEN **6**	**0** MALTA
03.09.05	SWEDEN **3**	**0** BULGARIA
07.09.05	HUNGARY **0**	**1** SWEDEN
08.10.05	CROATIA **1**	**0** SWEDEN
12.10.05	SWEDEN **3**	**0** ICELAND

EUROPE QUALIFYING GROUP 8 – FINAL TABLE							
TEAM	P	W	D	L	F	A	Pts
CROATIA	10	7	3	0	21	5	**24**
SWEDEN	10	8	0	2	30	4	**24**
BULGARIA	10	4	3	3	17	17	**15**
HUNGARY	10	4	2	4	13	14	**14**
ICELAND	10	1	1	8	14	27	**4**
MALTA	10	0	3	7	4	32	**3**

FINALS GROUP B		
SWEDEN	Date	Venue
Trinidad & Tobago	10 June	Dortmund
Paraguay	15 June	Berlin
England	20 June	Cologne

Zlatan IBRAHIMOVIC

THE RED-HOT 'YELLOW-AND-BLUE'

When, in the tense Euro 2004 tie against Italy, Ibrahimovic back-heeled a volley over the head of Christian Vieri and into an empty net, many dismissed the audacious chip as a fluke. Those who had watched the player develop at Malmo and Ajax knew better – the world would soon know about Zlatan.

Two years later, the Swedish son of Bosnian immigrants now stands as one of world's top stars. 'Zlatan is Sweden's Zorro', wrote the newspaper *Svenska Dagbladet* and so many of the hopes of the country seem stacked upon his shoulders. Eight goals in the qualifiers, top scorer in 2004–05 – his first season for Juventus – with 16 goals, Sweden have found a natural successor to Larsson – and Henrik is still there alongside him!

Under the colours of Ajax, Ibrahimovic often attracted more attention for his

Although he's a big man, Ibrahimovic posesses incredible skills with the ball at his feet.

'He is the greatest talent I have ever seen. And I have watched Tomas Brolin and Fredrik Ljungberg closely when they started. Zlatan has everything. He has the physique, the speed and the technique. If he has decided to win a fight over the ball, he does it.'

Lars Lagerback, Swedish coach

FACT FILE | STRIKER | 21 CAPS | 17 GOALS | JUVENTUS

Date of birth: **03.10.1981**
Height: **192 cm**
Weight: **84 kg**
Previous clubs: **Ajax, Malmo, FBK Balkan**
International debut: **10.11.2001 v England**
Previous World Cups: **2002**

STYLE GUIDE

⚽ Often compared to the great Marco van Basten, his height (1.92 m) and touch create an immediate impression. The *Observer* described Ibrahimovic as a Swedish Kanu: 'outrageously skilful with a full range of jinks, turns and backheels.' Big, strong, skilful and fast, Zlatan has proved in Italy he has all the qualities of a great striker.

temperament and off-the-field antics – some saying he has an ego the size of Stockholm – than his performances. But his developing talent was enough to attract interest from Arsène Wenger and for Ajax manager Ronald Koeman to nurture his wayward charge.

Word began to spread and soon after that impudent strike in Portugal, Juventus splashed out €16 million on the imposing centre forward. Battling for a starting place with David Trezeguet and Alessandro Del Piero, he settled into Serie A with amazing ease. The way he applied flair and self-discipline surprised even seasoned Zlatan fans and – scoring seemingly at will – he was voted the Scudetto winners' player of the year.

His leading role in the national side is now assured, although he is still dogged by a bad relationship with the Swedish press and, it is rumoured, with some of the senior players. But, while the team will never have

the arrogance of Zlatan himself, his emergence has given them a real belief that they can make a mark in Germany.

ARGENTINA

DON'T CRY FOR US

With one of their most talented squads for many years, Argentina can't afford another early exit from a competition they are desperate to win.

Olympic gold medallists in 2004, first qualifiers in the tough South American group and a strong showing in last year's Confederation Cup inevitably positions Argentina, once again, among the favourites to win the World Cup. Having had similar expectations in the last two tournaments, only to come unstuck fairly early, they will be hoping the stars who have endured an injury-dogged season – Roberto Ayala, Gabriel Heinze and Javier Mascherano – recover and key players such as Riquelme, Saviola, Crespo and Tevez produce their best at the right time.

Above *Argentina celebrate winning gold at the Athens Olympics in 2004 after beating Paraguay 1-0 in the Final with a goal from Carlos Tevez.*

Opposite *Juan Roman Riquelme looks delighted after scoring his team's second goal against Brazil during their World Cup qualifier at the Monumental in Buenos Aires on 8 June 2005. Joining him are Javier Mascherano (centre) and Juan Pablo Sorin (right).*

THE FABULOUS PEKER-BOYS

The style and success of Argentina's Under-20 team earned them a nickname – 'The Fabulous Peker-Boys'. So when coach Jose Pekerman took over the senior side it surprised no one to see many of them step up a level. What has amazed fans is the quality of Pekerman's production line that has consistently produced star performers from the likes of Fabricio Coloccini (aged 24), Mario Santana (23), Javier Mascherano (21), Javier Saviola (24), Carlos Tevez (21) and Cesar Delgado (24) to the latest sensation, 18-year-old Lionel Messi.

IDEAL PREPARATION

With Argentina winning gold at the Athens Olympics and riding high in the FIFA World Cup qualifiers, it was a complete surprise when manager Marcelo Bielsa resigned. The baton was, controversially, passed to Jose Pekerman who, despite criticism, masterfully chopped and changed his team to an

easy passage to Germany. To the delight of the fans, they secured their finals place, with three matches to spare, in a stylish and emphatic 3-1 victory over Brazil in Buenos Aires. Argentina then travelled to Germany for the FIFA Confederations Cup, where despite Brazil gaining revenge in the Final, they showed enough to issue a warning to the rest of the World Cup finalists.

HOW THEY'LL LINE UP
Throughout the squad, Argentina has quality established performers and exciting young

Fabricio Coloccini shields the ball from Brazil's Adriano during their World Cup qualifier.

GREAT MATCH

1986	ARGENTINA 2-1 ENGLAND

WORLD CUP QUARTER-FINAL
Azteca Stadium, Mexico City

Coming just four years after the Falklands War, *this match took on incredible significance with the defeated Argentinians battling for a nation's pride. And so it appeared as the match got underway with Beardsley and Lineker being tightly marked and Maradona eclipsing the quiet Hoddle in midfield. Despite failing to get a shot at goal, England reached half time on equal terms.*

The second-half was only six minutes old when Hodge sliced a clearance into his own penalty area. The two captains – Maradona and Shilton – contested the ball and amazingly the pint-sized genius seemed to outjump the towering keeper and the ball bounced towards the empty net. The whole stadium was fooled, only TV replays and Shilton knew Maradona had punched the ball. Four minutes later, the Argentinian hero created and scored one of the greatest World Cup goals ever, picking up the ball near the halfway line and going past three tackles before selling Shilton a dummy.

England attempted to rally, sending Waddle and Barnes on and the latter provided a great run

and cross for Lineker to nod in. Then in the dying minutes, he repeated the feat. This time, just as Lineker seemed poise to equalise, a defender pushed the ball away. Argentina celebrated madly, Maradona proclaimed the 'Hand of God' and the world realised that football had found a new king.

Back row (left to right): Juan Pablo Sorin, Roberto Abbondanzieri, Javier Zanetti, Roberto Ayala, Juan Roman Riquelme and Gabriel Heinze. Front row: Luis Gonzalez, Javier Saviola, Hernan Crespo, Esteban Cambiasso and Javier Mascherano before the World Cup qualifier against Colombia.

stars who just might take their chance. In defence, captain Juan Pablo Sorin is a tireless attacking left back, Javier Zanetti has over 100 caps, Ayala has been acknowledged as one of the finest central defenders in Europe, Walter Samuel has strengthened Real Madrid's leaking backline and, before his injury, Gabriel Heinze was looking like a world-class defender for Manchester United. Waiting in the wings are the likes of Deportivo's Coloccini, quick, skillful and tough as nails.

Their midfield looks equally formidable. In Mascherano, they possess one of the best holding players in the world, playmaker Riquelme is stylish and a true orchestrator, box to box, Esteban Cambiasso is the ideal disrupter and Tevez is a true magician with his slalom runs and great finishing.

Up front Hernan Crespo seems invigorated by his Chelsea exile and

subsequent return while Villarreal's Luciano Figueroa proved his finishing ability at the Confederations Cup.

POSSIBLE SQUAD

Goalkeepers: Roberto Abbondanzieri (Boca Juniors), **German Lux** (River Plate), **Franco Leonardo** (Atletico Madrid)

Defenders: Juan Pablo Sorin (Villarreal), **Roberto Ayala** (Valencia), **Diego Placente** (Celta Vigo), **Walter Samuel** (Inter Milan), **Martin Demichelis** (Bayern Munich), **Javier Zanetti** (Inter Milan), **Aldo Duscher** (Deportivo La Coruna), **Fabricio Coloccini** (Deportivo La Coruna)

Midfielders: Pablo Aimar (Valencia), **Juan Roman Riquelme** (Villarreal), **Cristian Gonzalez** (Inter Milan), **Mario Santana** (Palermo), **Javier Mascherano** (Corinthians), **Esteban Cambiasso** (Inter Milan)

Forwards: Hernan Crespo (Chelsea), **Luciano Figueroa** (Villarreal), **Lionel Messi** (Barcelona), **Cesar Delgado** (Cruz Azul), **Carlos Tevez** (Corinthians), **Javier Saviola** (Barcelona)

RIQUELME
SAMUEL
MASHERANO
AYALA
TEVEZ
ABBONDANZIERI
COLOCCINI
CRESPO
CAMBIASSO
ZANNETTI
SORÍN

VITAL STATISTICS

WORLD RANKING 4th   **KEEPER AND DEFENCE** 7/10   **MIDFIELD** 8/10   **ATTACK** 8/10

STRENGTHS AND WEAKNESSES

Pekerman's squad has experience, youth, tenacity, skill and strength in depth. However, he is still to settle on a regular keeper, and with defenders coming back from serious injuries, there could be a fissure at the back.

HOW FAR WILL THEY GO?

Nothing less than the semi-finals will do or they'll be some explaining required back home.

ONE TO WATCH

Lionel Messi

The latest in a line of 'new Maradonas' – could he be the real thing? Voted best player in the 2005 FIFA World Youth Championship, Lionel Messi – at only 18 – almost single-handedly took his country's Under-20 side to a fifth world title. A six-goal tally in the tournament belied his other attributes as a superb playmaker with technical skills, reminiscent of another diminutive Argentinian No. 10 – Diego Armando Maradona.

Having lived in Spain since he was 13, Messi had no hesitation in signing for Barcelona, making his debut for them at the age of 16, and then – at just 17 years, ten months and seven days – he became the youngest league scorer in the club's history. At 18, after becoming

his country's latest football darling, he came on as a substitute against Hungary for his debut, but he was sent off after just two minutes!

Manager Pekerman refuses to get over-excited saying, 'We're not going to see him as some kind of saviour. We just want to set him off on a journey which we're sure will turn out to be very good.' But the clamour is rising for a young man, who, given the chance, might just set the tournament alight.

COACH

Jose Nestor Pekerman

(born 3 September 1949)

Record: P18 W9 D5 L4

'He's never ever coached a club or a senior team in his life. How on earth can he lead our *Albiceleste* ['light blue and whites'] to the World Cup 2006?' Diego Maradona wasted no time in dismissing the former taxi driver and ice-cream salesman appointed Argentinian coach. Yet Pekerman does have considerable experience – eight years as a player at senior level, and seven years in charge of Argentina's national youth team. On three occasions – 1995, 1997 and 2001 – the 56-year-old guided the Under-20 team to the World Championship title. On taking over the senior side he showed he wasn't scared to drop big names, such as Veron, Samuel and Gonzalez, to make way for the talented new generation but equally he won over senior players like Zanetti, Crespo and his new captain, Sorin. The nation's huge footballing expectations are Pekerman's biggest problem, but if he brings home the big one, Maradona and the other carpers will be forced to eat some humble pie.

Coach Jose Pekerman (right) explains how its done to squad player Leandro Curfe. Pekerman has the confidence of the players, but will it be enough to get the best out of his talented squad?

SOUTH AMERICA QUALIFYING GROUP – FINAL TABLE							
TEAM	P	W	D	L	F	A	Pts
BRAZIL	18	9	7	2	35	17	**34**
ARGENTINA	18	10	4	4	29	17	**34**
ECUADOR	18	8	4	6	23	19	**28**
PARAGUAY	18	8	4	6	23	23	**28**
URUGUAY	18	6	7	5	23	28	**25**
COLOMBIA	18	6	6	6	24	16	**24**
CHILE	18	5	7	6	18	22	**22**
VENEZUELA	18	5	3	10	20	28	**18**
PERU	18	4	6	8	20	28	**18**
BOLIVIA	18	4	2	12	20	37	**14**

FINALS GROUP C

	Team	Date	Venue
	ARGENTINA	Date	Venue
	Ivory Coast	10 June	Hamburg
	Serbia & Montenegro	16 June	Gelsenkirchen
	Holland	21 June	Frankfurt

ROUTE TO THE FINALS

DATE			
06.09.03	ARGENTINA 2	2 CHILE
09.09.03	VENEZUELA 0	3 ARGENTINA
15.11.03	ARGENTINA 3	0 BOLIVIA
19.11.03	COLOMBIA 1	1 ARGENTINA
30.03.04	ARGENTINA 1	0 ECUADOR
02.06.04	BRAZIL 3	1 ARGENTINA
06.06.04	ARGENTINA 0	0 PARAGUAY
04.09.04	PERU 1	3 ARGENTINA
09.10.04	ARGENTINA 4	2 URUGUAY
13.10.04	CHILE 0	0 ARGENTINA
17.11.04	ARGENTINA 3	2 VENEZUELA
26.03.05	BOLIVIA 1	2 ARGENTINA
30.03.05	ARGENTINA 1	0 COLOMBIA
04.06.05	ECUADOR 2	0 ARGENTINA
08.06.05	ARGENTINA 3	1 BRAZIL
03.09.05	PARAGUAY 1	0 ARGENTINA
09.10.05	ARGENTINA 2	0 PERU
12.10.05	URUGUAY 1	0 ARGENTINA

What a feeling? Roberto Abbondanzieri (left), Javier Zanetti (No. 4) and captain Juan Pablo Sorin celebrate their 3-1 win over Brazil.

Javier MASCHERANO

TOUGH, HARD WORKING AND DISCIPLINED, 'THE LITTLE CHIEF' IS A SURPRISING ARGENTINIAN HERO

'Of all the youngsters to have come through in recent years, the one who impresses me most is Javier Mascherano.' That the great Maradona chose to single out, not a silky playmaker or a clinical finisher, but a biting midfield ranger who cites Edgar Davids and Patrick Vieira as his heroes, just added to the lustre on the 21-year-old.

A key member of the national side since his debut against Uruguay in 2003 and a star of the Confederations Cup, 'Jefecito' ('little chief') was expected to underline his reputation in Germany. So it came as a thundering blow to Pekerman's World Cup preparations when it was

> ### 'He is a monster of a player and destined for great things.'
> Diego Maradona

revealed that Mascherano was to miss the second half of 2005 after having surgery on his left foot.

Not that his career has ever followed the usual lines. First coming to attention in the national Under-17 side, he progressed with stunning notices through the Under-20 set up and into the senior team before making his debut with River Plate. Even after winning gold with the *Albiceleste* in Athens, he still found himself warming the bench for his club side.

And so Mascherano found himself at the centre of one of South American football's

Precocious talent? Mascherano played for the national team before making his club debut.

FACT FILE | DEFENSIVE MIDFIELDER | 12 CAPS | 0 GOALS | CORINTHIANS

Date of birth: **08.06.1984**
Height: **171 cm**
Weight: **66 kg**
Previous club: **River Plate**
International debut: **16.07.2003 v Uruguay**
Previous World Cups: **None**

STYLE GUIDE

Singled out for his maturity of play, sense of position and natural leadership, Mascherano has also been known to wield the hatchet with a predilection for a crunching tackle. But he is also a supremely gifted footballer and one of the hardest-working players around.

most intriguing transfer deals. He – along with fellow Argentinians Carlos Tevez and Sebastian Dominguez – signed, not for one of the rich European sides expressing interest, but for the Brazilian team Corinthians. The adventure had started out pretty badly with Corinthians struggling to gain results when Mascherano revealed his injury. Nevertheless, it didn't discourage the likes of Milan, Chelsea and Arsenal keeping tabs on the steely midfield dynamo.

Those who have watched his progress and appreciate the determined character of the quiet man, have little doubt that he will make a full recovery. And, if he returns to the kind of form he has showed over the past couple of seasons, even the buy-out clause of $150 million that Corinthians wrote into his contract, might not keep the likes of Roman Abramovich away.

A SHORT, STOCKY AND SKILFUL NO. 10 IN A BLUE-AND-WHITE STRIPED SHIRT – WHERE HAVE WE SEEN THAT BEFORE?

2004 was some year for 20-year-old Carlos Tevez. He helped Argentina win the South American Olympic qualifying tournament, and inspired Boca Juniors to the Final of the Copa Libertadores and to the Copa Sudamericana title. At the Copa America, he impressed press and public alike despite the *Albiceleste*'s heartbreaking Final defeat to Brazil on penalties.

In August the rest of the world discovered 'Carlito' as his fabulous performances and eight goals in six games helped Argentina win their first ever Olympic gold. Finally he was voted South American player of the year for the second year running. It seemed he had the world at his highly-prized feet.

'He's not only the best striker in Argentina, but the best striker in the world today.'

Antonio Lopes, Corinthians coach

Like many before him, Tevez was quickly given the 'new Maradona' label. But for once the comparisons run deeper than a well-filled shirt. Like Maradona, Tevez is from a tough barrio of Buenos Aires – Fuerte Apache – and endured a childhood of poverty and hunger. And, he too is finding the obsessive intrusions of the Argentine press hard to bear.

His year of glory ended with fights with photographers, a pregnant ex-girlfriend and coach Jose Pekerman insisting 'he should be

Barrel-chested and with a low centre of gravity, football fans will marvel at Tevez's skills in Germany.

 **FACT FILE** | ATTACKING MIDFIELDER | 17 CAPS | 2 GOALS  | CORINTHIANS

Date of birth: **05.02.1984**
Height: **168 cm**
Weight: **67 kg**
Previous clubs: **Boca Juniors**
International debut: **30.03.2004 v Ecuador**
Previous World Cups: **None**

more professional,' before dropping him from the Argentina squad for the last competitive match of the year against Venezuela. 2005 found 'Apache' (a nickname that reiterates his pride in his roots) leaving Boca Juniors for Brazilian club Corinthians in a record fee for a South American transfer deal ($20 million) and claiming 'I feel like I've been thrown out of my own country.'

Life in Brazil saw him fare little better – sendings off, outbursts at referees, fights with team-mates, even wearing a Manchester United shirt to a press conference, events that saw him in the headlines for the wrong reasons. Yet amidst all this his talent shone through and by the time the Confederations Cup in Germany

came around in June, Tevez was back in the side, and playing well.

Carlos Tevez is a player who can make goals, score goals and win games, but he can also make trouble, upset the dressing room and lose his temper. Can Pekerman risk playing him, or can he simply not afford to leave him out?

STYLE GUIDE

⚽ A short and stocky figure wearing the blue and white striped No. 10 shirt, endowed with superb dribbling skills complete with explosive bursts, tight ball control and top class finishing – Tevez is like a Maradona clone. But will Carlito share Diego's ability to shine on the world stage?

Hernan CRESPO

THERE'S NO SUBSTITUTE FOR TALENT

If Hernan Crespo finally makes Argentina's World Cup team sheet this time, defenders better beware; he is a man making up for lost time. Despite making his debut for the national side in 1995 and becoming a major star with his club River Plate, he was overlooked for the 1998 World Cup. Then, having led his country to the 2002 World Cup in Japan and Korea with nine goals during their South American qualifying campaign, he found himself playing back-up to the ageing Batistuta.

In the qualifiers for the 2006 tournament, the athletic forward has at last managed to get a foothold in the team. His chances of staying there may depend on making the first eleven for Chelsea – in a battle with Didier Drogba for the lone striker spot.

'I don't feel like I've booked my place for the World Cup yet. Experience tells me that right up until the last moment nobody gives you any presents.'

The £16 million signing disappointed in his first spell at Stamford Bridge (2003–04) and was packed off to AC Milan on loan for the following season. There, he soon found his goal touch again, eleven league goals and six in the Champions League, including two to help knock out Manchester United and two more in the tournament's astonishing Final against Liverpool which ended 3-3 and was eventually settled on penalties. It seemed he was destined to stay at Milan, but negotiations

FACT FILE | STRIKER | 55 CAPS | 28 GOALS | CHELSEA

Date of birth: **05.07.1975**
Height: **184 cm**
Weight: **78 kg**
Previous clubs: **River Plate, Parma, Lazio, Inter Milan, AC Milan (loan)**
International debut: **14.02.1995 v Bulgaria**
Previous World Cups: **1998, 2002**

stalled, and Crespo found himself back at the Bridge.

Those who have watched the lethal marksman over the years were not surprised to find him sharper and working hard to improve his English game. He takes a while to settle, but when he does... His first European club, Parma, were initially disappointed with his goal tally. Then, in the 1998–99 season, he fired in 28 goals. In 2000, he became the most expensive player in the world when Lazio paid £36.5 million for him. Again, he initially struggled to live up to his price-tag, but finished the season as Serie A's top scorer. Another big money move found him at Inter, but injuries ravaged his season and when Abramovich offered a way out both parties grabbed at it.

And so Crespo began the 2005–06 season back in blue, scoring a 90th-minute winner against Wigan Athletic on the opening day of the campaign. Once again the striker – who has proved himself time and time again – forced people to sit up and take notice. Not too different from the situation he might find himself in Germany, as Pekerman and the world wait to see what he is made of.

Crespo's talents do not lie in his pace or his stamina but in his timing and movement. A place in the starting line-up in Germany will undoubtedly bring the best out of him.

STYLE GUIDE

⚽ **Crespo is one of the most lethal finishers on the planet. Deadly with either foot and with his head, Crespo doesn't rely on pace or tricks, but on a sense of timing and position – arriving at the right spot at the right time. His big match temperament is second to none, scoring in his only World Cup appearance and grabbing two in the 2005 Champions League Final.**

Javier **ZANETTI**

THE ORIGINAL WING-BACK AND NOW ARGENTINA'S MOST-CAPPED PLAYER

For over ten years Javier Zanetti has been ploughing his furrow up and down the San Siro – little surprise he is referred to as 'The Tractor'. Still only in his early 30s, it seems that Zanetti, a veteran of the 1998 and 2002 World Cups, has been wearing Argentina's blue and white forever.

Strong and determined, Zanetti is a fearsome opponent. Despite being in his early 30s he shows no sign of slowing down and is as eager as always to get forward as soon as he wins the ball.

In 2005's Confederation Cup in Germany, having just been named by Pelé as one of the 125 greatest living footballers, Zanetti went on to put in a series of performances that made him one of the players of the tournament and in the process earned his 100th cap for the *Albiceleste* in the semi-final against Mexico.

When Zanetti arrived at the San Siro in 1995 having joined Italian giants Inter Milan from Argentinian outfit Banfield, few knew of the slender defender. But soon his combination of talent, reliability and hard work won over the Inter fans. In 1997 Mr Reliable was made captain and – having

'The best full back I've come up against in the Champions League. He's quick, he's tough, he's strong ... but he's also very experienced. He's a very difficult opponent because he keeps bombing forward, which makes you work extra hard.'
Ryan Giggs

FACT FILE | DEFENDER | 106 CAPS | 6 GOALS | INTER MILAN

Date of birth: **10.08.1973**
Height: **178 cm**
Weight: **75 kg**
Previous clubs: **Banfield, Atletico Talleres**
International debut: **16.11.1994 v Chile**
Previous World Cups: **1998, 2002**

STYLE GUIDE

⚽ Originally a traditional full back, Zanetti's speed and stamina enabled him to overlap into threatening positions. Soon, for club and country, he was proving as effective an attacking force as he was a defender – terrorizing opponents with well-timed runs, incisive passes and pin-point crosses. He was the prototype wing-back, a position soon copied throughout Europe but rarely as effectively as executed by the Tractor.

turned down offers from Real Madrid and Barcelona – he now stands unchallenged as the club's talisman and one of its finest ambassadors.

Making his international debut against Chile in 1994, Zanetti was a member of the Argentina side that won the silver medal at Olympic football tournament at Atlanta in 1996 and was a fixture in the team by the time the 1998 World Cup finals in France came around. His goal in the memorable match against England, though overshadowed by Michael Owen's wonder strike, was the result of a masterfully worked free-kick and a clinical finish.

Despite some reasonable personal performances, Zanetti was as disappointed as his team-mates with Argentina's poor showing in Japan and Korea in 2002. Yet, typically for Argentina's record appearance-maker, he pulled on the blue and white shirt again and helped them stroll through the qualifying competition for 2006.

In Germany, alongside a new generation of stars, he will find himself with one last chance of World Cup glory – and a realistic one at that.

VISION, FLAIR, SKILL, ROMI HAS EVERYTHING – EVEN CRITICS

It's a strange irony that 'Romi' finds himself heading for Germany as the lynchpin of the Argentina World Cup plan. Four years ago, as the darling of La Bombonera wowed his nation's fans, coach Marcelo Bielsa left him out of the squad for Japan and Korea claiming he was 'too slow'.

'Nearly everything he does is perfect, he hardly makes a mistake. That is something special.'

Jurgen Klinsmann

Germany 2006 will provide a world stage on which Riquelme, one of its brightest stars, can shine.

Not that it has been plain sailing for Romi since then. In 2002 a bitter parting with his boyhood favourites Boca Juniors led to him joining Barcelona for just over £7 million, but the dream move soon became a nightmare. New manager, Frank Rijkaard, gave the playmaker role to Ronaldinho and Riquelme was sidelined. Three goals in an unsettled season did little to enhance his reputation and he was ready to escape.

Riquelme's revival came as a result of the controversial appointment of Jose Pekerman as Argentina's national coach. Romi had played in Pekerman's triumphant Under-20 side which won the South American Youth Championship, and the Football World Youth Championship in 1997. Unlike previous coaches Bielsa and Passerella, Pekerman had never lost faith in the gifted playmaker.

Back in the national squad, Riquelme secured a loan deal to take him to Villarreal in Spain. There, Chilean coach Manuel Pellegrini was building a team with a South American style and flavour. Riquelme joined fellow Argentinian internationals Sorin and Figueroa alongside a host of Brazilians and Chileans. It was clearly an atmosphere in which he felt secure and his natural game re-emerged.

Suddenly everything fell into place. At Villarreal, Romi proved a huge hit, helping them to the Intertoto Cup and UEFA Cup

FACT FILE | ATTACKING MIDFIELDER | 27 CAPS | 7 GOALS | VILLARREAL

Date of birth: **24.06.1978**
Height: **182 cm**
Weight: **75 kg**
Previous clubs: **Barcelona, Boca Juniors, Argentinos Juniors**
International debut: **16.11.1997 v Colombia**
Previous World Cups: **None**

STYLE GUIDE

Riquelme is the engine of the Argentina team, the origin of most of their attacks. Flawless vision and ball control, pin-point passing and finishing and a devastating free-kick taker and 100 per cent penalty converter, he is the complete playmaker. If he has a flaw, it is that his pace is suspect and if he's not switched on, he tends to lumber through a game.

semi-finals. His loan was extended and he enjoyed another sensational season, scoring 15 league goals, providing numerous assists for strikers Forlan and Guayre and helping the 'Yellow Submarines' to a Champions League place. At the end of the season, he accepted an offer to join the club permanently.

With the *Albiceleste*, he was making similar headlines. In the World Cup qualifiers he orchestrated a 4-2 win against Uruguay, and showed moments of pure brilliance in their last qualifier against Venezuela. His performances in the Confederations Cup earned comparisons with Ronaldinho.

It seemed that when Riquelme was on song, Argentina were unbeatable. A magic left foot that gave him time and space saw him creating chance after chance for his strikers. 'Riquelme is extraordinary,' says Chelsea striker Hernan Crespo. 'I put myself in position and wait for the pass which I know will come and give me the chance to score.' Yet, he still has critics out there who point to his inconsistency and some lacklustre displays and there is only one way he will permanently put them behind him: by helping to bring the World Cup home.

IVORY COAST

BEWARE THE CHARGE OF THE AFRICAN ELEPHANTS

Affectionately known as 'The Elephants', Ivory Coast are facing their first World Cup finals with confidence. They have overcome Cameroon and Egypt to qualify and in Didier Drogba they have a world-class striker.

If ever a nation needed World Cup qualification, it is the war-torn state of Ivory Coast, but a defeat to Cameroon in their penultimate qualifier looked to have robbed them of it. Then, as they won their last tie in Sudan, the news came through – Cameroon had missed an injury-time penalty and drawn with Egypt. The Elephants were going to Germany after all.

Coach Henri Michel knows a bit about World Cups and a lot about African football: he took France to the 1986 World Cup semi-finals and later led both Morocco and Cameroon to the tournament. He took charge of Ivory Coast in 2004 and turned them into formidable opposition at any level.

Michel was fortunate in having a settled squad with both French-born players, such as Drogba and Bakiri Kone, and homegrown talent, like Aruna Dindane and Kolo Toure. The new coach also had a wealth of emerging talent to consider including Arsenal's Emmanuel Eboue, Messina's Marc-Andre Zoro and Kolo's brother, Yaya Toure.

Striker and national hero Didier Drogba holds the line with great power, has fantastic pace and his natural goalscorer's instinct made him top scorer in the qualifiers with nine goals. He is teamed up with Lens frontman Aruna Dindane whose speed and dribbling skills often dazzle defenders. Meanwhile, 23-year-old Bakari Kone seems set to be more than a bench-warmer for Michel.

Highly-experienced: coach Henri Michel.

VITAL STATISTICS

WORLD RANKING 42nd **KEEPER AND DEFENCE** 6/10
MIDFIELD 4/10 **ATTACK** 8/10
STRENGTHS AND WEAKNESSES
A tough group will find a weak midfield severely tested, but the forwards will stretch most defences.
HOW FAR WILL THEY GO?
The best of the African nations, they are the most likely to cause a shock and could send a big name out.

PSG's extravagantly skilled Bonventure Kalou is the team's playmaker and captain and he is usually joined in midfield by the attack-minded Gilles Yapi-Yapo. At the back, Arsenal's ever-improving Kolo Toure is joined by two veteran defenders in Cyrille Domoraud and Blaise Kouassi, with youngsters Eboue, Meite and Zoro also contesting a place.

Already through a 'group of death' qualifying group, the World Cup finals draw has landed Ivory Coast with incredibly tough group stage matches. But these Elephants are no circus act and they could take some stopping if they start a charge.

Above *Didier Drogba: abundant pace and power.*

Right *Back row (left to right): Arouna Kone, Boubacar Barry, Yaya Toure, Marc-Andre Zoro, Abdoulaye Meite, Kolo Toure. Front row: Aruna Dindane, Didier Zokora, Didier Drogba, Arthur Boka and Gilles Yapi-Yapo.*

POSSIBLE SQUAD

Goalkeepers: Jean-Jacques Tizie (Esperance Tunis), **Gerard Gnanhouan** (Montpellier), **Boubacar Barry** (Beveren)

Defenders: Cyrille Domoraud (Creteil), **Kolo Toure** (Arsenal), **Emmanuel Eboue** (Arsenal), **Abdoulaye Meite** (Marseille), **Blaise Kossi Kouassi** (Guingamp), **Marc-Andre Zoro** (Messina), **Arthur Boka** (Strasbourg)

Midfielders: Christian Koffi Ndri (Le Mans), **Didier Zokora** (St Etienne), **Bonaventure Kalou** (Paris St Germain), **Gilles Yapi-Yapo** (Nantes), **Gneri Yaya Toure** (Olympiakos), **Emerse Fae** (Nantes), **Siaka Tiene** (St Etienne), **Guy Roland Demel** (Borussia Dortmund), **Kanga Akale** (Auxerre)

Forwards: Didier Drogba (Chelsea), **Aruna Dindane** (Lens), **Bakari Kone** (Nice), **Arouna Kone** (PSV Eindhoven)

FINALS GROUP C			
	IVORY COAST	Date	Venue
	Argentina	10 June	Hamburg
	Holland	16 June	Stuttgart
	Serbia & Montenegro	21 June	Munich

AFRICA QUALIFYING GROUP 3 – FINAL TABLE							
TEAM	P	W	D	L	F	A	Pts
IVORY COAST	10	7	1	2	20	7	**22**
CAMEROON	10	6	3	1	18	10	**21**
EGYPT	10	5	2	3	26	15	**17**
LIBYA	10	3	3	4	8	10	**12**
SUDAN	10	1	3	6	6	22	**6**
BENIN	10	1	2	7	9	23	**5**

SERBIA & MONTENEGRO

NEWCOMERS WITH A PROUD HERITAGE

With a new name and a new young team Serbia & Montenegro aim to spring a few surprises on the bigger names in Germany 2006. Unbeaten in qualifying, conceding only one goal in the process, Serbia's high levels of motivation will make them hard to beat.

Until 2003 Serbia & Montenegro played under the name Yugoslavia and has assimilated that nation's proud tradition of football. Regular participants in the World Cup finals prior to 1990, political upheavals saw the national sport take a back seat for a few years.

But they qualified for the World Cup again in 1998 where they reached the last 16 before being beaten 2-1 by Holland. The same happened at Euro 2000 but this time it was in the quarter-finals. Failure to qualify for the 2002 World Cup saw an ageing team, featuring players such as Pedrag Mijatovic and Sinisa Mihajlovic, dismantled.

In July 2003 – after failing to qualify for Euro 2004 – former member of the 1974 World Cup side Ilija Petkovic was appointed coach for the second time. He has since built a winning team, blooding new talent alongside experienced heads like Savo Milosevic, Darko Kovacevic and Mateja Kezman, who all play their club football in Spain.

Above The players celebrate their 1-0 win over Bosnia-Herzegovina that ensured their berth in the World Cup 2006.

Above right Coach Ilija Petkovic is confident of his team's abilities.

VITAL STATISTICS

WORLD RANKING 47th
KEEPER AND DEFENCE 7/10
MIDFIELD 6/10
ATTACK 6/10
STRENGTHS AND WEAKNESSES
Very solid at the back, mobile, agile and tough, they conceded only one goal in ten games during the qualifying campaign. Need to score more goals.
HOW FAR WILL THEY GO?
Pushed Spain into second spot in the qualifying campaign, will be unlucky if they don't qualify for the knockout stage.

His team is built on a solid defence that has remained almost the same as when he was appointed coach. With the dependable Dragoslav Jevric in goal, the back four of Gavrancic, Vidic, Krstajic and Dragutinovic form a solid back line. In young Red Star Belgrade wing back Aleksandar Lukovic they have another star in the making. In midfield, Inter Milan's experienced Dejan Stankovic pulls the strings and up front old heads Savo Milosevic and Darko Kovacevic are joined by the rejuvenated Mateja Kezman who is now scoring regularly for Atletico Madrid after a

season on the subs' bench at Chelsea. Young Lecce striker Mirko Vucinic, one of the brightest talents in Serbian football, is also staking a claim with some marvellous performances for his club.

Solid at the back, experienced in the middle, it is imperative that the *Plavi* (the Blues) start scoring more regularly. If they do, they might spell danger for the other teams in their group in Germany.

POSSIBLE SQUAD

Goalkeepers: Dragoslav Jevric (Ancaraspor), **Oliver Kovacevic** (unattached), **Vladimir Stajkovic** (Red Star Belgrade)

Defenders: Goran Gavrancic (Dynamo Kiev), **Mladen Krstajic** (Schalke), **Aleksandar Lukovic** (Red Star Belgrade), **Marko Basa** (Le Mans), **Ivica Dragutinovic** (Seville), **Nemanja Vidic** (Manchester United), **Milan Dudic** (Red Star Belgrade)

Midfielders: Dejan Stankovic (Inter Milan), **Predrag Djordjevic** (Olympiakos), **Ognjen Koroman** (Terek Grozny), **Igor Duljaj** (Shakhtar Donetsk), **Zvonimir Vukic** (Portsmouth), **Dragan Mladenovic** (Rangers), **Sasa Ilic** (Galatasaray), **Albert Nadj** (Partisan Belgrade)

Forwards: Mateja Kezman (Atletico Madrid), **Daniel Ljuboja** (Stuttgart), **Nikola Zigic** (Red Star Belgrade), **Savo Milosevic** (Osasuna), **Darko Kovacevic** (Real Sociedad)

Back row (left to right): Dragan Mladenovic, Ivica Dragutinovic, Goran Gavrancic, Savo Milosevic, Dragoslav Jevric, Pedrag Djordjevic. Front row: Dejan Stankovic, Ognjen Koroman, Zvonimir Vukic, Marjan Markovic and Nemanja Vidic.

EUROPE QUALIFYING GROUP 7 – FINAL TABLE							
TEAM	P	W	D	L	F	A	Pts
SERBIA & MONTENEGRO	10	6	4	0	16	1	22
SPAIN	10	5	5	0	19	3	20
BOSNIA-HERZEGOVINA	10	4	4	2	12	9	16
BELGIUM	10	3	3	4	16	11	12
LITHUANIA	10	2	4	4	8	9	10
SAN MARINO	10	0	0	10	2	40	0

FINALS GROUP C			
	SERBIA & MONTENEGRO	Date	Venue
	Holland	11 June	Leipzig
	Argentina	16 June	Gelsenkirchen
	Ivory Coast	21 June	Munich

HOLLAND

TOTAL FOOTBALL OR A TOTAL WASTE OF TIME?
– IT'S ALL IN THE HANDS OF AN OLD MASTER

First-time coach Marco van Basten prepares to lead his team into his first major championship.

Unbeaten in their qualifying group, unseeded for the finals, drawn alongside Argentina, Serbia & Montenegro and Ivory Coast in what many people think is the toughest group, new coach van Basten is undaunted by the task ahead. 'I don't think this is the group of death,' he said, 'it's a group with good opponents, who all want to play football.' Holland are in good form under their new coach and, despite their absence from the last tournament, are solid contenders to lift the trophy in Berlin on 9 July.

Holland's recent footballing history is nothing to be proud of. Since the early 1990s, ethnic divisions within the national squad have simmered and often boiled over into open conflict. Coupled with what many see as a movie star attitude from some of the top players who don't seem too bothered to play for their country, this has been to the detriment of a team that was on top of the world for almost 20 years with the likes of Johan Cruyff, Johan Neeskens, Ruud Gullit, Frank Rijkaart and, of course, Marco van Basten. The result has meant a period of complete under-achievement that has seen a wealth of Dutch talent go unfulfilled on the international stage culminating in their failure to qualify for the 2002 World Cup finals.

Cue the returning hero, a man who had scoffed at the idea of coaching when he left his then club side AC Milan in 1995. But football was too important to van Basten and he underwent a coaching course and took charge of the Ajax second team in 2003. A year later he was appointed national team coach. Since his appointment, there have been changes, but things have gone well and a revitalised Holland cruised through their qualifying group, unbeaten.

Clarence Seedorf: experienced but out of favour.

It was all a bit of a breeze for Holland, beating the Czech Republic – the only other strong side in the group – 2-0 in Amsterdam in the first game, they then lost two points in a 2-2 draw away in Macedonia, and that was it, until the final game when they lost another two points in a home draw with Macedonia. They scored goals galore at one end, 27 in all, and conceded only 3 at the other. Van Basten's tenure as boss yielded an unbeaten run of 16 games after he took over – a Dutch record. Coupled with that, van Basten has promised that his teams will play attractive football. Although that remains to be seen, Holland are undoubtedly the best of the unseeded teams in the 2006 World Cup.

HOW THEY'LL LINE UP

Van Basten has already used 38 players in his teams, 18 of them making their international debuts since he took over. Several of the old guard have now gone, Clarence Seedorf and Patrick Kluivert in particular, but Edgar Davids, Roy Makaay and Mark van Bommel – all major stars at their clubs – also rarely make the starting line-up. Instead van Basten has insisted on a policy of selecting players on merit. As a result of

Above and right *Van Basten's policy of using in-form players from the Dutch league has unearthed a number of gems, such as Dirk Kuyt of Feyenoord (left), but he has also been fortunate that Hamburg's Rafael van der Vaart, has hit form at just the right time.*

VITAL STATISTICS

KNVB

WORLD RANKING 3rd
KEEPER AND DEFENCE 8/10
MIDFIELD 8/10
ATTACK 8/10
STRENGTHS AND WEAKNESSES
Talented in every department, but the Dutch have a habit of playing as a collection of individuals rather than as a team.
HOW FAR WILL THEY GO?
They will expect to get through the group stage and will be a danger to anyone in the knockout rounds. A good outside bet for a place in the Final.

Denny Landzaat of AZ Alkmaar hit form in the qualifiers.

this many Dutch league players have made the squad among whom are some unfamiliar names: Dick Kuyt, Hedwiges Maduro and Khalid Boulahrouz included.

POSSIBLE SQUAD

Goalkeepers: Henk Timmer (AZ Alkmaar), **Edwin van der Sar** (Manchester United), **Edwin Zoetebier** (PSV)

Defenders: Urby Emanuelson (Ajax), **Ron Vlaar** (AZ Alkmaar), **Nigel de Jong** (Ajax), **Giovanni van Bronckhorst** (Barcelona), **Andre Ooijer** (PSV), **Joris Mathijsen** (AZ Alkmaar), **Khalid Boulahrouz** (Hamburg), **Jan Kromkamp** (Liverpool)

Midfielders: Hedwiges Maduro (Ajax), **Rafael van der Vaart** (Hamburg), **Wesley Sneider** (Ajax), **Denny Landzaat** (AZ Alkmaar), **Phillip Cocu** (PSV), **George Boateng** (Middlesbrough), **Mark van Bommel** (Barcelona)

Forwards: Ruud van Nistelrooy (Manchester United), **Robin van Persie** (Arsenal), **Dirk Kuyt** (Feyenoord), **Jan Vennegoor of Hesselink** (PSV), **Arjen Robben** (Chelsea)

Back row (left to right): Hedwiges Maduro, Ruud van Nistelrooy, Edwin van der Sar, Dirk Kuyt Khalid Boulahrouz. Front row: Giovanni van Bronckhorst, Rafael van der Vaart, Nigel de Jong, Barry Opdam, Robin van Persie and Denny Landzaat.

While van Basten's line-up is still not decided, it seems likely that Edwin van der Sar will be No. 1. Van Bronckhorst is a sure starter at full back while in midfield Landzaat played very well in the qualifiers as did Rafael van der Vaart. Up front there is no doubt that if fit then Robin van Persie will team up with Ruud van Nistelrooy in a potent strikeforce.

ONE TO WATCH
Robin van Persie

A top class striker with everything to play for, so thought Arsène Wenger when he bought the youngster from Feyenoord in 2004. Tall and strong, very much in the van Basten mould, van Persie has superb technical ability and is deadly at set pieces. He did well at Feyenoord, winning runners-up medals in both the league and cup. But he did have something of a reputation for over confidence and fell out with then coach Bert van Marwijk. However, his transfer to Arsenal confirmed his huge potential and van Basten was quick to give him his senior international

The boy who has everything: Robin van Persie has pace, strength, agility and a keen eye for goal.

debut. Many feel that he has been recruited by Arsenal as a replacement for Dennis Bergkamp; perhaps van Basten has the same role in mind for him in the national team. Whatever the case, expect some explosive play in Germany from one of the most precocious talents in world football.

COACH

Marco van Basten

(born 31 September 1964)
Record: P17 W11 D5 L1

Van Basten: great player, good coach?

Widely regarded as one of the finest strikers in the world, Marco van Basten's playing career was ended in 1995 by an ankle injury. A magnificent career took him from Ajax to AC Milan with whom he won three league titles and two European Cups. He was voted European Player of the Year three times in six years. The highlight of his international career came in 1988 when Holland beat everyone, including England, to win the European Championships. When he retired from football, he was sure he had retired for good.

But after a year's rest and three years of golf and tennis, van Basten realised that he wanted to use his experiences in football to put something positive back. He contributed to a FIFA task force that outlawed the tackle from behind, he did his coach's course and

took up a post as boss of the Ajax second XI. A year later he was offered the top job for the national team and the rest is history: played 17, won 11, drawn 5 and lost 1, a friendly against Italy in Amsterdam in November 2005. Expect nothing more than the best in Germany 2006 at the hands of a Dutch master.

ROUTE TO THE FINALS				
DATE				
08.09.04	HOLLAND	**2**	**0**	CZECH REPUBLIC
09.10.04	MACEDONIA	**2**	**2**	HOLLAND
13.10.04	HOLLAND	**3**	**1**	FINLAND
17.11.04	ANDORRA	**0**	**3**	HOLLAND
26.03.05	ROMANIA	**0**	**2**	HOLLAND
30.03.05	HOLLAND	**2**	**0**	ARMENIA
04.06.05	HOLLAND	**2**	**0**	ROMANIA
08.06.05	FINLAND	**0**	**4**	HOLLAND
03.09.05	ARMENIA	**0**	**1**	HOLLAND
07.09.05	HOLLAND	**4**	**0**	ANDORRA
08.10.05	CZECH REPUBLIC	**0**	**2**	HOLLAND
12.10.05	HOLLAND	**0**	**0**	MACEDONIA

EUROPE QUALIFYING GROUP 1 – FINAL TABLE							
TEAM	P	W	D	L	F	A	Pts
HOLLAND	12	10	2	0	27	3	**32**
CZECH REPUBLIC	12	9	0	3	35	12	**27**
ROMANIA	12	8	1	3	20	10	**25**
FINLAND	12	5	1	6	21	19	**16**
MACEDONIA	12	2	3	7	11	24	**9**
ARMENIA	12	2	1	9	9	25	**7**
ANDORRA	12	1	2	9	4	34	**5**

FINALS GROUP C			
	HOLLAND	Date	Venue
	Serbia & Montenegro	11 June	Leipzig
	Ivory Coast	16 June	Stuttgart
	Argentina	21 June	Frankfurt

NATURAL-BORN GOALSCORER – READY TO TAKE ON THE WORLD

A world-class striker, Ruud van Nistelrooy still has to prove himself on the world stage. First capped after the 1998 World Cup, he missed out on the 2002 tournament in Japan and Korea as Holland failed to qualify for the finals. However, he has proved himself capable of scoring at every other level: in the Premiership, in the Champions League, in the European Championships and in World Cup qualifying. There's only one big stage left on which he has to perform … watch out Argentina!

Goals, goals, goals – it's been raining them for the big Dutchman since moving from Den Bosch, for whom he signed on as a midfielder, to Heerenveen in 1998 where he was converted into a striker. He scored 13 league goals in his only season there and also scored his first international goal against Morocco, and then moved on to PSV in 1999.

'Ruud is the best in Europe. His record is incredible ever since he joined Manchester United. He is a big game player.'

Sir Alex Ferguson

His first season in Eindhoven was a revelation as he scored 31 goals in 34 games – Ruud was flying! He scored another 29 goals the following year and was all set for a big move to Manchester United when disaster struck. He collapsed in training with a cruciate knee ligament injury and the

Heads, hands and feet: its all the same to Ruud van Nistelrooy as long as the ball ends up in the net. Here he scores against Cyprus with a bullet header.

FACT FILE | STRIKER | 49 CAPS | 25 GOALS | MANCHESTER UNITED

Date of birth: **01.07.1976**
Height: **188 cm**
Weight: **79 kg**
Previous club: **PSV, Heerenveen, Den Bosch**
International debut: **18.11.1998 v Germany**
Previous World Cups: **None**

move broke down. However, Sir Alex Ferguson was determined to get his man and a year later, when Ruud had recovered from his terrible injury and proved his fitness, the £19 million move was completed.

He scored a further 43 goals for club and country in 2002–03 and a phenomenal 47 the following season, including in a run of ten consecutive matches, and is now one of the deadliest strikers in the Premiership.

In the World Cup qualifying campaign for Germany 2006, Ruud scored seven goals in 12 matches: right-foot volleys, left-foot tap-ins, half-volleys, headers and penalties … Ruud doesn't care how he scores and one look at the stats – 25 goals in 49 games for the national team – and a quick look at his face when he's celebrating another goal tells you why.

STYLE GUIDE

⚽ Selfish, doesn't tackle back, shoots on sight – these qualities are always part of the makeup of the world's greatest strikers. He can score with his head, both feet and any other part of his anatomy that it takes to get the ball into the net. Second top scorer at Euro 2004, van Nistelrooy will be desperate to register as soon as possible in Germany.

MEXICO

TURBULENT QUALIFYING CAMPAIGN LEAVES
LOS TRICOLORES WITH NEW SCORES TO SETTLE

So long the dominant team in Central American football, Mexico now faces a stiff challenge from the USA. The new rivals faced each other in a World Cup second round match in 2002 and the USA won 2-0. It was a bitter pill for the green-white-and-reds to swallow. The rivalry continued during qualifying for Germany 2006, the USA again victorious, finishing above Mexico on head-to-head results after two explosive encounters which ended in a bitter war of words. The rivalry will be renewed in Germany.

Mexico is a country in love with the beautiful game. By far the most successful footballing nation in the region, this will be their 13th World Cup tournament, they have won the Gold Cup four times (in 1993, 1996, 1998 and 2003) and were even runners-up in the Copa America in 2001. The country's economic stability means that its national sport is in a more healthy state than many of its neighbours'. The Mexican league is the best outside Europe and many players make the trip north from Brazil and Argentina to seek fame and fortune. Local players have benefited from this and the standard of football in Mexico is high.

POOR RETURN

Despite their credentials Mexico have never really done well at the World Cup. Two quarter-finals, in 1970 and 1986 when they hosted the tournament, have been the total return. But hopes were high for Germany 2006 – indeed coach Ricardo Lavolpe's attacking style saw them score freely, easily qualifying from the first two rounds. The third and final round was contested by six teams including Costa Rica and the USA.

Opposite *Franciso Fonseca in action against the USA. Striker 'Kikin', as he is known, scored ten goals in Mexico's World Cup qualifying campaign.*

Left *Brazilian-born Antonio Naelson's inclusion in the Mexico squad has caused great controversy.*

Things went well here too with 2-1 wins over the Ticos in San Jose and the USA in Mexico City.

A break in the summer of 2005 for the Confederations Cup, which saw victories over Japan and the world champions Brazil, has enhanced the team's reputation.

Mexico's first defeat in qualifying came against their nemesis, the USA, and the war of words began again. 'They suck,' said Landon Donovan. 'My mother, my grandmother or my great grandmother could play in a team like that,' replied Lavolpe. Three points saw the USA book their tickets to Germany, Mexico needed to beat Panama to qualify, they duly won 5-0 and qualified with two games to play.

Mexico keep a close guard on Michael Ballack during their 2005 Confederations Cup match against Germany.

1998	HOLLAND 2-2 MEXICO	WORLD CUP GROUP E
		Stade Geoffroy, Guichard, St Etienne

Needing a point from their last *and toughest group game to qualify for the knockout rounds, Mexico went 2-0 down within the first 19 minutes with goals from Phillip Cocu and Ronald de Boer. They had been behind in both games played so far. But roared on by a vociferous crowd, many uncommitted fans supporting them because of an outrageous stamp on a Mexican defender by Dennis Bergkamp and others because they had witnessed the famous Blanco 'bunny hop', Mexico did not give up. With 15 minutes remaining substitute striker Ricardo Palaez headed in from a corner. With Holland unable to rouse themselves after sitting on their lead for so long, Mexico pushed forward again. In the 92nd minute the Dutch defence failed to deal with a routine punt upfield and the blond haired Luis Hernandez, El Matador to his fans, who had been a thorn in*

the Dutch side all game, squeezed in the equaliser. It was a tremendous end to a dramatic encounter, both sides going through to the knockout rounds.

Midfielder Luis Perez of Monterrey provides much of the guile in midfield and chips in with the odd goal.

HOW THEY'LL LINE UP

An experienced spine runs through Lavolpe's side. Oswaldo Sanchez in goal, Rafael Marquez and Pavel Pardo in the centre and the World Cup qualifiers' top goalscorer Jared Borgetti up front – all are indispensable. Around them is a group of up-and-coming youngsters led by the superb full back Carlos Salcido and also including Ricardo Osorio at the back, Gonzalo Pineda and Luis Perez in midfield and strikers Jaime Lozano and Francisco Fonseca, one of whom will partner Borgetti.

The one real problem that Lavolpe has is whether to include the legendary Cuauhtemoc Blanco in the squad. Dropped from the Confederations Cup squad because he 'needed a rest', Blanco's performances for his club America have prompted calls for his return. Many suspect that personal differences between Blanco and the coach are the real reasons for his absence.

Back row (left to right): Oswaldo Sanchez, Jose Fonseca, Ricardo Osorio, Jaime Lozano, Pavel Pardo.
Front row: Luis Perez, Juan Pablo Rodriguez, Mario Mendez, Carlos Salcido, Ramon Morales and Gonzalo Pineda line up for the Confederations Cup in Germany in 2005.

Formation diagram:
- SALCIDO
- ZINHA
- ROJAS
- PINEDA
- FONSECA
- SANCHEZ
- PARDO
- MARQUEZ
- BORGETTI
- R. MORALES
- OSORIO

A potential superstar in the making, Carlos Salcido (left) is an outstanding prospect for Germany 2006.

POSSIBLE SQUAD

Goalkeepers: Oswaldo Sanchez (Guadalajara), **Moises Munoz** (Morelia), **Oscar Perez** (Cruz Azul)

Defenders: Rafael Marquez (Barcelona), **Ricardo Osorio** (Cruz Azul), **Hugo Sanchez Guerrero** (UANL), **Francisco Rodriguez** (Guadalajara), **Carlos Salcido** (Guadalajara), **Oscar Rojas** (America), **Israel Lopez** (Toluca)

Midfielders: Juan Pablo Rodriguez (UAG), **Pavel Pardo** (America), **Gerardo Torrado** (Cruz Azul), **Gonzalo Pineda** (UNAM), **Luis Perez** (Monterrey), **Ramon Morales** (Guadalajara), **Zinha** (Toluca)

Forwards: Jared Borgetti (Bolton Wanderers), **Jesus Arellano** (Monterrey), **Francisco Fonseca** (Cruz Azul), **Jaime Lozano** (UANL), **Guillermo Franco** (Monterrey), **Cuauhtemoc Blanco** (America)

ONE TO WATCH
Carlos Salcido
Young, solid and aggressive and armed with an engine that keeps him going for 90 minutes, Carlos Salcido of Guadalajara is a top-quality left back. Adept at man marking,

Salcido also has great pace and vision when coming forward and has an uncanny knack of finding the right players with his passes.

He made himself something of a national hero in the Confederations Cup in 2005 when, in extra time, he ran the whole length of the pitch dribbling past three Argentinian defenders before scoring. Since making his debut for the national team against Trinidad & Tobago in 2004 he has been a regular starter.

COACH
Ricardo Lavolpe
(born 6 February 1952)
Record: P59 W31 D16 L12
Born in Argentina, Ricardo Lavolpe has a World Cup-winner's medal. He was third-choice goalkeeper when Argentina won the championship on home soil in 1978. Coach of Mexico since his appointment in the summer

of 2002 a few months after that defeat to the USA in Japan and Korea, Lavolpe has a difficult job. His every move is dissected in the press, he is the subject of intense criticism whatever the results and he has made an enemy of Mexican footballing legend Hugo Sanchez, former manager of Mexican club side Pumas UNAM, who feels he should have the coach's job. Their dispute came to a head when Mexico lost to the USA and Lavolpe found himself defending his job and worrying that he might be replaced by Sanchez. However, things change quickly in football and Sanchez has since been sacked by his club while Lavolpe basks in the glory of World Cup qualification.

Ricardo Lavolpe – often a lonely figure in a coach's job similar to that of the England boss.

ROUTE TO THE FINALS

DATE			
09.02.05	COSTA RICA **1**	**2** MEXICO	
27.03.05	MEXICO **2**	**1** UNITED STATES	
30.03.05	PANAMA **1**	**1** MEXICO	
04.06.05	GUATEMALA **0**	**2** MEXICO	
08.06.05	MEXICO **2**	**0** TRINIDAD & TOBAGO	
17.08.05	MEXICO **2**	**0** COSTA RICA	
03.09.05	MEXICO **0**	**2** UNITED STATES	
07.09.05	MEXICO **5**	**0** PANAMA	
08.10.05	MEXICO **5**	**2** GUATEMALA	
12.10.05	TRINIDAD & TOBAGO **2**	**1** MEXICO	

CONCACAF FINAL STAGE – FINAL TABLE

TEAM	P	W	D	L	F	A	Pts
USA	10	7	1	2	16	6	**22**
MEXICO	10	7	1	2	22	9	**22**
COSTA RICA	10	5	1	4	14	16	**16**
TRINIDAD & TOBAGO	10	4	1	5	10	15	**13**
GUATEMALA	10	3	2	5	16	18	**11**
PANAMA	10	0	2	8	4	21	**2**

VITAL STATISTICS

WORLD RANKING 5th=
KEEPER AND DEFENCE 7/10
MIDFIELD 7/10
ATTACK 7/10
STRENGTHS AND WEAKNESSES
Free-scoring against weaker opponents, Mexico will need to keep this up against top quality defences.
HOW FAR WILL THEY GO?
A place in the quarter-finals would equal their best-ever World Cup return. Any further would be marvellous.

FINALS GROUP D

		Date	Venue
	MEXICO		
	Iran	11 June	Nuremberg
	Angola	16 June	Hanover
	Portugal	21 June	Gelsenkirchen

Oswaldo SANCHEZ

DEPENDABLE GOALKEEPER FINALLY FINDS HIS FEET AND HEADS FOR GERMANY AT THE PEAK OF HIS GAME

So long the number two between the sticks for the international *seleccion* to the famous Jorge Campos, including the 1998 World Cup, and then on the bench at the 2002 World Cup because of the fantastic form of understudy Oscar Perez, it has been a long road for the 32-year-old keeper from Guadalajara. But having made the No.1 jersey his own, coach Lavolpe then offered him the captaincy.

Oswaldo Sanchez first came to prominence at the FIFA World Youth Championships in Australia in 1993, the same year he signed for Mexican club Atlas. His international career took off during qualifying for the 1996 Olympics in Atlanta but was ousted by his more flamboyant counterpart Campos before the quarter-final. Campos was famous for wearing the most garish goalkeeping shirts he could find and also for dribbling the ball out of his penalty area and upfield as far as he would dare. However, a move to America, Mexico's most famous club side, saw Sanchez given a run in the national team, and he had made more than 30 appearances by the time the next World Cup arrived in 2002. Unfortunately, the good form shown in the run up to the tournament by his understudy Oscar Perez of Cruz Azul, saw Sanchez relegated to the bench again.

In 2000 Sanchez had joined his hometown club Guadalajara, and this move saw him settle down and become a more consistent performer. Though settling down did not stop him from emulating his contemporary, Jorge Campos, when Sanchez left his penalty area for a corner and crashed home the

Sanchez uses his great shot-stopping abilities to halt Argentina striker Javier Saviola during their Confederations Cup semi-final in 2005.

FACT FILE | GOALKEEPER | 58 CAPS | 0 GOALS | GUADALAJARA

Date of birth: **21.09.1973**
Height: **184 cm**
Weight: **84 kg**
Previous clubs: **America, Atlas**
International debut: **08.08.1996 v Bolivia**
Previous World Cups: **1998, 2002**

equalising goal with a right-foot volley in a 3-3 draw against El Nacional of Ecuador during a Copa Merconorte match.

He was rewarded for his good club form with a run in the national team, a position that he has not relinquished since then. His performances in the Confederations Cup in 2005 were spectacular, particularly in the match against Greece, when he was named man of the match, and in the semi-final against Argentina. He received rave notices and was named keeper of the tournament.

Now aged 32 and long regarded as one of the best goalkeepers in Latin America, Sanchez has made no secret of the fact that he would like to play in Europe. Germany 2006 will see this dependable goalkeeper at the peak of his game, and will be the perfect shop window for his talents.

'We've seen with Sanchez just how valuable it can be when a goalkeeper finds his rhythm.'

Oliver Kahn

STYLE GUIDE

⚽ Solid rather than spectacular, Sanchez is nevertheless very agile and a dependable shot stopper as well as being good in the air. Famed for his reflex saves and speed of thought he is nevertheless prone to the odd handling error. However, one thing's for sure, he will not let the side down.

Rafael MARQUEZ

THE 'KAISER OF MICHOACAN' IS FINALLY MAKING A NAME FOR HIMSELF

Nicknamed the 'Kaiser' in homage to his hero Franz Beckenbauer, Marquez is a key figure in coach Ricardo Lavolpe's team. He is the team leader. With a good sense of timing, he is a tenacious tackler, is supremely strong in the air and has great vision. Now playing for Barcelona in Spain, Marquez is only the second Mexican player to make a big impression in Europe – the first was the legendary Hugo Sanchez.

'Marquez is one of the best defenders in the world ... and also has excellent ball skills – only time will tell whether he will become as great a player as Beckenbauer.'

Ricardo Lavolpe

Mature, solid and extremely gifted, Rafael Marquez played a great part in Barcelona's La Liga title in 2004–05. Having become the first Mexican player to win titles in two major European leagues he is hoping to establish his international credentials with a fine performance in Germany 2006. Making his professional debut for Atlas as the age of 17, Marquez made his debut for the national team a year later. In 1999 he moved abroad, to France, to play for Monaco. A year later he had won his first title and had been voted the French league's top defender.

In 2003 he moved to Barcelona and immediately established himself in the

FACT FILE | DEFENDER | 62 CAPS | 7 GOALS | BARCELONA

Date of birth: **13.02.1979**
Height: **182 cm**
Weight: **74 kg**
Previous clubs: **Monaco, Atlas**
International debut: **02.05.1997 v Ecuador**
Previous World Cups: **2002**

STYLE GUIDE

⚽ Can either play as a central defender or in the holding role. Only uses his considerable power when necessary, preferring to deny strikers the ball by stealth. Brings the ball out well and can distribute it with precision and with an eye to the counter attack. Adept at feints and delicate touches. However, he does have a temper and has a poor disciplinary record which might let him down.

No quarter is given and none expected when Mexico play against the USA. Here Marquez stops Eddie Johnson in his tracks during their qualifier in Mexico City in March 2005. Mexico won 2-1.

starting line-up alongside Brazil's Ronaldinho. Runners-up in La Liga in his first season, Barcelona won first prize the following year for the first time since 1999.

His international career has also been impressive. He was a member of the team that won the 1999 Confederations Cup on home soil, he played at the 2002 World Cup, though he was sent off for a dreadful tackle on Cobi Jones when they were eliminated by the USA, and was a key figure in Mexico's 2004 Copa America campaign.

As for his nickname, it's very simple. 'I have always admired Beckenbauer's game,

especially his elegance. And I come from Zamora in the Michoacan region.' There is no doubt then that Rafael Marquez will be out to impress in Germany, and where better to perform than in the home of his hero and the man he is named after.

Pavel PARDO

VETERAN LINKMAN WITH OVER 100 CAPS TO HIS NAME READY TO MAKE ONE LAST BID FOR WORLD CUP GLORY

Although less pacy than he was, Pardo more than makes up for it with experience and a superb positional sense. A tough tackling ball-winner, Pardo is the central linkman in the team, dependable under pressure and superb at distributing the ball from deep. Although not a prolific scorer, he waited until his 60th game before scoring his first international goal, he also possesses a lethal long-range shot. Now 30 years old it seems likely that Germany 2006 will see his last tilt at international success.

In June 2004 in the 8-0 win over Guatemala in a World Cup qualifier, Pavel Pardo won his hundredth international cap. In doing so he enrolled himself in an exclusive club of five Mexican players who have achieved a century of appearances for the national team.

Born in Guadalajara, Pardo signed professional forms for local club Atlas as a 17-year-old right-sided wing-back. He was called up for the national team three years later and played his part in qualification for the 1998 World Cup. His impressive form saw him selected for three of Mexico's four matches in

'I'm proud of what my team-mates have accomplished so far ... our goal is to win the tournament and we can beat anyone.'

FACT FILE | MIDFIELDER | 118 CAPS | 5 GOALS | AMERICA

Date of birth: **26.07.1976**
Height: **175 cm**
Weight: **67 kg**
Previous clubs: **Tecos UAG, Atlas**
International debut: **31.08.1996 v France**
Previous World Cups: **1998**

STYLE GUIDE

A reliable midfield ball-winner and a master of distribution. Not as quick as he used to be and can sometimes get caught in possession, but Pardo makes up for his mistakes with an uncanny sense of positioning. Good on the ground and in the air, Pardo plays his part both in defence and in building attacks.

the finals in France in 1998. At the end of the tournament he moved across the city of Guadalajara to join Tecos UAG where he was moved into the centre of midfield. The move did not affect his form and he continued to appear regularly for club and country although he moved on to join America in Mexico City in 1999 and still plays there today.

Although he did not make the trip to Japan and Korea because of injury, Pardo is a veteran of several Copa Americas, Gold Cups and four Confederations Cup tournaments, including in 1999 when the Mexicans won the trophy on home soil.

Reliable and solid Pardo will bring his considerable experience to the Mexico midfield and together with Rafael Marquez will give coach Lavolpe a solid base on which to work. It may be his last chance for international glory, but Pardo fully intends to give it his best shot.

Pardo leaps over Japanese player Takashi Fukunishi during their Confederations Cup match in 2005. Mexico won 2-1.

MEXICO'S 'GOAL KING' – NOW PLYING HIS TRADE WITH BOLTON IN THE PREMIERSHIP – IS READY TO SET THE WORLD ALIGHT

No team scored more goals in qualifying for Germany 2006 than Mexico, and no one scored more times for Mexico than the tall and lanky striker Jared Borgetti. Known to the national team's fans as *El Zorro del Desierto* ('the desert fox') Borgetti has an unerring knack of scoring which has brought him the tremendous strike rate of 37 goals in 72 appearances. Borgetti will be Mexico's main threat in this year's World Cup.

Now more familiar to English football fans since signing for Bolton Wanderers in August 2005, Jared Borgetti is a legend in his own country. One of the finest headers of the ball in world football, Borgetti played for several clubs in Mexico but never for any of the big-name teams preferring to play for small provincial sides – much like Bolton in England.

> 'Borgetti is a superb goalscorer... able to get away from defenders and find the goal at will.'
>
> Ricardo Lavolpe

Signed as a youth by Atlas from Guadalajara where he failed to make an impression, he was soon sold to Santos Laguna who were languishing at the bottom of the league. His goals transformed the club. He was top scorer in the Mexican league in three of his seven years there, winning two league titles and reaching two cup finals before moving to

FACT FILE | STRIKER | 72 CAPS | 37 GOALS | BOLTON WANDERERS

Date of birth: **14.08.1973**
Height: **182 cm**
Weight: **78 kg**
Previous clubs: **Pachuca, Dorados, Santos Laguna, Atlas**
International debut: **05.02.1997 v Ecuador**
Previous World Cups: **2002**

his hometown club Dorados from Sinaloa and then on to Pachuca.

His international career started in 1997 but he was not chosen for the World Cup squad in 1998 despite being the league's top scorer that year. However, who can ever forget his magnificent header against Italy in Mexico's final group game of the 2002 tournament when he set the pulses racing by out-jumping Paulo Maldini to meet Blanco's cross. Borgetti has rarely missed a game for *El Tri* since then.

His prolific goalscoring in qualifying for Germany 2006 began in the first qualifying round when he scored four goals in an 18-0 aggregate victory against the Dominican Republic. He scored five of eight against St Vincent and the Grenadines in the second round and top scored again in the third round with 14 of Mexico's 22 goals to finish the campaign with his name at the top of the list of the World Cup's leading goalscorers.

STYLE GUIDE

⚽ Tall and strong, Borgetti is one of the best headers in the world. But that's not all, he has an unerring sense of where the goal is, can make space for himself even in a crowded penalty box and is a lethal finisher with either foot. Mexico's greatest ever goalscorer will be a handful for any defence.

One of Mexico's most famous victories in recent years came in the Confederations Cup in 2005 when they beat world champions Brazil 1-0 courtesy of this right-foot shot from the prolific Jared Borgetti.

RECENTLY VOTED MEXICO'S GREATEST EVER PLAYER ... BUT WILL HE MAKE IT INTO THE 2006 WORLD CUP SQUAD?

2005 was a big year for Cuauhtemoc Blanco. He won his first ever club championship as a player with his current club America, he was voted Mexico's greatest ever player by the Mexican FA and was dropped from the national side because he asked to be excused from the Confederations Cup claiming he needed the rest. Now Mexico's favourite son's international future hangs in the balance.

His career has been littered with spats with club officials, coaches, the press and others, but never with the fans. Blanco is universally adored both for his attitude and for his sumptuous skills. Perhaps most famous for his *cuauteminha* or 'Cuauhtomoc hop', a trick where he jumps over tackles with the ball trapped between his feet, something he showed to a worldwide audience in Mexico's vital last group game against Holland in the 1998 World Cup in France, Blanco's stature is about much more than that.

Brought up in Tepico, a tough neighbourhood of Mexico City known as the Bronx because of its high murder rate, Blanco started his career aged 17 in Mexico City with America, the country's biggest club. During more than 15 years in top-

'[Blanco] is undoubtedly the greatest footballer that Mexico has ever produced ... and the only player to have a dribbling manoeuvre named after him.'

The Raven's Desk, US football website

FACT FILE | FORWARD | 83 CAPS | 30 GOALS | AMERICA

Date of birth: **17.01.1973**
Height: **177 cm**
Weight: **72 kg**
Previous clubs: **Necaxa, Veracruz, Real Valladolid**
International debut: **01.02.1995 v Uruguay**
Previous World Cups: **1998, 2002**

STYLE GUIDE

⚽ Fast and unpredictable, Blanco also possesses one of the fiercest shots in football. Can be temperamental and has a reputation for being hot headed. However, he has already proved himself on the world stage and is a lethal goalscorer, able to shoot with both feet.

flight football he has played either as an out-and-out striker or in the hole behind them for Mexican clubs Necaxa and Veracruz as well as Real Valladolid in Spain. Since his rise to fame in the 1998 World Cup he has rarely been out of the news or the treatment room as arguments and injuries have blighted his career.

In between though, the player named after a legendary Aztec warrior has scored over 100 goals in league football, made over 80 appearances for the national team, scoring 30 goals. He has also, as they say, done it his way, never worrying who he upsets and always saying what he thinks. Most recently this has been a disaster for his international career, and when he criticised national team coach Ricardo Lavolpe for leaving him out of the World Cup qualifying

Excellent ball skills and pace make Blanco a dangerous player.

squad following his requested rest during the Confederations Cup, things came to a head. It is now up to the coach what he does, but it would be a shame if football's greatest tournament were not graced by one of its most colourful characters.

IRAN

UNDERDOGS KEEN TO PROGRESS

Along with Japan, Iran was the first nation to qualify for Germany 2006 following a controversial qualification campaign. But Croatian coach Branko Ivankovic is confident that 'Team Melli' – as they are known – will go further in the competition than ever before, 'We will go to the World Cup to achieve something, not just to participate.'

Iran first qualified for the World Cup finals in 1978 but failed to progress from the group stage with only one point from a draw with Scotland. They qualified again in 1998 with a team that included players like Ali Daei and Karim Bagheri, and recorded their first World Cup win in France, beating the USA 2-1 on a memorable night in Lyon. Despite this they still failed to progress to the knockout rounds.

The qualification competition for Germany 2006 saw highs and lows. The lows both came in the final group stage. The first after a 2-1 home win against Japan at the Azadi stadium in Tehran when panic started among the 110,000-strong crowd at the end of the match which led to deaths and injuries. Five days later there was also crowd violence in North Korea when the referee turned down a penalty appeal for the home side with Iran winning 2-0.

Below Bayern Munich's influential Ali Karimi (right).

Above Croatian-born coach Branko Ivankovic.

VITAL STATISTICS

WORLD RANKING 19th
KEEPER AND DEFENCE 6/10
MIDFIELD 6/10
ATTACK 6/10
STRENGTHS AND WEAKNESSES
Very strong going forward. Technically good in midfield but it's hard to know how well the defence will cope up against world-class strikers.
HOW FAR WILL THEY GO?
Hard to disagree with the Kaiser, but Iran's draw is a pretty tough one, will do very well to progress from the group stage.

Back row (left to right): Jalal Kameli, Ali Daei, Ebrahim
Mirzapour, Ali Karimi, Alireza Vahedi, Javad Nekounam.
Front row: Mojtaba Jabarik, Hossein Kaebi, Arash
Borhani, Mohammad Alavi and Mohammad Nosrati.

The highs came courtesy of an easy ride
to Germany 2006. In the final group games
four wins, one draw and one defeat, against
Japan in the meaningless last fixture, saw
Iran through to the finals in second place
to Japan. Stars of the successful campaign
were 36-year-old leading appearance
maker Ali Daei, who contributed nine goals,
and influential midfielder Ali Karimi.

Coach Ivankovic has support for his
confidence from none other than the
Kaiser himself. 'With a little luck Iran can
successfully overcome the first group phase,'
said Franz Beckenbauer on a visit to the
Iranian capital Tehran in October 2005.
There are close footballing ties between
Iran and Germany with four of Iran's top stars
currently playing in the Bundesliga: Karimi
at Bayern Munich, Vahid Hashemian at
Hannover, Asian footballer of the year in
2003 Mehdi Mahdivikia at Hamburg and
Ferydoon Zandi at Kaiserslautern. 'These four
players will form the backbone of Iran's World
Cup squad,' added Beckenbauer. Add to that
the talents of home-based youngsters like
Hossein Kaebi and Iman Mobali and it's hard
to disagree with either of them, though
Mexico and Portugal might have something
to say about the matter.

POSSIBLE SQUAD

Goalkeepers: **Ebrahim Mirzapour** (Foolad),
Vahid Taleblou (Esteghlal), **Mahdi Vaezi** (Peykan)

Defenders: **Yahya Golmohammadi** (Saba Battery),
Rahman Rezaei (Messina), **Mohammad Nosrati**
(Pas), **Hossein Kaebi** (Foolad), **Sattar Zar'e**
(Bargh Shiraz), **Hamidreza Azizzadeh** (Zob Ahan),
Mehdi Amirabadi (Esteghlal), **Mohammad Alavi** (Foolad)

Midfielders: **Javad Nekounam** (Pas), **Moharram
Navidkia** (Bochum), **Ferydoon Zandi**
(Kaiserslautern), **Mehdi Mahdavikia** (Hamburg),
Mehdi Rajabzadeh (Zob Ahan), **Iman Mobali**
(Foolad), **Javad Kazemian** (Persepolis)

Forwards: **Ali Daei** (Saba Battery), **Ali Karimi**
(Bayern Munich), **Vahid Hashemian** (Hannover 96),
Arash Borhani (Pas), **Reza Enayati** (Esteghlal)

ASIA QUALIFYING FINAL GROUP 2 – FINAL TABLE							
TEAM	P	W	D	L	F	A	Pts
JAPAN	6	5	0	1	9	4	**15**
IRAN	6	4	1	1	7	3	**13**
BAHRAIN	6	1	1	4	4	7	**4**
NORTH KOREA	6	1	0	5	5	11	**3**

FINALS GROUP D			
	IRAN	Date	Venue
	Mexico	11 June	Nuremberg
	Portugal	17 June	Frankfurt
	Angola	21 June	Leipzig

ANGOLA

EXPECT THE UNEXPECTED

Of all the surprises that the World Cup qualifying competition provided, Angola's was the greatest. Ranked 62nd in the world at the start of the competition Angola weren't even dark horses. Instead the *Palancas Negras* ('Black Antelopes') overcame the formbook and qualified as top dogs in African Qualifying Group 4 on the same points as favourites Nigeria but in front on a head-to-head basis.

In a country that only achieved independence from Portugal 30 years ago, 27 of which have seen bitter civil war, there has always been one unifying force, football. Another constant, for the past ten years or so, has been coach Luis Oliveira Goncalves who took charge of the country's Under-17 team in 1997 before winning the African Under-21 championship with the same players in 2001.

The team that clinched qualification with a 1-0 away win in Rwanda in October 2005 includes many of the players that Goncalves has brought along during his career: top star Pedro Mantorras, who plays for Benfica, and captain Fabrice Akwa Maieko, the oldest member of the squad, who has a record of 32 goals in 67 matches including the winner against Rwanda in Kigali.

But the team's greatest achievement was in qualifying ahead of African giants Nigeria. A 1-0 home win, thanks to another goal from Akwa, and a 1-1 draw away in Kano, courtesy of a goal from midfield dynamo Paulo Figueiredo, eventually saw both teams end the group stage on 21 points, Angola going through on the head-to-head results.

VITAL STATISTICS

WORLD RANKING 61st   **KEEPER AND DEFENCE** 5/10
MIDFIELD 4/10   **ATTACK** 5/10
STRENGTHS AND WEAKNESSES
Enthusiasm will get them some goals and they might surprise an unwary opponent, but it is vital that they remain organised and avoid shipping goals.
HOW FAR WILL THEY GO?
Will make many friends along the way, but are unlikely to progress from the group stage.

Permanent fixture? Coach Luis Goncalves (left).

Above *Captain fantastic: Fabrice Akwa (right) celebrates after scoring against Rwanda.*

Above right *Back row (left to right): Joao Ricardo Castro Freddy, Antonio Lebo Lebo, Joao Pereira, Miloy, Fabrice Akwa. Front row: Paulo Figueiredo, Mendonca, Jacinto Pereira, Yamba Asha and Gilberto.*

Little is expected of Angola in Germany, which will not only be their first ever World Cup finals but until 2006 they had also never won an African Nations Cup match. However, it is clear that they deserve their place in the tournament and that their opponents in Group D, which include former colonists Portugal, who they face in an enticing first game, Mexico and Iran will underestimate them at their peril.

POSSIBLE SQUAD

Goalkeepers: Joao Ricardo (Unattached), **Lama** (Petro Atletico), **Goliath** (Sagrada Esperanca)

Defenders: Luis Delgado (Primeiro Agosto), **Jacinto Pereira** (AS Aviacao), **Antonio Lebo Lebo** (Sagrada Esperanca), **Loco** (Benfica Luanda), **Marco Abreu** (Portimonense), **Jamba** (AS Aviacao), **Castro Freddy** (Uniao Leiria)

Midfielders: Andre (Kuwait), **Edson** (Pacos Ferreira), **Paulo Figueiredo** (Varzim), **Gilberto** (Al Ahli), **Mendonca** (Varzim), **Miloy** (InterClube), **Ze Kalanga** (Petro Atletico)

Forwards: Fabrice 'Akwa' Maieko (Al Wakra), **Amado Flavio** (Al Ahli), **Arsenio Love** (AS Aviacao), **Pedro Mantorras** (Benfica), **Maurito** (Al Wahda), **Santana** (Sagrada Esperanca)

AFRICA QUALIFYING GROUP 4 – FINAL TABLE

TEAM	P	W	D	L	F	A	Pts
ANGOLA	10	6	3	1	12	6	21
NIGERIA	10	6	3	1	21	7	21
ZIMBABWE	10	4	3	3	13	14	15
GABON	10	2	4	4	11	13	10
ALGERIA	10	1	5	4	8	15	8
RWANDA	10	1	2	7	6	16	5

FINALS GROUP D

		Date	Venue
	ANGOLA	Date	Venue
	Portugal	11 June	Cologne
	Mexico	16 June	Hanover
	Iran	21 June	Leipzig

PORTUGAL

BIG PHIL'S MEN JUST GET BETTER AND BETTER

Flops in the last World Cup, thwarted at the last in Euro 2004, coach Phil Scolari is back with an improved, better-organised and potentially devastating team.

It seems a sweet irony that having seen their 'Golden Generation' (winners of the 1989 and 1991 Under-20 World Cups) come of age to no avail in Japan and Korea and their hosting of Euro 2004 end in ultimate disappointment, Portugal enter the 2006 tournament with perhaps a better-prepared team than ever before.

While Luis Figo and Pauleta remain from the 1990s teams, the rest of the positions have been filled with emerging talent and proven competitors. Coach Scolari turned the team around from near disaster in Euro 2004 to finish as runners-up and has carried on where he left off, building a team that is watertight at the back, creative and forward-thinking in midfield and clinical in front of goal. Pragmatic to the last, he thought nothing of leaving out ageing heroes Fernando Couto and Rui Costa, but also tempted Figo back from retirement.

The strength of the team is evident in the household names that litter the squad including Manchester United's magician Cristiano Ronaldo and Barcelona's inspirational Deco. Figo, now at Inter Milan, is still capable of turning a match and in Pauleta they have Portugal's all-time leading goalscorer, his 11 goals in the qualifiers helping him pass the great Eusebio's total of 41 international goals.

PROLIFIC AND MEAN TO THE END

The Portuguese took no time to get into their stride in the qualifiers, despite the trauma of their defeat by Greece in the Final of Euro 2004. Convincing victories over Latvia and Estonia put them on their way and unbeaten throughout, they won all of their

Pauleta (left), of Paris Saint-Germain in France, is now Portugal's all-time leading goalscorer.

Jorge Andrade (right) forms half of an iron-hard central defence with Chelsea's Ricardo Carvalho.

home games and all but three away. Even their one slip-up, a 2-2 draw in Liechtenstein, was followed just four days later by a 7-1 thrashing of Russia. They averaged nearly three goals a game, but a more telling statistic is the goals against tally – just five. This is a team that means business.

HOW THEY'LL LINE-UP

Scolari likes to employ a 4-2-3-1 formation, placing great emphasis on building from a secure defence. Fortunately he has been blessed with some of the best defenders in the world. Chelsea knew who was who when they invested in Paulo Ferreira and Ricardo Carvalho and alongside the majestic Jorge Andrade they provide a tremendous shield for long-standing keeper Ricardo.

The defensive and short-passing midfield duties are conducted by Tiago, Maniche or Petit – all excellent players, and they will be challenged by Benfica's fast-improving

Luis Figo, now at Inter Milan, has been tempted out of retirement for one last chance of international glory.

VITAL STATISTICS

WORLD RANKING 10th   **KEEPER AND DEFENCE** 7/10
MIDFIELD 8/10   **ATTACK** 7/10
STRENGTHS AND WEAKNESSES
Devastating in the qualifiers, but can they thrive against the big boys? Friendlies suggest they just might.
HOW FAR WILL THEY GO?
They will have to be on top form to get further than the quarter-finals.

19-year-old Manuel Fernandes. In front of them, the flair kicks in with three magnificent ball-players. Apart from Brazil, no team will enjoy such a fount of creativity with Deco exploring the angled through ball, Cristiano Ronaldo tormenting the full

backs and the imperious Figo orchestrating play. Hugo Viana, the Newcastle United flop now impressing at Sporting Lisbon, could also make the trip, although his younger team-mate, Joao Moutinho, threatens his place in the squad.

Goals are expected from the head of Ronaldo, the sublime boot of Figo, but mainly from Pauleta. The 'Eagle of the Azores', was the leading goalscorer in the European qualifiers and is an instinctive finisher. At 32, this will be his last chance to impress on the world stage. If he fails, he'll have the highly-rated Nuno Gomez breathing down his neck.

Back row (left to right): Jorge Andrade, Fernando Meira, Pauleta, Tiago, Quim. Front row: Maniche, Deco, Miguel, Luis Figo, Caneira and Cristiano Ronaldo.

ONE TO WATCH
Deco
He is the typical Brazilian No. 10 – imaginative, clever and magical on the ball – except this Brazilian plays No. 20 for Portugal after being granted citizenship in

POSSIBLE SQUAD

Goalkeepers: Paulo Santos (Sporting Braga), **Ricardo Pereira** (Sporting Lisbon), **Quim** (Braga)

Defenders: Fernando Meira (Stuttgart), **Jorge Andrade** (Deportivo La Coruna), **Jorge Ribeiro** (Dynamo Moscow), **Miguel** (Valencia), **Caneira** (Valencia), **Paulo Ferreira** (Chelsea), **Ricardo Carvalho** (Chelsea)

Midfielders: Costinha (Dynamo Moscow), **Petit** (Benfica), **Tiago** (Lyon), **Simao** (Benfica), **Maniche** (Dynamo Moscow), **Cristiano Ronaldo** (Manchester United), **Manuel Fernandes** (Benfica), **Joao Moutinho** (Sporting Lisbon), **Deco** (Barcelona)

Forwards: Pauleta (Paris Saint-Germain), **Nuno Gomes** (Benfica), **Helder Postiga** (Porto), **Luis Boa Morte** (Fulham)

Deco is Portugal's playmaker supreme. However, he can make himself unpopular with the fans if he goes overboard with his play acting and diving.

March 2003. He took Rui Costa's place in the line-up during Euro 2004 and his tackling, vision and skill proved irreplaceable. At his club, Barcelona, many thought he would be eclipsed by Ronaldinho, but dropping back where necessary and perfectly complimenting the Brazilian's forward runs, he became an essential part of their La Liga winning team. Deco is fast becoming the hub of Portugal's moves – if he meets his Brazilian compatriot this summer, don't expect him to play second fiddle.

COACH
Luis Felipe Scolari
(born 11 September1948)
Record: P38 W23 D9 L6

'Big Phil' – Luis Felipe Scolari – took over the Brazilian side in 2001 when they were struggling to qualify for the 2002 World Cup. Just over a year later they won the tournament. The 57-year-old then took charge of the Portuguese side in time for 'their' Euro 2004 tournament and despite a disastrous start, still ended it as a national hero. Renowned for his disciplinarian tendencies, he instilled a physical and mental toughness – a will to win that

seemed missing in the 'Golden Generation' teams. Like all his teams, Portugal know when to defend, but can attack with pace and invention.

Success in Germany in 2006 will make Phil Scolari a Portuguese hero for life.

EUROPE QUALIFYING GROUP 3 – FINAL TABLE							
TEAM	P	W	D	L	F	A	Pts
PORTUGAL	12	9	3	0	35	5	30
SLOVAKIA	12	6	5	1	24	8	23
RUSSIA	12	6	5	1	23	12	23
ESTONIA	12	5	2	5	16	17	17
LATVIA	12	4	3	5	18	21	15
LIECHTENSTEIN	12	2	2	8	13	23	8
LUXEMBOURG	12	0	0	12	5	48	0

ROUTE TO THE FINALS			
DATE			
04.09.04	LATVIA 0	2 PORTUGAL	
08.09.04	PORTUGAL 4	0 ESTONIA	
09.10.04	LIECHTENSTEIN 2	2 PORTUGAL	
13.10.04	PORTUGAL 7	1 RUSSIA	
17.11.04	LUXEMBOURG 0	5 PORTUGAL	
30.03.05	SLOVAKIA 1	1 PORTUGAL	
04.06.05	PORTUGAL 2	0 SLOVAKIA	
08.06.05	ESTONIA 0	1 PORTUGAL	
03.09.05	PORTUGAL 6	0 LUXEMBOURG	
07.09.05	RUSSIA 0	0 PORTUGAL	
08.10.05	PORTUGAL 2	1 LIECHTENSTEIN	
12.10.05	PORTUGAL 3	0 LATVIA	

FINALS GROUP D			
	PORTUGAL	Date	Venue
	Angola	11 June	Cologne
	Iran	17 June	Frankfurt
	Mexico	21 June	Gelsenkirchen

Cristiano **RONALDO**

HE MADE HIS PROFESSIONAL DEBUT AT 16, JOINED MANCHESTER UNITED AT 18 AND TOOK EURO 2004 BY STORM AT 19

Cristiano Ronaldo makes an impact. Few can forget the first time they saw his step-overs, close control and lightning change of pace. For some it was on his Manchester United debut, for others it was as a starring sub for Portugal in Euro 2004; and for the lucky ones, it was as a teenage prodigy at Sporting Lisbon.

'He has so much skill and speed it is frightening. If the opposition gets physical, he just comes back for more.'
Paul Scholes

For his Manchester United team-mates, it was in a summer friendly against Sporting. Sir Alex Ferguson tells how, on the plane home, his players begged him to sign the skinny winger. As other chasing clubs forced Sir Alex's hand, he splashed out £12 million for the unproven talent.

No one in Portugal was surprised. Cristiano Ronaldo dos Santos Aveiro (his second name is a tribute to Ronald Reagan!) had been under the spotlight since the boy from Madeira joined Sporting at the age of 11. He made his debut for the senior side at 16 and played a starring role for the Portuguese Under-17 side at the European Championships. Now he has taken over United's No. 7 shirt – as worn by Best, Robson, Cantona and Beckham – and wears it with pride.

A debut appearance as a substitute against Bolton introduced the new star. He duly obliged with his trademark step-overs, tricks

FACT FILE | MIDFIELDER | 26 CAPS | 7 GOALS | MANCHESTER UNITED

Date of birth: **05.02.1985**
Height: **185 cm**
Weight: **75 kg**
Previous club: **Sporting Lisbon**
International debut: **20.08.2003 v Khazakhstan**
Previous World Cups: **None**

and light-footed manoeuvres, but Ronaldo found his first season in England tough. Some supporters decided he was little more than a showboating luxury, others disagreed and he was voted player of the season by Manchester United fans.

Euro 2004 was a watershed for the teenager. Forcing his way into the team, he produced exciting, mature performances – including two goals – that rejuvenated the host side. The tricks were still there, but this time they were there for a purpose; a pin-point cross, a vicious shot or a delicious through ball. Back in England, Ronaldo's progress continued, his vastly improved upper-body strength ensuring he was no longer easily shrugged off the ball.

Since Euro 2004 he has become an essential member of the national side, fitting in alongside Deco, providing countless assists for Pauleta and chipping in with seven goals of his own in 26 appearances. In Portugal they've watched him develop for over a decade, now they are ready for him to take on the world.

STYLE GUIDE

⊕ His distinctive 'twinkle-toes' running style only serves to emphasise Cristiano Ronaldo's turn of pace and ability to bemuse defenders. Equally comfortable on either foot, he favours the step-over but has a bag of tricks at his disposal. Perhaps his weakness is his eye for goal, but he is a danger in the air at corners and set pieces.

Flying winger: Ronaldo ghosts past Phil Neville during England's quarter-final meeting with hosts Portugal at Euro 2004.

ITALY

PROUD WORLD CUP HERITAGE

The new-look *Azzurri* are unproven on the big stage, but are still among the favourites.

Though they finished top of their qualifying group, in reality Italy were less than convincing in a fairly average collection of teams including Norway, Scotland, Slovenia, Belarus and Moldova. Their away form in particular, losing to Slovenia and drawing with both Norway and Scotland, did not impress their notoriously impatient supporters. However, Italy have been there before in the run-up to the finals.

IMPRESSIVE PEDIGREE

Italy has an impressive World Cup pedigree, they have won the trophy three times (1934, 1938 and 1982) and hosted a very impressive tournament in 1990. Qualifying for the finals has long been the norm for the national side. Though Serie A remains one of the most competitive leagues in Europe, the *Azzurri* performed poorly in Japan and Korea in 2002 and failed to qualify for the knockout stages of Euro 2004. However, coach Marcello Lippi, who took over from Giovanni Trapattoni after the last European Championships, has pledged to change all that and has started to dismantle an ageing and predictable team with a younger, more vibrant one.

Above *Fabio Grosso shoots past the Scotland keeper Craig Gordon during the 1-1 draw at Hampden Park.*

Opposite *Mauro Camoranesi in action during the qualifier against Belarus in Minsk. Italy won 4-1.*

Emerging in top spot from an easy qualification group has not convinced anyone, though the group was not without its fair share of drama. But perhaps Lippi's new team came of age toward the end of 2004 when they were beaten in Slovenia and then faced Belarus in Parma four days later. Two goals from Francesco Totti and one each from new boys Alberto Gilardino and Daniele De Rossi helped them home in a nail-biting seven-goal thriller.

Lippi, whose credentials for the job as national team coach are based on a hugely successful spell as manager of Juventus, likes his teams to play a passing game and to play the ball forward before they play it square or behind. He doesn't like to see the ball in the air and he does like to use the width of the pitch. He is also at pains to ensure that each player contributes to attack when they go forward and to defence when they lose the ball. Though the team performances in the qualifiers were lacklustre it is hoped that Italy will play a more attractive style of football when the tournament proper begins in June.

HOW THEY'LL LINE UP

It seems likely that 2006 will see the end of the international careers of players like Christian Vieri, Alessandro Del Piero, Filippo Inzaghi and even, though it should be said quietly, Paolo Maldini. Though he is likely to stick with a 4-4-2 formation, Lippi has found new vibrancy up front from Antonio Cassano and Alberto Gilardino though Luca Toni and Cristiano Lucarelli are also pushing for places, and in midfield he has the experience of Francesco Totti and Andrea

1982 ITALY 3-2 BRAZIL	WORLD CUP SECOND ROUND, GROUP STAGE
	Estadio Sarria, Barcelona

With in-form Brazil only needing a draw to qualify for the semi-finals, Italy had it all to do in this final group game. The Azzurri's poor form in the first round was blamed on striker Paolo Rossi just returning from a lengthy ban over a betting scandal. However, Rossi found his feet after just five minutes and put the Italians in front. A few minutes later Zico fed Socrates to shoot past Dino Zoff for the equaliser. On 25 minutes Rossi scored again, punishing a Brazilian defensive mistake and Italy went into the break 2-1 ahead.

Twenty minutes into the second half Brazil's Falcao pulled it back to 2-2, a result that would have been enough to see the South Americans through. But almost immediately Rossi scored a third, his hat-trick, to put the Italians back in front.

The final few minutes were breathtaking with both sides having goals ruled out and the 40-year-old Italian keeper Dino Zoff making several remarkable saves. In the end the Italians held on to win, and went on to beat Poland in the semi-final and Germany in the Final to claim their third World Cup victory.

Back row (left to right): Giorgio Chiellini, Alberto Gilardino, Daniele Bonera, Marco Materazzi, Gianluigi Buffon.
Front row: Gennaro Gattuso, Andrea Pirlo, Mauro Camoranesi, Fabio Cannavaro, Antonio Cassano, Francesco Totti.

Pirlo as well as the new talent of Daniele De Rossi, Manuel Blasi and Simone Barone.

However, in central defence things remain the same with Fabio Cannavaro and Alessandro Nesta as permanent fixtures.

POSSIBLE SQUAD

Goalkeepers: Gianluigi Buffon (Juventus), **Morgan De Sanctis** (Udinese), **Angelo Peruzzi** (Lazio)

Defenders: Daniel Bonera (Parma), **Fabio Cannavaro** (Juventus), **Alessandro Nesta** (AC Milan), **Gianluca Zambrotta** (Juventus), **Fabio Grosso** (Palermo), **Giorgio Chiellini** (Juventus), **Cristian Zaccardo** (Palermo)

Midfielders: Francesco Totti (Roma), **Gennaro Gattuso** (Milan), **Andrea Pirlo** (AC Milan), **Daniele De Rossi** (Roma), **Manuel Blasi** (Juventus), **Mauro Camoranesi** (Juventus), **Simone Barone** (Palermo), **Aimo Diana** (Sampdoria)

Forwards: Antonio Cassano (Real Madrid), **Alberto Gilardino** (AC Milan), **Vincenzo Laquinta** (Udinese), **Luca Toni** (Fiorentina), **Cristiano Lucarelli** (Livorno)

The legendary mean defence might be stretched should either of these stalwarts get injured. In goal Gianluigi Buffon has missed much of the season with a serious shoulder injury and has been replaced between the sticks by Morgan De Sanctis of Udinese. Palermo's Fabio Grosso has been used as right back during the qualifiers with the impressive Gianluca Zambrotta at left back.

ONE TO WATCH
Giorgio Chiellini

Powerful and pacy, this 21-year-old Juventus left back has earned himself the nickname 'The Armoured Truck'. At his best when pushing forward, Chiellini has also worked hard on improving his defensive skills and earned himself a permanent berth in Fabio Capello's team. Brought in to the national team in November 2004, Chiellini was a regular in the squad for the qualifying campaign and offers coach Lippi several new options, most obviously to free up Zambrotta for a midfield role.

Tall and good in the air, Chiellini also has quick feet and an eye for goal. He spent the 2004–05 season on loan at Fiorentina, missing only one game of the full league season. His form persuaded Juve to bring him back to Turin in the summer of 2005.

With a powerful engine that gets him up and down the field at pace, Lippi seems likely to give Chiellini a place in the pre-tournament friendlies. If he performs well, he could find himself in the starting line-up in Germany 2006.

A place in the starting XI for Giorgio Chiellini might see Gianluca Zambrotta pushed up into midfield.

VITAL STATISTICS

WORLD RANKING 12th   **KEEPER AND DEFENCE** 7/10   **MIDFIELD** 7/10   **ATTACK** 7/10

STRENGTHS AND WEAKNESSES

A blend of experienced defenders and midfielders and other younger players – particularly in attack – unproven at the highest level might provide the balance that recent Italian sides have lacked. But the squad is a little light in defence if Cannavaro and Nesta are injured and unless Totti and Pirlo play to their full potential then goals might be hard to come by.

HOW FAR WILL THEY GO?

A place in the semi-finals is the least that Italian fans will expect from their national team.

COACH
Marcello Lippi
(born 11 April 1948)

Record: P19 W11 D6 L2

Associated as a player and as a fledgling coach with Sampdoria, Marcello Lippi made his mark during an incredibly successful ten years at Juventus. His tenure as boss (1994–2004) saw the club as one of the giants of Europe and he led them to five Italian league championships, other cups and the Champions League in 1996. During his last season in charge at the Turin club he made no secret of the fact that he would like to manage the national team and after Italy's poor showing in Portugal in the summer of 2004 he replaced Giovanni Trapattoni in the hot seat.

Lippi's skills are as a motivator but he also has a reputation for refusing to let sentiment cloud his judgement. Tactically flexible, he likes to construct his teams carefully allowing each player to play to his strengths and the opposition's weaknesses. Lippi inherited a team of experienced players but many saw them as too old, too predictable and complacent. Lippi has pledged a clearout of the older players and is blessed with new talent, especially in attack where he has an embarrassment of riches. However, he is a loyal man and it may be hard for him to ignore Del Piero and Veiri when he choses his squad for Germany 2006.

Coach Marcello Lippi smiles during the qualifiers – but will the Azzurri come good at the right time?

ROUTE TO THE FINALS		
DATE		
04.09.04	ITALY **2**	**1** NORWAY
08.09.04	MOLDOVA **0**	**1** ITALY
09.10.04	SLOVENIA **1**	**0** ITALY
13.10.04	ITALY **4**	**3** BELARUS
26.03.05	ITALY **2**	**0** SCOTLAND
04.06.05	NORWAY **0**	**0** ITALY
03.09.05	SCOTLAND **1**	**1** ITALY
07.09.05	BELARUS **1**	**4** ITALY
08.10.05	ITALY **1**	**0** SLOVENIA
12.10.05	ITALY **2**	**1** MOLDOVA

EUROPE QUALIFYING GROUP 5 – FINAL TABLE							
TEAM	P	W	D	L	F	A	Pts
ITALY	10	7	2	1	17	8	**23**
NORWAY	10	5	3	2	12	7	**18**
SCOTLAND	10	3	4	3	9	7	**13**
SLOVENIA	10	3	3	4	10	13	**12**
BELARUS	10	2	4	4	12	14	**10**
MOLDOVA	10	1	2	7	5	16	**5**

FINALS GROUP E		
ITALY	Date	Venue
Ghana	12 June	Hanover
USA	17 June	Kaiserslautern
Czech Republic	22 June	Hamburg

Alessandro NESTA

POWERFUL AND EXTREMELY MOBILE, NESTA IS WIDELY REGARDED AS ONE OF THE BEST CENTRAL DEFENDERS IN EUROPE

One half of one of the most dependable defensive partnerships in world football – together with Fabio Cannavaro – Nesta is an elegant footballer with a superb positional sense. He has been part of the Italian national squad since the mid-1990s and played a big part in the *Azzurri*'s march to the Final of Euro 2000, where they lost to World Cup holders France. For Nesta, now in his early 30s, Germany 2006 will probably be his last World Cup but football fans will be able to see a fine defender playing at his peak.

Born in Rome in 1976 Alessandro Nesta signed for local team Lazio aged nine. He played for the junior teams at various levels before joining the first-team squad in 1993. Three years later he was also playing for the Italian national Under-21 team which won the European Championships in 1996. Later that year he made his senior international debut against Moldova.

'We will do everything we can to win in Germany next summer ... Brazil are strong, but in a one-off match anything can happen.'

In 2002 Nesta was the subject of a bidding war with all the major European teams interested in his signature including Manchester United and Real Madrid. He eventually signed for AC Milan and has remained with the *Rossoneri* ever since. During his four years at the San Siro he has won the Italian league title, the Italian cup, the European Super Cup and the Champions League. Not a bad haul of silverware.

Though the national team has not performed well during his time, Nesta has been a consistently important member of the

FACT FILE | CENTRAL DEFENDER | 72 CAPS | 0 GOALS | AC MILAN

Date of birth: **19.03.1976**
Height: **187 cm**
Weight: **79 kg**
Previous club: **Lazio**
International debut: **05.10.1996 v Moldova**
Previous World Cups: **1998, 2002**

STYLE GUIDE

Nesta's elegance hides his strength in the tackle and his tenacity. He also has pace, stamina and the ability to mark an opponent out of the game. But at the centre of his game is an uncanny positional sense that allows him to be first to the ball on most occasions. Nesta is also renowned for his excellent passing ability not only when defending but also when going forward. Expect to see exemplary defending from the Italian centre-back pairing.

side at Euro 96, the World Cup in 1998, Euro 2000, the World Cup in 2002 and Euro 2004.

In 2005 Nesta had to have treatment on a ruptured tendon in his left index finger and faced a barrage of criticism from fans and journalists who claimed that his injury was due to his hobby of playing video games. Surgery meant that he missed two World Cup qualifiers, but Nesta strenuously denied any connection between the injury and his hobby.

Nesta's experience, he now has over 70 caps, and his partnership with Fabio Cannavaro will provide the *Azzurri* with a solid base on which to work. If the 'new wave' of players can perform well then the Italians have a good chance of progressing to the knockout rounds.

Strong in the air as well as on the ground –
Alessandro Nesta is a fearsome opponent for anyone.

Francesco **TOTTI**

ITALIAN PLAYMAKER WITH EVERYTHING TO PROVE

Francesco Totti is the most iconic footballer in Italy. Captain and inspiration for both Roma and the national team, Totti is the playmaker supreme. With quicksilver feet and a lighting brain, he is the master of the defence splitting pass, whether over 50 yards or five yards. In recent years he has added goalscoring to his armoury, scoring regularly from penalties and free-kicks but also adding scores from open play. In the past, such as the 2002 World Cup, indiscipline has let him down. He now feels that in Germany 2006 he has something to prove.

Perhaps the most famous player in Italy, brilliant on the ball, fiercely loyal to one club – Roma – Totti is also a best-selling author. He had long been the butt of comedians' jokes, probably because he talks in a guttural local accent, and in 2003 he collected these jokes together and published them. The book, of which all proceeds went to UNICEF, was a huge success, selling 150,000 copies in its first few months on the bookshelves instantly turning Totti from a laughing stock into a national hero.

'We've simply got to atone for that World Cup failure as well as wiping out the bitter finish to Euro 2000.'

Germany 2006 presents Francesco Totti with a golden opportunity to prove that he is one of the best playmakers in the world.

FACT FILE
 | MIDFIELDER | 49 CAPS | 8 GOALS | ROMA

Date of birth: **27.09.1976**
Height: **180 cm**
Weight: **82 kg**
Previous clubs: **None**
International debut: **10.10.1998 v Switzerland**
Previous World Cups: **2002**

Born in 1976 in Rome, Totti joined Roma's junior team in 1989. He made his debut for the senior team aged 16 and has played there ever since, helping them, in 2001, to their first Italian league title in almost 20 years.

Like Alessandro Nesta, Totti was also part of the Italian Under-21 team that won the European Championships in 1996. He was promoted to the senior team during the qualifying campaign for Euro 2000. But his time on the international stage has been disappointing. Apart from reaching the Final at Euro 2000, which they lost to France, the World Cup in 2002 was a disaster. Totti was sent off in their match against South Korea as Italy failed to get through the second round. At Euro 2004 things got worse as Totti was suspended until the semi-finals for spitting at an opponent during their opening match against Denmark. In the event, Italy failed to qualify for the knockout rounds.

Fabulously talented, like all great footballers Totti needs a big stage on which to parade his skills, let's hope Germany 2006 proves to be that stage.

STYLE GUIDE

Totti is the player that makes Italy tick. Playing in the space just behind the strikers, he provides the essential link between central defence and the forward players. Totti is perfect for coach Lippi's intentions. With tremendous passing ability, speed of thought and vision, Totti is adept at opening up even the tightest defences – and he can score regularly from free-kicks and penalties. If he can keep his temper and find the sort of form he has showed for Roma in the past few seasons then Germany 2006 could finally see Totti get the credit he deserves as one of the world's true footballing geniuses.

Andrea **PIRLO**

THE SILENT LEADER QUIETLY MAKING HIS WAY TO THE TOP OF HIS GAME BY KEEPING IT SIMPLE

It is only since Marcello Lippi became coach that Andrea Pirlo has become a key player in the national team. But he, like Pirlo's club manager Carlo Ancelotti at Milan, had trouble deciding where to play this cultured midfielder. Again like Ancelotti, Lippi decided to play him in front of the back four. His performances since then, including both goals in the 2-0 home win against Scotland, have earned him a permanent place in the new-look *Azzurri*.

Starting as a youngster at Brescia, Pirlo made his debut in Serie A in 1995. He performed well, especially in tandem with the great Roberto Baggio, and in 1998 he was transferred to Inter Milan. But his career at Inter was disappointing, the then coach, Marcello Lippi, unsure where to best use his obvious talents. A loan spell at Reggina followed, as did a second spell at Brescia, then in 2001 Inter decided to sell him. In came city neighbours AC Milan who, in retrospect, got the bargain of all bargains.

It was just before the start of the 2002–03 season that Ancelotti decided to employ

Pirlo (second left) scores one of his two free-kicks as Italy beat Scotland 2-0 during the qualifying campaign.

FACT FILE | MIDFIELDER | 21 CAPS | 4 GOALS | AC MILAN

Date of birth: **19.05.1979**
Height: **177 cm**
Weight: **68 kg**
Previous clubs: **Reggina, Inter Milan, Brescia**
International debut: **07.09.2002 v Azerbaijan**
Previous World Cups: **None**

Pirlo as a deep-lying playmaker, the position he had been so successful with at Brescia, and it worked. Milan won the Champions League and the Italian cup that season. But the Italian coach at the time, Giovanni Trapattoni, was a great admirer of Pirlo's offensive qualities and was reluctant to play him deep, 'it would be like having Zico just in front of the defence,' he claimed. But Pirlo's performances at Euro 2004, while consistent, were nothing to write home about.

However, the qualifying campaign for Germany 2006 has given Pirlo the chance to show off his talents and he has taken that chance. Superb passing, great vision, a positional sense that allows him to be where he needs to be to win the ball and tremendous set-piece skills have made him indispensable for coach Lippi. 'Pirlo is a silent leader on the pitch. His feet do the talking for him,' said Lippi after one match.

For Pirlo himself, 'the secret is to keep it simple. Keep possession and keep the ball moving quickly so you tire out opponents.' If he can do that and find the form that has been so impressive in the *Azzurri*'s run to the finals then we may see the best from this midfield maestro in Germany 2006.

'When I see what Andrea can do with the ball I have to ask myself whether I am a footballer.'

Gennaro Gattuso

STYLE GUIDE

Now employed just in front of the back four, Pirlo allows Lippi to use two wide midfielders with Totti playing just behind the two front men. Though a bit lightweight for this anchor role, Pirlo makes up for it with his positional sense which allows him to win the ball, often without diving in to the tackle. His vision allows him to spray passes all round the pitch and his accuracy at free-kicks is always a danger to opposing defences.

Alberto **GILARDINO**

NATURAL-BORN GOALSCORER SET TO MAKE A BIG IMPACT IN GERMANY 2006

Transferred from Parma to AC Milan in the summer of 2005 Alberto Gilardino is considered one of the best strikers to have emerged in Italy for many years. He can shoot with both feet, is good in the air and possesses explosive pace. At 23 years of age he remains the great hope for the Italian national team's future.

Starting his career at Piacenza, where he made his Serie A debut, Gilardino then spent two years at Hellas Verona. But 23 goals in two consecutive seasons playing for Parma have been the making of Alberto Gilardino. The first season, 2003–04, was a good one on the pitch for Parma as they finished fifth in Serie A with Gilardino's goal tally second only to Milan's Andrei Shevchenko. Though off the pitch the club suffered badly as the size of

'The 2006 World Cup is definitely my main ambition and I will be working very hard to be there.'

its debt became apparent leading to wholesale changes in management and playing staff. The following season was awful, a much-weakened Parma only avoided relegation on the final day, but Gilardino again recorded 23 goals.

In the summer of 2005 it seemed inevitable that cash-strapped Parma would be looking to sell the young marksman. Interest was

Alberto Gilardino's club form for AC Milan is good news for Lippi's new-look Azzurri.

FACT FILE | STRIKER | 12 CAPS | 5 GOALS | AC MILAN

Date of birth: **05.07.1982**
Height: **184 cm**
Weight: **79 kg**
Previous clubs: **Parma, Verona, Piacenza**
International debut: **04.09.2004 v Norway**
Previous World Cups: **None**

STYLE GUIDE

With a tremendous temperament for the high-pressure world of football Gilardino is a natural leader of the line. Able to shoot with both feet, he is also an exceptional header of the ball and a fantastic exponent of the shot-on-the turn. Much will also depend on how he links up with his likely strike parter in the *Azzurri* starting XI. His partner at Milan is the ageing Christian Vieri, so if Vieri is chosen then the partnership will be a tried and tested one, but the most likely paring will be with the mercurial Antonio Cassano. If so, opposing defences need to be on their guard.

high with Milan, Inter and Juve all making enquiries and Chelsea, Real Madrid and Manchester United joining the throng from outside Italy. Gilardino chose Milan and joined the *Rossoneri* for a reported £18 million.

Gilardino has played and scored at every level for the national team. He captained the Under-21 side to victory in the 2004 European Championships, won a bronze medal at the 2004 Olympics and made his debut for the senior team in September 2004.

Though five goals in his first 12 games for the *Azzurri* represent a dream start for the young striker he makes no bones about his ultimate objective on the international stage, 'I really hope to play in the World Cup finals. I want to be there, be in the squad. I know I am still relatively young but I hope to be ready for it.'

Antonio **CASSANO**

IT'S MAKE OR BREAK TIME FOR THE BAD BOY OF ITALIAN FOOTBALL

Antonio Cassano burst onto the Italian football scene in 1999 playing for his hometown club Bari. He was almost immediately linked with a big-money move to Juventus. However, he remained loyal to his local club for two more seasons during which time he put in tremendous performances for club and for country at Under-21 level. In 2001 Roma won the auction for his services where he linked up with his idol Francesco Totti. A goal against Poland on his international debut in 2003 earned him a place in the squad for Euro 2004. For many Cassano is the future of Italian football.

Two-footed, fast and direct and with an eye for goal Antonio Cassano has the world at his feet. The perfect strike partner for Francesco Totti he should have a bright future for club and country. However, his career has been blighted by the periodic descent of the red mist. He has had several disciplinary problems since he left Bari, having spats with his coaches at both club and international level, and with referees.

'He's the greatest young talent in the Italian game.'

Fabio Capello, Juventus coach

Often out of the team and at odds over money with his club side Roma, Cassano also had run-ins with his Under-21 coach Claudio Gentile, who eventually threw him out of the side, and former Roma boss Fabio Capello who nicknamed his now famous losses of temper as *Cassanate*. But the time has come for Cassano to sort himself out. Current Italian coach Marcello Lippi has said that Cassano has to be playing

Antonio Cassano dribbles past a Scottish defender during their World Cup qualifier at the San Siro in Milan, Italy won 2-0.

FACT FILE | FORWARD | 8 CAPS | 3 GOALS | REAL MADRID

Date of birth: **12.07.1982**
Height: **175 cm**
Weight: **81 kg**
Previous club: **Roma, Bari**
International debut: **12.11.2003 v Poland**
Previous World Cups: **None**

first-team football to be considered for the World Cup squad. His move, in January 2006, to Real Madrid shows just how much he took the coach's words to heart.

After a superb season in 2003–04 for Roma, scoring 14 goals in Serie A, he also played well at Euro 2004, scoring two of Italy's three goals and almost seeing them through to the knockout rounds. He did play a part in World Cup qualification but he is not sure of his place in the starting line-up. A good start to his career at new club Real Madrid would do a lot for his chances.

Whatever his problems may be, 'Peter Pan', as he is nicknamed, has a supreme

footballing ability. 'Players like him are born only once every 30 years,' said Bari boss Eugenio Fascetti when he left the club. With balance, guile and speed, Cassano can unlock the tightest defences and has plenty of other admirers too. 'I was always struck by this boy who dribbled past players as if they were skittles,' says Sir Alex Ferguson's current assistant coach Carlos Queiroz, 'He will be a star at the next World Cup'. It's in Cassano's hands now.

STYLE GUIDE

Superbly skilled on the ball, Cassano plays as an out-and-out striker for the *Azzurri*. His lightning pace troubles even the swiftest defenders but he also has great positional sense and can make space even in tight situations. He developed a great understanding with Roma club-mate Francesco Totti. Whether they can still reproduce this at international level remains to be seen.

GHANA

THE BLACK STARS MAKE THEIR WORLD CUP BOW

On 8 October 2005 the streets of Ghana's main cities Accra and Kumasi were packed with celebrating football fans. A 4-0 victory away at the Cape Verde Islands had secured the Black Stars a first ever qualification for the World Cup finals.

Ghana emerged from a group that included the favourites South Africa and strong teams from DR Congo and Burkina Faso, but with six wins – including home and away wins against South Africa – and only one defeat saw them finish five points clear. Serbian coach Radomir Dujkovic takes a great deal of credit for harnessing a set of talented individuals and turning them into a team using his so-called 'rod of iron'. 'My players displayed a lot of commitment throughout and that, for me, is our secret,' he said, 'They played as a unit with every player doing his best in all the qualifying games.'

Producing good players has never been a problem for Ghana: Abedi Pele was a Champions League winner with Marseille in 1993 and African Footballer of the Year three times (1991–93), Anthony Yeboah had a fine career in Germany with Frankfurt and Hamburg and in England with Leeds United. But a good international team has long been coming. 'We always had good players, but

Back row (left to right): Godwin Attram, John Pantsil, Sammy Adjei, Isaac Boakye, John Mensah, Stephen Appiah. Front row: Abubacar Yahuza, Laryea Kingston, Matthew Amoah, Sulley Ali Muntari and Mohammed Hamza.

VITAL STATISTICS

WORLD RANKING 50th=
KEEPER AND DEFENCE 5/10
MIDFIELD 8/10
ATTACK 6/10

STRENGTHS AND WEAKNESSES
Very powerful in midfield where they have world-class players. However, it is debatable whether the defence will be strong enough to deal with top-class strikers or whether the forwards will be able to supply their fair share of goals.

HOW FAR WILL THEY GO?
A supreme effort might see them through to the knockout stages, but an early exit seems most likely.

only our generation has moulded into an excellent team,' says Ghana's new superstar Michael Essien of Chelsea.

Alongside Essien in a strong midfield there is inspirational captain Stephen Appiah and their partnership was the driving force behind the team's qualification. Another player to watch is Sulley Ali Muntari, a 21-year-old who has been receiving rave notices for his club form in Italy with Udinese. With Sammy Kuffour also back in the squad after differences with the coach, the defence looks solid too. Up front the goals come

from Asamoah Gyan of Modena, who scored four times in the qualifying campaign. He is likely to be partnered by the less experienced Matthew Amoah of Vitesse Arnhem.

However, it is in midfield that Ghana are at their strongest, with Appiah (four) and Michael Essien (three) contributing most goals in qualifying as well. Other teams will underestimate Ghana at their peril.

POSSIBLE SQUAD

Goalkeepers: Sammy Adjei (Moadon Sport Ashdol), **George Owu** (Ashanti Gold), **Philemon McCarthy** (Feyenoord)

Defenders: Aziz Ansah (Asante Kotoko), **Issa Ahmed** (Asante Kotoko), **Samuel Kuffour** (Roma), **Daniel Edusei** (Egaleo), **John Mensah** (Cremonese), **John Pantsil** (Hapoel Tel Aviv)

Midfielders: Francis Dickoh (Nordsjaelland), **Godwin Attram** (Al Shabab), **Michael Essien** (Chelsea), **Laryea Kingston** (Terek Grozny), **Stephen Appiah** (Fenerbahce), **Anthony Obodai** (Sparta Rotterdam), **Sulley Ali Muntari** (Udinese), **Abubacar Yahuza** (King Faisal Babes), **Haminu Dramani** (Red Star Belgrade)

Forwards: Prince Tagoe (Hearts of Oak), **Isaac Boakye** (Armenia Bielefeld), **Asamoah Gyan** (Modena), **Joe Tex Frimpong** (Enyimba), **Matthew Amoah** (Vitesse Arnhem)

Above *Germany 2006 will be the first chance to see new superstar Michael Essien in action on the world stage.*

Above right *Ghana's Serbian coach Radomir Dujkovic.*

AFRICA QUALIFYING GROUP 2 – FINAL TABLE							
TEAM	P	W	D	L	F	A	Pts
GHANA	10	6	3	1	17	4	**21**
DR CONGO	10	4	4	2	14	10	**16**
SOUTH AFRICA	10	5	1	4	12	14	**16**
BURKINA FASO	10	4	1	5	14	13	**13**
CAPE VERDE IS	10	3	1	6	8	8	**15**
UGANDA	10	2	2	6	6	15	**8**

FINALS GROUP E			
	GHANA	Date	Venue
	Italy	12 June	Hanover
	Czech Republic	17 June	Cologne
	USA	22 June	Nuremberg

USA

IT'S THE BILLION-DOLLAR QUESTION – ARE THE USA REALLY ANY GOOD AT FOOTBALL?

With their best-ever coach and their best-ever players, it's time for the USA national football team to stand up and be counted.

The World Cup in Japan and Korea saw a magnificent performance from the Americans. They played well in a difficult group, including co-hosts South Korea, but emerged following a superb 3-2 victory over Portugal. They beat local rivals Mexico 2-0 in the first knockout round and only fell 1-0 to eventual finalists Germany in the quarter-final. It is essential for a game developing fast across the nation that the USA do well in the 2006 World Cup. However, a difficult draw has left them sweating in a group also containing Italy, the Czech Republic and Ghana.

Above Team USA players celebrate qualification after beating Mexico to confirm their World Cup berth for Germany 2006.

Right Experienced midfielder and captain Claudio Reyna.

It may seem hard to believe but the USA made the semi-finals of the inaugural World Cup in 1930. More amazing still is the fact that there has been a professional football league in the USA since the 1920s. However, it didn't last. They had another go in the 1960s and that lasted for 20 years. The latest incarnation, Major League Soccer, began in 1996 and is still going strong.

But it is a strange beast. There are only 12 clubs across the nation, the major competition is organised badly and allows endless pointless matches in a labyrinthine series of play-offs and the sports organising body is continually trying to develop the rules of a game which is more popular than any other in the rest of the world.

However, in the real world Team USA's stock has never been higher. Since Bruce Arena's appointment following a disappointing World Cup in 1998 when they went out at the group stage following a 2-1 defeat by Iran, the USA have been on the up. They played well in qualifying, confirming their place with three games to go and finishing above new and bitter rivals Mexico.

There is no denying it, the USA is on the rise. With players now playing regularly in England, Germany and Holland as well as a sustainable national league producing players like Landon Donovan, DaMarcus Beasley and wunderkind Freddy Adu, it's only a matter of time before the USA win a major tournament. Their terrible draw for Germany 2006 makes it look unlikely that this will be their year, but their time will come.

HOW THEY'LL LINE UP

Though coach Arena has been keen to include as many US-based players as possible, the team is likely to be made up mostly of players already playing in Europe. In goal, however, he has to decide between Tim Howard, who never gets a game for Manchester United, and Kasey Keller, who was voted Honda's Player of the Year in 2005. Keller seems most likely to get the nod.

At the back, Arena is likely to favour Bocanegra and Spector as the full backs with Berhalter and the 6-foot-4-inch Onyewu as the centre backs. In midfield he has the talented DaMarcus Beasley, who has

VITAL STATISTICS

WORLD RANKING 8th   **KEEPER AND DEFENCE** 6/10
MIDFIELD 7/10   **ATTACK** 7/10
STRENGTHS AND WEAKNESSES
Reasonably solid in goal, the defence is inexperienced. Strong in midfield, but how many goals are they going to score against world-class defences.
HOW FAR WILL THEY GO?
It will take a titanic effort for them to emerge from the group stage. If they do… watch out the rest of the world.

been in such fine form for Dutch club PSV, and Landon Donovan as well as the experienced Claudio Reyna. And up front it seems likely that Brian McBride will lead the line. Who will partner him will probably depend on the form of the other contenders during a series of friendlies which have been arranged for 2006, including games against Canada, Japan and Germany.

Victory over Panama in the Final saw the USA win the Gold Cup in 2005.

POSSIBLE SQUAD

Goalkeepers: Tim Howard (Manchester United),
Kasey Keller (Borussia Moenchengladbach),
Kevin Hartman (Los Angeles Galaxy)

Defenders: Jonathan Spector (Charlton Athletic),
Gregg Berhalter (Energie Cottbus), **Heath Pearce**
(FC Norjælland), **Carlos Bocanegra** (Fulham), **Jim
Conrad** (Kansas City Wizards), **Steve Cherundolo**
(Hannover 96), **Oguchi Onyewu** (Standard Liege)

Midfielders: DaMarcus Beasley (PSV Eindhoven),
Brian Carroll (DC United), **Kerry Zavagnin** (Kansas
City Wizards), **Benny Feilhaber** (Hamburger SV),
Landon Donovan (Los Angeles Galaxy), **Eddie
Gaven** (MetroStars), **Claudio Reyna** (Manchester
City), **Santino Quaranta** (DC United), **Freddy Adu**
(DC United)

Forwards: Brian Ching (San Jose Earthquakes),
Brian McBride (Fulham), **Chris Rolfe** (Chicago Fire),
Josh Wolff (Kansas City Wizards)

Above Back row (left to right): Jonathan Spector, Kasey Keller, Carlos Bocanegra, Greg Berhalter, Brian Ching, Eddie Gaven. Front row: Brian Carroll, Josh Wolff, DaMarcus Beasley, Steve Cherundulo and Kerry Zavagnin.

Right Talented full back Jonathan Spector in action against Scotland.

Superstar Landon Donovan returned to the USA after a disappointing spell in Europe with Bayer Leverkusen.

ONE TO WATCH
Jonathan Spector

A tough tackling and energetic full back, Spector rose to prominence as a member of the USA Under-17s at the World Championships in 2003. His performances during the tournament saw him signed by Manchester United from his hometown club, Chicago Soccers. He made his debut for the senior USA team aged 18 in November 2004 against Jamaica.

Though he had played several times for the Manchester United first-team, 2005–06

saw him out on loan at Charlton Athletic, for whom he has made regular appearances in the Premiership. A place in the USA squad for Germany 2006 would be a major step on the career path of this talented youngster.

COACH
Bruce Arena
(born 21 September 1951)
Record: P118 W67 D26 L25

A superb college sports record saw Bruce Arena embark on a career as a football coach in a country crying out for one. Regarded as the distant fourth to American football, baseball and basketball, soccer – as it is known across the Atlantic – is still looked at with curiosity. A short career as a professional player with Tacoma Tides, earning one cap

Bruce Arena, a talented and much-liked coach, is likely to move on following the 2006 World Cup.

for the national team, was followed by his appointment as soccer coach at various universities but ending up at the University of Virginia, where he stayed for 18 highly successful years.

He turned to the world of professional football in 1996 with DC United from Washington, adding to that duties as coach to the national team at the Olympics in 1996, before being appointed national coach in 1998. Since then, two victories in the Gold Cup and a quarter-final placing in the 2002 World Cup have catapulted the USA into the FIFA top ten world rankings and the coach felt they were unlucky not to receive a seeding this time around. Arena will be the longest serving coach in Germany 2006 and is the first American coach to have been in charge for more than 100 games. However, the USA's record against the top teams is poor and a tough draw has left Arena a worried man.

ROUTE TO THE FINALS

DATE			
09.02.05	TRINIDAD & TOBAGO **1**	**2**	USA
27.03.05	MEXICO **2**	**1**	USA
30.03.05	USA **2**	**0**	GUATEMALA
04.06.05	USA **3**	**0**	COSTA RICA
08.06.05	PANAMA **0**	**3**	USA
17.08.05	USA **1**	**0**	TRINIDAD & TOBAGO
03.09.05	USA **2**	**0**	MEXICO
07.09.05	GUATEMALA **0**	**0**	USA
08.10.05	COSTA RICA **3**	**0**	USA
12.10.05	USA **2**	**0**	PANAMA

CONCACAF FINAL STAGE – FINAL TABLE

TEAM	P	W	D	L	F	A	Pts
USA	10	7	1	2	16	6	22
MEXICO	10	7	1	2	22	9	22
COSTA RICA	10	5	1	4	14	16	16
TRINIDAD & TOBAGO	10	4	1	5	10	15	13
GUATEMALA	10	3	2	5	16	18	11
PANAMA	10	0	2	8	4	21	2

FINALS GROUP E

		Date	Venue
	USA		
	Czech Republic	12 June	Gelsenkirchen
	Italy	17 June	Kaiserslautern
	Ghana	22 June	Nuremberg

DaMarcus **BEASLEY**

FAST, SKILFUL AND AT THE TOP OF HIS GAME, DAMARCUS BEASLEY IS THE FIRST OF HIS KIND – A REAL ALL-AMERICAN 'SOCCER' STAR

Transferred in a multi-million dollar deal from Chicago Fire to PSV in Holland in 2004, DaMarcus Beasley has gone from strength to strength. In his first season in Eindhoven, 'Jitter' (short for 'Jitterbug'), helped PSV to the league and cup double, and top scored in the team's run to the semi-finals of the Champions League where they narrowly lost to AC Milan. A mainstay of the USA national team, Beasley's skills and experience helped ensure World Cup qualification and victory in the 2005 Gold Cup.

Born in the American heartland of Fort Wayne, Indiana, DaMarcus Beasley is now treading in uncharted waters for an American footballer, winning tournaments and plaudits in Europe and becoming the first American to play in the semi-finals of the Champions League. 'It's something not many Americans have done,' he says with modesty, 'but I'm sure I won't be the last. This just goes to show that Americans are moving in the right direction.' Equally at home in midfield, on the wing or as an out-and-out striker Beasley has done well in the last two years for both club coach Guus Hiddink and national coach Bruce Arena. His superb performances for the USA at the World Cup in 2002 brought him to the notice of several European clubs and he jumped at the chance of a move to Holland. Beasley turned professional in 1999 with Los Angeles Galaxy but, without playing a game in LA, he moved to Chicago Fire in February 2000. Playing as a midfielder, using his speed and strength as a 'two-way' player moving from 'offense to defense' with ease, he helped Chicago become one of the MLS's leading teams. He starred in

FACT FILE | MIDFIELDER | 54 CAPS | 11 GOALS | PSV EINDHOVEN

Date of birth: **24.05.1982**
Height: **175 cm**
Weight: **57 kg**
Previous clubs: **Chicago Fire, Los Angeles Galaxy**
International debut: International debut: **27.01.2001 v China**
Previous World Cups: **2002**

the USA's 2002 World Cup campaign and continued his good form for both club and country in 2003. PSV manager Guus Hiddink bought him in 2004 to replace Arjen Robben who moved to Chelsea. Playing as a central striker in Holland Beasley added stamina to a game based on strength and speed, scoring 12 goals in 43 games in his first season and proving that American footballers can cut it with the best that Europe has to offer.

His international credentials are also impressive and have brought him more than 50 caps since his debut in January 2001. He played a major part in the USA's victory in the 2005 Gold Cup and in their qualification campaign for Germany 2006 despite suffering a major injury towards the end of the 2004–05 season.

'It doesn't get any better than playing in the World Cup ... the speed, the skill level ... everything ... Everybody's talking about it, and we'll be ready for it.'

STYLE GUIDE

⚽ Playing as a left-sided midfielder for the national team Beasley uses strength and speed to fetch and carry in a 'box-to-box' style. Also has the ability to beat players and cross the ball for the strikers. Has recently added trickery with free-kicks to his armoury of skills. Can also score important goals as he showed with his spectacular left-footed strike against Mexico in the World Cup qualifier in September 2005 that clinched their World Cup berth.

Mexico keeper Oswaldo Sanchez is powerless to stop DaMarcus Beasley scoring the USA's second goal in their 2-0 qualifying victory.

CZECH REPUBLIC

UNSEEDED AND UNFANCIED, THE CZECHS ARE DESPERATE TO TAKE THEIR EURO 2004 FORM ONTO THE WORLD STAGE

Agonisingly beaten 1-0 by eventual winners Greece, the Czech Republic were almost everyone's favourite team at the European Championships in Portugal.

With an attractive brand of attacking football, full of flowing moves and resourcefulness, the Czech Republic breezed through the group stage of Euro 2004, winning all their group games, beating Denmark in the quarter-finals and narrowly losing to Greece in the semi-finals courtesy of a 'silver goal' despite hitting the bar towards the end of normal play – 'a Greek Tragedy' – shouted the newspapers.

Twice runners-up in the World Cup as Czechoslovakia, in 1934 and 1962, their first qualification campaign as the Czech Republic came in 1998. They failed to qualify for that tournament and for the next one four years later. The appointment of coach Karel Bruckner in November 2001, at the end of that second unsuccessful campaign proved to be something of a watershed for the national team. Led by the effervescent Pavel Nedved and Karel Poborsky, both of whom had left their native country to ply their trade in more lucrative European Leagues, Nedved with Juventus and Poborsky with Manchester United, the team began to believe in themselves.

The coach abandoned the more cautious approach of his predecessors and urged

VITAL STATISTICS

WORLD RANKING 2nd   **KEEPER AND DEFENCE** 8/10
MIDFIELD 7/10   **ATTACK** 7/10
STRENGTHS AND WEAKNESSES
With the best keeper in the tournament they will be hard to beat. Solid in midfield, it will be up to the strikers to perform on the biggest stage they have ever experienced.
HOW FAR WILL THEY GO?
Despite not being seeded, they would be disappointed not to reach the quarter-finals.

his team to use their speed to pressurise opponents in their own half. Stressing discipline, demonstrated in full by the admirable Nedved, he dropped various more volatile players like Tomas Repka and Patrik Berger, and brought in new ones like Milan Baros, Marek Heinz and Jaroslav Plasil. It worked as his team embarked on a 20-match unbeaten run which ended just before the start of Euro 2004.

Though often successful in the European Championships their performance at Euro 2004 and since then has earned them the No. 2 spot in the FIFA world rankings but was not enough to earn them a seeding for Germany 2006. This makes them dangerous opponents for their fellow members in Group E: USA, Ghana and Italy, none of whom were happy with the draw. Germany 2006 will prove whether Karel Bruckner's blend of ageing stars and young bloods can keep the Czech Republic on their upward trajectory in the list of football's world powers.

HOW THEY'LL LINE UP

Whether Bruckner will play his favoured 4-5-1 or go for the more fashionable 4-4-2, one thing's for sure – Petr Cech will be between the sticks. A magnificent keeper, commanding and with good handling, he has been superb for club and country for a number of years. He played a great part in Euro 2004 where a series of top-notch displays helped the Czech Republic into the semi-finals. The dynamic Marek Jankulovski is a certain starter in defence but it is in midfield that Bruckner has enviable

Opposite *Pavel Nedved (right) came out of international retirement to help the Czech's qualify.*

Right *Striker Milan Baros was impressive at Euro 2004, scoring five goals on the way to the semi-finals.*

Chelsea's Petr Cech: one of the world's finest keepers.

strength. With Tomas Galasek and Tomas Rosicky providing a solid and flexible barrier, old stagers Poborsky and the inspirational Nedved can produce the flair needed to unlock the tightest defences. However, Nedved has yet to decide whether to play or not.

Bruckner also has choices up front with Milan Baros, one of Euro 2004's best performers, and the giant Jan Koller the probable starters, but with Marek Heinz, who also starred in Portugal, providing an alternative style of goalgetting.

Back row (left to right): Marek Jankulovski, Tomas Ujfalusi, Zdenek Grygera, Petr Cech, David Rozehnal. Front row: Karel Poborsky, Vladimir Smicer, Milan Baros, Tomas Rosicky, Pavel Nedved and Jan Polak.

POSSIBLE SQUAD

Goalkeepers: Petr Cech (Chelsea), **Jaromir Blazek** (Sparta Prague), **Antonin Kinsky** (Saturn Ramensko)

Defenders: Zdenek Grygera (Ajax), **Martin Jiranek** (Spartak Moscow), **Tomas Ujfalusi** (Fiorentina), **Rene Bolf** (Auxerre), **Marek Jankulovski** (AC Milan), **David Rozehnal** (Paris St-Germain), **Pavel Mares** (Zenit St Petersburg)

Midfielders: Karel Poborsky (Ceske Budejovice), **Tomas Galasek** (Ajax), **Tomas Rosicky** (Borussia Dortmund), **Pavel Nedved** (Juventus), **Vladimir Smicer** (Bordeaux), **Tomas Hubschman** (Shakhtar Donetsk), **Jan Polak** (Nuremberg), **Jaroslav Plasil** (Monaco), **Jiri Jarosik** (Birmingham City)

Forwards: Milan Baros (Aston Villa), **Jan Koller** (Borussia Dortmund), **Marek Heinz** (Galatasaray), **Vratislav Lokvenc** (Red Bull Salzburg)

ONE TO WATCH
Jaroslav Plasil

Jaroslav Plasil: a quality passer of the ball.

Spotted by Monaco playing for the Czech Under-16 team in 1999, Plasil was signed up straight away. Two years later he made his first-team debut, but progress was slow in a troubled team. A spell on loan at second division Creteil sharpened up the youngster and on his return to the Principality he was given a run in the first-team by coach Didier Deschamps. His technical skills in midfield were a revelation and he played a major part in a marvellous season for Monaco when they reached the Champions League Final defeating Real Madrid and Chelsea, among others, along the way.

His form prompted a call-up to the national squad for Euro 2004 and he scored in one of the warm-up games against Bulgaria. A regular in the squad since then, apart from a lengthy layoff through injury, Plasil is aiming high for Germany 2006.

COACH

Karel Bruckner

(born 13 November 1939)

Record: P46 W33 D7 L6

Appointed team coach in November 2001 after the Czech Republic's failure to qualify for the World Cup in 2002, Bruckner has used his renowned tactical ability to build one of his country's most successful teams ever.

A long playing career with club side Sigma Olomouc was followed by his appointment as coach of the same club in 1973 where he honed his tactical skills. After coaching at various other clubs he was appointed coach of the national Under-21 team in 1997 where his charges included Petr Cech, Tomas Ujfalusi and Milan Baros. His familiarity with the players guaranteed him their respect when he took over the senior team and must have influenced Pavel Nedved's decision to come out of international retirement to ensure qualification for Germany 2006.

His appointment had an immediate effect on the national team and they embarked on a 20-match unbeaten run until they lost to the Republic of Ireland in March 2004. The team's flowing performances at Euro 2004 enhanced his reputation for fielding a team bursting with attacking flair who want to push forward and score goals.

Karel Bruckner has built a strong attacking team.

ROUTE TO THE FINALS

DATE			
08.08.04	HOLLAND **2**	**0**	CZECH REPUBLIC
09.09.04	CZECH REPUBLIC **1**	**0**	ROMANIA
13.09.04	ARMENIA **0**	**3**	CZECH REPUBLIC
17.11.04	MACEDONIA **0**	**2**	CZECH REPUBLIC
26.03.05	CZECH REPUBLIC **4**	**3**	FINLAND
30.03.05	ANDORRA **0**	**4**	CZECH REPUBLIC
04.06.05	CZECH REPUBLIC **8**	**1**	ANDORRA
08.06.05	CZECH REPUBLIC **6**	**1**	MACEDONIA
03.09.05	ROMANIA **2**	**0**	CZECH REPUBLIC
07.09.05	CZECH REPUBLIC **4**	**1**	ARMENIA
08.10.05	CZECH REPUBLIC **0**	**2**	HOLLAND
12.10.05	FINLAND **0**	**3**	CZECH REPUBLIC

EUROPE QUALIFYING GROUP 1 – FINAL TABLE

TEAM	P	W	D	L	F	A	Pts
HOLLAND	12	10	2	0	27	3	**32**
CZECH REPUBLIC	12	9	0	3	35	12	**27**
ROMANIA	12	8	1	3	20	10	**25**
FINLAND	12	5	1	6	21	19	**16**
MACEDONIA	12	2	3	7	11	24	**9**
ARMENIA	12	2	1	9	9	25	**7**
ANDORRA	12	1	2	9	4	34	**5**

PLAY-OFFS

DATE			
12.11.05	NORWAY **0**	**1**	CZECH REPUBLIC
16.11.05	CZECH REPUBLIC **1**	**0**	NORWAY

Czech Republic won 2-0 on aggregate

FINALS GROUP E

		Date	Venue
	CZECH REPUBLIC	Date	Venue
	USA	12 June	Gelsenkirchen
	Ghana	17 June	Cologne
	Italy	22 June	Hamburg

Tomas **ROSICKY**

DIMINUTIVE AND SLIGHT, ROSICKY IS A GIANT IN MIDFIELD FOR ONE OF THE DARK HORSES OF GERMANY 2006

Nicknamed 'Dumpling' after his favourite food, Rosicky scored six goals during the qualifying campaign. After finishing the group stage in second place behind Holland, the Czechs had to face Norway in a play-off. Having won the first leg 1-0 in Oslo, Rosicky, who had been doubtful because of an ankle and knee injury, played and scored the only goal of the game to secure a first World Cup finals place for the Czech Republic.

From a footballing family, his father Jiri played for Sparta Prague, Tomas Rosicky joined the same club as a youngster in 1988. He made his first-team debut aged 17 and won two league titles with them (1999 and 2000) earning himself a reputation as the 'football Mozart' because of his artistic playmaking. His performances also earned him a debut for the international team against the Republic of Ireland in 2000. The following year he moved to Borussia Dortmund for a Czech Republic record fee of £8 million.

In his second season with the German club they won the Bundesliga and reached the UEFA Cup Final, and just to prove that he hadn't been forgotten at home he was voted the Czech Republic's player of the year in 2001 and 2002.

In 2004 he played a major part in the European Championships in Portugal – his country's first major international tournament. Playing what was regarded by many as the tournament's most attractive football – coming from behind to beat both Germany and Holland in the group stage –

FACT FILE | MIDFIELDER | 37 CAPS | 8 GOALS | BORUSSIA DORTMUND

Date of birth: **14.10.1980**
Height: **178 cm**
Weight: **68 kg**
Previous club: **Sparta Prague**
International debut: **23.02.2000 v Republic of Ireland**
Previous World Cups: **None**

and with Rosicky in outstanding form they reached the semi-final only to be beaten by eventual winners Greece.

During the last year Rosicky has suffered several injuries, had an appendix operation and broken his arm. However, having recovered from his injuries and not lost his form it seems wholly appropriate that he scored the winning goal in the play-off against Norway that secured the Czech Republic their tickets to their first ever World Cup. Rosicky, still only 25 years old, is looking to Germany 2006 for recognition that he is one of the finest midfielders not only in Europe, but in the world.

'Tomas has sensational vision and all the qualities you need from a playmaker of international class.'

Josef Chovanec, former national coach of the Czech Republic

STYLE GUIDE

⚽ Plays a more defensive role with the national team than with his club side, doing his fair share of the legwork beside captain Galasek. Composed even under pressure, Rosicky has good control and has an eye for the right pass at the right time. His unique technical abilities can be seen in how comfortable he is with the ball at his feet.

Rosicky (right) battles with Greece's Angelos Basinas during their tense semi-final at Euro 2004.

BRARZIL

PERENNIAL WINNERS

The five-times World Champions – and the world's favourite football team – are once again hot favourites to lift the trophy in Berlin on 9 July.

As the only team to have appeared in all World Cup finals since the competition began in 1930 it is no surprise that Brazil is the nation most closely associated with the world's greatest sporting competition. The current World Cup holders, winners of the 2004 Copa America and the 2005 Confederations Cup, also held in Germany, and top dogs in a tough South American qualifying group, Brazil are strongly tipped to mount a successful defence of their world crown.

EXPORTS BRING PRESSURE

It all seems a far cry from 1998 in Paris when Ronaldo's shambolic appearance in the Final saw Brazil humbled 3-0 by France, and from 2002 when Brazil almost failed to qualify for the finals in Japan and Korea. However, victory in the 2002 Final over Germany and

their fantastic record in the years since then, including a tremendous 2006 World Cup qualifying campaign in which Brazil had to compete despite being the holders of the trophy, have banished any doubts that Brazil are the best team in the world.

Ironically the last few years have seen Brazilian domestic football take a dive, crumbling stadiums, violence before, during and after matches and allegations of corruption have all led to a serious decline in attendances – the average crowd at a top-flight game is down to about 7,000. This has meant that hundreds of players have fled the country and now play in Europe. Brazilian national team coach Carlos Alberto Parreira has said that the majority of the squad he will assemble for the finals in Germany will be made up of players who play in Europe. This has not gone down well

Adriano (left) heads the ball past Argentina's goalkeeper German Lux to score his side's fourth goal during the Confederations Cup Final in 2005. Much to their delight, Brazil won 4-1.

Opposite Roberto Carlos (top) celebrates a goal in the World Cup qualifier at home to Venezuela. Ronaldinho (left) and Kaka are also delighted as their 3-0 victory took the favourites a step closer to Germany.

among football fans in Brazil where press and public take a huge interest in the doings of the *Seleção* – as they are known in Brazil – and are always clamouring for players in form in domestic football to be given a chance at international level.

However, Parreira has great tactical awareness and has used this skill to great effect during the last few years. His current team is based around a tight defence, a midfield that features some of the most exciting players in the world, topped off with fast and direct strikers.

HOW THEY'LL LINE UP

It is reported that coach Parreira is likely to favour the 4-2-2-2 formation that he tried out in the qualification match against Peru in March and has used ever since. After the final group match against Venezuela in October he said, 'For the start of the World Cup, I can't see us changing the system we are using now, with two holding midfielders, two attacking midfielders and two forwards. In principle, the formation for the opening match of the World Cup has practically been determined.'

In goal Parreira seems to have found a favourite in the gigantic Dida. His defence has been consistent throughout the last few years with Cafu, going in to his fourth World Cup with over 140 caps to his name, and Roberto Carlos as the wing-backs and Lucio and Juan in the centre of a

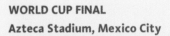

1970 BRAZIL 4-1 ITALY

WORLD CUP FINAL
Azteca Stadium, Mexico City

Besides being one of the most exciting World Cup Finals ever played, *Brazil's third world championship victory earned them the right to keep the Jules Rimet trophy forever. The legendary Pelé's last World Cup appearance proved to be one of the best displays of attacking football ever witnessed.*

On top in the opening exchanges Italy went behind when Pelé outjumped Burgnich to head in a cross from Rivelino after 17 minutes. Fittingly, it was Brazil's 100th World Cup goal. Italy equalised soon after when Boninsegna seized on a mistake by Clodoaldo and steered the ball home.

But the Italian cause was lost as the Brazilians scored three goals in 25 second-half minutes. First Gerson scored with a powerful left-footer from outside the box, then a back-header across goal by Pelé following a Gerson free-kick allowed Jairzinho to put them further ahead. Matters were finally sealed when Pelé fed the onrushing Carlos Alberto to blast a right-foot shot past the hapless Italian keeper Albertosi.

mobile defence. However, teenage sensation Cicinho, who left Sao Paulo for Real Madrid during the January transfer window, will be looking to start his career with some spectacular performances in Spain in the hopes of replacing the ageing Cafu.

In terms of team selection, the manager has more problems going forward, but they are great problems to have. In the midfield the holding players are likely to be Emerson and Ze Roberto, with Kaka and Ronaldinho looking to get forward to support strikers Robinho and Adriano. This team means there's no place for either Julio Baptista or Ronaldo, though Adriano's shoulder fracture

picked up in Inter's Serie A match against Udinese in October 2005 will give Ronaldo the opportunity to prove his continuing worth to the team.

POSSIBLE SQUAD

Goalkeepers: Dida (AC Milan), **Julio Cesar** (Inter Milan), **Rogerio Cenni** (Sao Paulo)

Defenders: Cafu (AC Milan), **Roberto Carlos** (Real Madrid), **Cicinho** (Real Madrid), **Gilberto** (Hertha Berlin), **Lucio** (Bayern Munich), **Juan** (Bayer Leverkusen), **Alex** (PSV), **Luisao** (Benfica)

Midfielders: Kaka (AC Milan), **Ronaldinho** (Barcelona), **Juninho Pernambucano** (Lyon), **Ze Roberto** (Bayern Munich), **Emerson** (Juventus), **Alex** (Fenerbahce), **Renato** (Seville), **Gilberto Silva** (Arsenal), **Julio Baptista** (Real Madrid)

Forwards: Ronaldo (Real Madrid), **Adriano** (Inter Milan), **Robinho** (Real Madrid), **Ricardo Oliveira** (Real Betis)

COACH
Carlos Alberto Parreira
(born 27 February 1943)
Record: P106 W54 D39 L13
Unusually in modern football Parreira never played the game professionally. But no one can doubt his abilities as a coach as he prepares to lead a team into the World Cup finals for the fourth time in his career. Trained as a physical education instructor, he began to specialise in football training in the late 1960s. He worked alongside

Back row (left to right): Ronaldinho, Dida, Adriano, Roque Junior, Lucio, Emerson. Front row: Robinho, Kaka, Ze Roberto, Maicon and Gilberto line-up before the 2005 Confederations Cup semi-final against Germany. Brazil won 3-2.

Coach Alberto Parreira keeps an eye on Robinho (centre) and Roberto Carlos during training.

manager/coach Mario Zagallo for the Brazil team that won the World Cup in Mexico in 1970 and took his own first tentative steps in coaching soon afterwards, quickly developing his unique tactical style. He coached Kuwait for four years, taking them to the World Cup in 1982 and then took charge of the Brazilian national team for the first time the following year. He was in charge of the United Arab Emirates team that took part in Italia 90 and then returned to the Brazilian hot seat for the qualifiers for USA 94 with Zagallo as his technical director. After a tough qualifying competition, Brazil won the tournament in convincing if unspectacular fashion, beating Italy on penalties in the Final. Parreira then stood aside again.

Following Brazil's victory in the 2002 World Cup in Japan and Korea under Luis Felipe Scolari, Brazil needed a steady pair of hands to guide the team through what has become one of the most difficult qualifying competitions and they turned once again to Parreira. His record since then has been marvellous, victory in the Copa America in 2004, victory in the Confederations Cup in 2005 and top of the pile in the South American World Cup qualifying group. Parreira has nothing more to prove.

ONE TO WATCH
Cicinho
The latest recruit of the Real Madrid *Galacticos* Cicinho seems likely to replace Michel Salgado as the club's right back and will eventually take Cafu's place in the Brazilian national team. The youngster enjoyed a meteoric rise during 2005. His performances at right back for his club Sao Paulo were instrumental in their winning

---

VITAL STATISTICS

WORLD RANKING 1st   **KEEPER AND DEFENCE** 7/10   **MIDFIELD** 9/10   **ATTACK** 9/10
STRENGTHS AND WEAKNESSES
Parreira's conservative approach, once considered a weakness of his management style, has produced a team that is solid at the back combined with the usual flair in midfield and speed and strength up front.
HOW FAR WILL THEY GO?
Expect to see Brazil in the Final, bet against them winning it at your peril.

Cicinho moved from Sao Paulo to Real Madrid during the January 2006 transfer window.

the Paulista and the Copa Libertadores earlier in the year and earned him a call up at national level for the friendly against Guatemala in April.

The veteran Cafu was given a rest for the Confederations Cup, and Cicinho grabbed his chance with some memorable performances that illustrated his tenacious tackling and his attacking qualities. His finest moments came in the Final when he had a hand in all four of Brazil's goals against arch enemies Argentina.

A small man, he more than makes up for it with speed and strength. Strong in the tackle, the main characteristics of his game are in supporting the attack with powerful forward thrusts, superb crosses and a thunderous shot. Expect to hear a lot more of the latest talent to roll off the Brazilian production line.

ROUTE TO THE FINALS

DATE			
07.09.03	COLOMBIA **1**	**2** BRAZIL	
10.09.03	BRAZIL **1**	**0** ECUADOR	
16.11.03	PERU **1**	**1** BRAZIL	
19.11.03	BRAZIL **3**	**3** URUGUAY	
30.03.04	PARAGUAY **0**	**0** BRAZIL	
02.06.04	BRAZIL **3**	**1** ARGENTINA	
06.06.04	CHILE **1**	**1** BRAZIL	
05.09.04	BRAZIL **3**	**1** BOLIVIA	
09.10.04	VENEZUELA **2**	**5** BRAZIL	
13.10.04	BRAZIL **0**	**0** COLOMBIA	
17.11.04	ECUADOR **1**	**0** BRAZIL	
27.03.05	BRAZIL **1**	**0** PERU	
30.03.05	URUGUAY **1**	**1** BRAZIL	
05.06.05	BRAZIL **4**	**1** PARAGUAY	
08.06.05	ARGENTINA **3**	**1** BRAZIL	
04.09.05	BRAZIL **5**	**0** CHILE	
09.10.05	BOLIVIA **1**	**1** BRAZIL	
12.10.05	BRAZIL **3**	**0** VENEZUELA	

SOUTH AMERICA QUALIFYING GROUP – FINAL TABLE

TEAM	P	W	D	L	F	A	Pts
BRAZIL	18	9	7	2	35	17	**34**
ARGENTINA	18	10	4	4	29	17	**34**
ECUADOR	18	8	4	6	23	19	**28**
PARAGUAY	18	8	4	6	23	23	**28**
URUGUAY	18	6	7	5	23	28	**25**
COLOMBIA	18	6	6	6	24	16	**24**
CHILE	18	5	7	6	18	22	**22**
VENEZUELA	18	5	3	10	20	28	**18**
PERU	18	4	6	8	20	28	**18**
BOLIVIA	18	4	2	12	20	37	**14**

FINALS GROUP F

		Date	Venue
	BRAZIL		
	Croatia	13 June	Berlin
	Australia	18 June	Munich
	Japan	22 June	Dortmund

RENOWNED FOR HIS PENALTY SAVING, *MURALHA* ('THE WALL') – AS HE IS KNOWN – IS ONE OF THE FINEST KEEPERS IN THE WORLD TODAY

Though he made his debut for the national team in 1995 against Ecuador it was not until after the 2002 World Cup victory that Dida made the Brazilian No. 1 jersey his own. A hugely successful season with club side AC Milan in Italy in 2003, which included victory in the Champions League over Juventus after a penalty shoot-out in which Dida saved three spot kicks, saw him elevated once again to Parreira's team and position that he has not since relinquished.

Dida's career has had its ups and downs. Successful seasons in goal for Vitoria and Cruzeiro led to his call-up for the national team and a trip to Atlanta for the Olympic tournament in 1996. Crucial errors tarnished his reputation as Brazil finished a disappointing third. His club form for Cruzeiro saw him win medals during the mid-1990s but he could not get back into the national team. In 1999 he moved to Milan but could not hold down a regular place and returned to Brazil this time under coach Wanderley Luxemburgo at Corinthians.

Dida dives to save David Trezeguet's spot kick during Milan's 2003 Champions League Final penalty shoot-out against Juventus.

'When things go against me, I find a way to overcome the disappointment through hard work and self-belief.'

His performances, including crucial penalty saves in the Brazilian championship play-offs and in the inaugural (and only) FIFA Club World Championship in 2000, earned him a second crack of the whip at Milan. In and out of the Milan team, in and out of the national team, Dida received a near fatal

FACT FILE GOALKEEPER | 85 CAPS | 0 GOALS | AC MILAN

Date of birth: **07.10.1973**
Height: **195 cm**
Weight: **85 kg**
Previous clubs: **Corinthians, Lugano, Cruzeiro, Vitoria**
International debut: **07.07.1995 v Ecuador**
Previous World Cups: **1998, 2002**

STYLE GUIDE

⚽ **A big man whose presence makes his team's goal look small, Dida's reputation is based on his legendary ability to save penalties. During his club career, with Vitoria, Cruzeiro and Corinthians in Brazil, and Lugano and AC Milan in Europe, Dida has worked hard on his tactics and skills. Once prone to errors, or *frangos* ('chickens' as they are called in Brazil after the farmer left groping at thin air when trying to catch them in the farmyard), Dida has improved his positioning and the timing of his moves from the goal line as well as his ability in the air and on crosses in particular.**

blow in 2001 when he was charged with having a forged EU passport and received a one-year European ban from FIFA.

Despite all these setbacks, Dida was growing in confidence as a person and as a keeper. Quietly spoken and renowned for his shyness, he began to show leadership abilities as he returned to Corinthians to play out his ban. More silverware followed. Though an important member of the national squad for the 2002 World Cup, Dida's role was confined to the dressing room where his easy-going manner and calmness helped Ronaldo overcome the memories of 1998.

The following year Dida seemed to have matured and hit his peak. Milan's victory in the Champions League in 2003 was followed by the Italian League title in 2004. Despite the horrors he experienced after being hit by a flare during the Champions League quarter-final between city rivals AC and Inter and the disappointment of losing the Final to Liverpool having been 3-0 up at half-time, Dida knows that he has achieved something rare for a Brazilian goalkeeper, a guaranteed place in the starting line-up.

BRAZIL'S ALL-TIME RECORD APPEARANCE MAKER IS KEEN TO LEAD HIS COUNTRY INTO HIS FOURTH WORLD CUP

Twice a World Cup winner, in 1994 and 2002, Cafu is the only man in the history of football to have played in three consecutive World Cup Finals and fully intends to lead his country into the tournament in Germany at the age of 36. He has played his club football in Italy since 1997, first for Roma and now for AC Milan; this dependable full back is renowned for the engine that keeps him bombing up and down the right flank for club and country.

Born in a hospital on the outskirts of Sao Paulo on 7 June 1970 while Brazil were playing England in the World Cup in Mexico, Cafu has grown up to become his country's leading appearance maker and captain. His first appearance came against Spain in September 1990. He went to the 1994 World Cup as a squad player and came on as a substitute in the Final earning a winner's medal in the process. He was on the losing side in the Final against France in 1998 and he led his country to victory in the 2002

'If there is one man who has made sacrifices and lent himself to the cause of the Brazil team, this man is Cafu. He has been my commander on the field. He is a great example of dedication and humility.'

Luis Felipe Scolari, former Brazil coach

Despite being a full back, Cafu's legendary 'engine' means he is as likely to worry the opposition's defence as he is to dispossess their attackers.

FACT FILE | FULL BACK | 137 CAPS | 5 GOALS | AC MILAN

Date of birth: **07.06.1970**
Height: **176 cm**
Weight: **75 kg**
Previous clubs: **Roma, Palmeiras, Real Zaragoza, Sao Paulo**
International debut: **12.09.1990 v Spain**
Previous World Cups: **1994, 1998, 2002**

Final in Korea and Japan providing a defining image of sporting triumph standing on a dais holding the trophy up to the heavens.

The nickname 'Cafu' is in honour of his childhood hero, Cafuringa, a right-winger who played for Fluminense and Atletico Mineiro. Cafu earned a call up to the national team through his performances for his local club Sao Paulo. Not always the most popular player among Brazilian fans, Cafu has endured his fair share of criticism during his career. But the brickbats have taken their place alongside a plethora of titles, medals and other honours at both club and international level.

In 1995 Cafu moved to Europe to play for Real Zaragoza with whom he won the Cup-Winners' Cup. A brief spell with Brazilian club Palmeiras was followed by a move to Roma and a spell of great popularity for the newly nicknamed *Il Pendolino* ('The express train').

In 2003 he moved on to AC Milan where he dominates the right flank as he has done at all the clubs for whom he has played, though at 35 years old he has to be careful not to get caught out of position. 'I have changed quite a lot since I came to Milan and I think I have become a more all-round footballer … Here, I am a right back and have had to improve my defending. Only if I defend well can I think about attacking,' he says.

STYLE GUIDE

At his most effective, like in Milan's 1-0 win in the 2004–05 Champions League match against Manchester United at Old Trafford, Cafu will control his flank so completely that the opponents will not get a look in down that side of the pitch. Add to that his ability to come forward at high speed and then get back in time to defend and you can begin to see why Cafu is on target to reach 150 caps for the 'best football team in the world'.

HUGELY TALENTED ATTACKING MIDFIELDER WITH THE WORLD AT HIS FEET

Virtually unknown in Europe when he signed for AC Milan in 2003 on the recommendation of his fellow countryman Rivaldo, Kaka is now universally regarded as one of the finest midfielders in the world. His first European season ended with the Italian league championship, and his second ended with a Champions League runners-up medal. Now Kaka is looking to the world stage to show off his explosive skills.

Born in 1982 Kaka was given his nickname by his youngest brother who was unable to say Ricardo, instead saying 'Ka-Ka'. He signed for São Paulo at the age of nine and worked his way up through the junior teams. He made his first team debut in 2001 and was voted Brazilian player of the season in 2002. In his two years for the senior team he played 131 games and scored 48 goals, not a bad record for someone just starting out in the professional game.

He made his debut for the Brazilian national team in 2002 and was included in the squad for the World Cup that year though he only played for 19 minutes against Costa Rica. However, the experience and the fact that he left Japan and Korea with a winner's medal set him up beautifully for a bargain £5.8 million move to Italian giants Milan in 2003.

There had been interest in the youngster from other European clubs, including Chelsea and Real Madrid, but it was Milan who secured his signature. His first season was a revelation: beautiful footwork, spectacular skills and a blistering shot that brought 10 goals in 30 Serie A appearances. An equaliser in the Milan derby that AC went on to win 3-2 earned him a place in the fans' hearts, a place that was secured when they won the title, beating Rome 2-1 at the San Siro in April 2004.

Kaka strikes home Brazil's second goal despite the challenge of Argentina's Esteban Cambiasso and Lucas Bernardi during the 2005 Confederations Cup Final in Frankfurt.

 **FACT FILE** | MIDFIELDER | 36 CAPS | 11 GOALS | AC MILAN

Date of birth: **22.04.1982**
Height: **183 cm**
Weight: **73 kg**
Previous clubs: **Sao Paulo**
International debut: **31.01.2002 v Bolivia**
Previous World Cups: **2002**

'Someone of his talent comes along once every fifty years.'

Carlos Alberto Parreira

A devout Christian, Kaka's clean lifestyle has made him a favourite among those looking for celebrities to endorse products. His good looks also persuaded Giorgio Armani to use him as a model. His modesty has made him a favourite among journalists used to footballers with monstrous egos, and his generosity of spirit – illustrated when he publicly supported Liverpool's efforts to defend their European title in 2005 even though they had beaten Milan in the Final and they were technically not entitled to do so – has endeared him to many football fans around the world.

Kaka is aware of the growing pressure that comes with Brazil being made favourites to win the World Cup in Germany. 'On paper, that looks to be the case, but just remember what happened in Istanbul. The 2006 World Cup will be seen by the national team as another competition that it simply has to win'. He is also modest about his own chances of making the team for the finals, 'The national team is going through a change. There is a new generation coming in. Myself, Adriano, Ronaldinho, Robinho … The time has come to stand up and confirm their place in the Brazilian team.'

STYLE GUIDE

⚽ Though he claims that he can play anywhere in midfield, Kaka is most effective playing on the right-hand side just behind the strikers. Skilful on the ball, Kaka also possesses an explosive shot and uses his body to great effect when tackling. Since arriving at Milan he has added consistency and stamina to his game. Expect him to make his mark on world football in Germany 2006.

RONALDINHO (Ronaldo de Assis Moreira/Ronaldinho Gaúcho)

FIFA'S WORLD PLAYER OF THE YEAR IS ONE OF THE TRULY GREAT FOOTBALLING ICONS OF THE OPENING DECADE OF THE NEW MILLENNIUM

Already well known to European fans as the player who has brought glory back to the Nou Camp with Barcelona, Ronaldinho is perhaps best known for the incredible free-kick goal he scored for Brazil against England in the 2002 World Cup quarter-final, and the subsequent red card he received. His buck-toothed grin has graced the covers of thousands of football magazines and newspapers since then and is likely to do so again in the run up to Germany 2006.

From the favelas of Porto Alegre to the grandeur of the Nou Camp in Barcelona might seem like a long journey, but it has been a relatively simple one for the hugely talented Ronaldinho. From a footballing family, his dad played at amateur level and his elder brother Roberto starred for local club Gremio, there was never any doubt about his future other than on the football field.

His own debut for Gremio came in 1998 and three years of spectacular performances for club and country brought him to the attention of clubs throughout the world and in 2001 he signed for Paris Saint-Germain where he struggled to find his touch and live up to expectations. He reserved his best form for the 2002 World Cup where his fine performances, including goals against China and England, were capped with a winner's medal. The following year, his relationship with the Parisian club at an all time low, he was on the move again. All the big clubs were interested: Manchester United, Real Madrid, Juventus and Internazionale were all strongly tipped to sign him, but Barcelona proved irresistible. 'I was a Barcelona fan as a boy because of

Ronaldinho slots the ball past Jens Lehmann from the penalty spot during the Confederations Cup semi-final against Germany in Nuremberg in June 2005.

FACT FILE

 MIDFIELDER | 62 CAPS | 27 GOALS | BARCELONA

Date of birth: **21.03.1980**
Height: **181 cm**
Weight: **80 kg**
Previous clubs: **Paris St Germain, Gremio**
International debut: **26.06.1999 v Latvia**
Previous World Cups: **2002**

STYLE GUIDE

⚽ **A brilliant and unpredictable player, Ronaldinho is capable of doing the most amazing things with a football. Best employed on the left just behind the strikers, Ronaldinho can pick out a pass or dribble through any defence himself with lightning speed. Superb at free-kicks, reliable at taking penalties, Ronaldinho is a true match-winner.**

'We lived for football when I was a kid. My mother wanted me to pay more attention to school but it wasn't possible. I even "dribbled" a football between my feet when we sat down to meals.'

the Brazilian players who came here [Romario, Rivaldo, Ronaldo]. I want to do as well as they did – and better if possible,' he said on his arrival at the Nou Camp.

He didn't disappoint. In his first season at Barcelona he scored 22 goals and guided the team to second place. The following season they went one better and clinched the La Liga title for the first time since 1999. But domestic success has merely spurred Ronaldinho on and his dreams are now centred on European and, of course, more world honours.

Success in the national team came early for Ronaldinho. He scored in his second match against Venezuela in the 1999 Copa America, which Brazil went on to win. Since then he has played 62 matches and scored 27 goals, a tremendous record for a midfielder.

Graceful and quick with a great footballing brain, Ronaldinho possesses a special brand of footballing magic, one that has endeared him to fans all over the world. Expect to see much more of this in Germany from the man voted World Player of the Year in 2004 and 2005.

THE 'NEW PELÉ' STANDS ON THE EDGE OF GREATNESS

Following his recent move from Santos to Real Madrid the interest on this 21-year-old from São Vicente has reached fever pitch. His Spanish debut in the La Liga match against Cadiz was the subject of unprecedented press coverage ... and he only played for 24 minutes as a substitute. However, he was impressive, performing all his tricks and then laying on the winning goal. Though coach Carlos Alberto Parreira has been cautious over whether he will be selected for the World Cup squad, it seems highly unlikely that he will not be included.

Though there have already been several 'new Pelés' over the years, Robinho may yet prove to be the real one. In 1999 the veteran footballer returned to his former club Santos to coach the youngsters. After his first training session he picked out a scrawny, stick thin youngster and said, 'this kid reminds me of myself when I was younger.' Praise indeed from the King of Football himself.

Three years later Robinho, by then 18 years old, steered his club to the 2002 Brazilian championship for the first time in over 20 years. Together with team-mate Diego, aged 17, the pair were the stars of the season. In the match that clinched the championship, against Corinthians, Robinho entertained the watching millions with a magnificent display. He scored once, then went on a mazy dribble which included eight *pedaladas* – a trick in which his feet dummy around the ball as if he was pedalling a bicycle – which ended when

Robinho gets away from Mexico's Zinha during their Confederations Cup match in 2005.

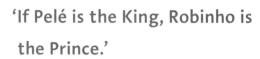

'If Pelé is the King, Robinho is the Prince.'

Betinho, youth coach

 **FACT FILE** | FORWARD | 22 CAPS | 5 GOALS | REAL MADRID

Date of birth: **25.01.1984**
Height: **172 cm**
Weight: **60 kg**
Previous clubs: **Santos**
International debut: **05.09.2004 v Bolivia**
Previous World Cups: **None**

STYLE GUIDE

⚽ Robinho is known as the king of the dribble in Brazil. His box of tricks includes the *pedalada* as explained opposite, the *bicicleta* ('step over'), the sombrero ('hat') where he flicks the ball over an opponent's head and several other moves which have made him one of the most exciting players to watch in world football. Normally playing in the space behind the strikers, Robinho may be played up front in a more offensive role. Given a place in the team in Germany expect to see some Samba football of the highest quality.

Corinthians' defender Rogerio brought him down for a penalty. The move was replayed on television over and over again and made Robinho the most famous player in Brazil bringing comparisons with another of Brazil's most famous players Garrincha.

His next and final season in Brazil was marred when his mother was kidnapped. She spent 40 days in captivity but was eventually released unharmed. Naturally Robinho's form slumped and criticism of his effectiveness under pressure, coupled with his lack of strength and consistency were aired. However, these events did not stop a big-money transfer to Real Madrid in 2005, the euphoria of which has only been dented by his poor form and the fact that the Madrid giants were having a very poor season.

Though doubts do remain about his physique, Robinho has made great efforts to improve his all-round skills including his tackling and his dedication to the team ethic, 'before, the highpoint of my game was my dribbling. I didn't score so many goals. Now the highpoint of my football is winning the game.' He made his debut for the national team in September 2004 scoring twice in the Confederations Cup and twice more in the World Cup qualifying campaign. It remains to be seen whether his move to Real Madrid will strengthen his game but it seems more likely that football fans will get to judge Robinho's qualities for themselves if he is awarded his rightful place in the Brazilian squad.

CROATIA

UNDERRATED – AND INTENT ON PROVING THEIR WORTH

Croatia sailed through their World Cup qualification group unbeaten, winning home and away against group favourites Sweden and conceding only five goals in ten games. Germany 2006 will be their third World Cup finals in a row, not bad for a country that only got its independence from the former Yugoslavia in 1991.

Their run of success started at Euro 96 when they reached the quarter-finals, and really took off in France in 1998 when the team, playing a refreshing brand of free-flowing football with players like Robert Prosinecki, Alen Boksic and Davor Suker, finished in third place only losing to the hosts and eventual winners in a tight semi-final.

Although the team was packed with good players the star of the show in France, Croatia's first appearance in the World Cup finals, was undoubtedly striker Davor Suker. His six goals, including the goal that clinched third place in a play-off against Holland, won him the Golden Boot as the tournament's top scorer.

The ageing team disbanded soon afterwards and coach Jozik Mirko seemed

Left *Captain fantastic: Niko Kovac (right) led Croatia through ten qualifying matches unbeaten.*

Above *Brother Robert (left) plays the libero role.*

VITAL STATISTICS

WORLD RANKING 20th   **KEEPER AND DEFENCE** 8/10
MIDFIELD 7/10   **ATTACK** 6/10
STRENGTHS AND WEAKNESSES
Kept six clean sheets in ten qualifying games, the team is full of running but don't really score enough goals.
HOW FAR WILL THEY GO?
It would be a good result for Croatia if they qualified from the group stage – within their grasp following a favourable draw.

Dario Srna (left) is congratulated by Igor Tudor after scoring the only goal against Sweden in Zagreb.

unable to build another one. They did poorly in Japan and Korea in 2002 under new coach Otto Baric where a single victory, against Italy, and defeats to both Mexico and Ecuador saw them leave early. Euro 2004 witnessed similar listless displays and after the tournament Baric was replaced by ex-Dinamo Zagreb coach Zlatko Kranjcar.

The effect was immediate with the team's dour defensive outlook replaced by an altogether more offensive attitude. Through organisation, tactical nous and technical ability, Kranjcar has instilled a team spirit right through the squad. A 1-0 win away in Sweden in the second match of the qualifying competition for Germany 2006, a goal scored by Dario Srna, set the tone of the group, and apart from a disappointing 1-1 draw in Malta, Croatia were unstoppable, despite Sweden matching them win-for-win. The crunch came in the return match in Zagreb when another goal from Srna settled matters

Tall, commanding in his area and adept at dealing with set pieces, Tomislav Butina (in blue) has made the No. 1 jersey his own since 2003.

with another 1-0 win. Level on points, Croatia took top spot thanks to the head-to-head results.

With a team now solid in all departments, many of the players based outside Croatia and particularly in Germany, the future looks bright for the red-and-whites. Croatia are now better drilled, fitter and ready to do themselves justice in Germany 2006. 'We can do well,' says skipper Niko Kovac, 'but we have to be more consistent.'

HOW THEY'LL LINE UP

Nominally playing a 1-2-4-1-2 formation featuring a libero behind two stoppers, two central holding midfielders, two wide midfielders, one creative midfielder and two strikers. The team is based on a sound

Back row (left to right): Josip Simunic, Stjepan Tomas, Jerko Leko, Dado Prso, Tomislav Butina, Marko Babic. Front row: Darijo Srna, Niko Kranjcar, Niko Kovac, Bosko Balaban and Robert Kovac.

POSSIBLE SQUAD

Goalkeepers: Tomislav Butina (Club Bruges), **Joseph Didulica** (Austria Vienna), **Stipe Pletikosa** (Shakhtar Donetsk)

Defenders: Robert Kovac (Juventus), **Igor Tudor** (Juventus), **Josip Simunic** (Hertha Berlin), **Stjepan Tomas** (Galatasaray), **Mario Tokic** (Austria Vienna), **Dario Simic** (AC Milan)

Midfielders: Dario Srna (Shakhtar Donetsk), **Ivan Bosnjak** (Dinamo Zagreb), **Mario Babic** (Bayer Leverkusen), **Anthony Seric** (Panathinaikos), **Niko Kovac** (Hertha Berlin), **Jerko Leko** (Dynamo Kiev), **Niko Kranjcar** (Hajduk Split), **Ivan Leko** (Club Bruges), **Jurica Vranjes** (Werder Bremen)

Forwards: Dado Prso (Rangers), **Ivan Klasnic** (Werder Bremen), **Bosko Balaban** (Club Bruges), **Eduardo Da Silva** (Dinamo Zagreb), **Ivica Olic** (CSKA Moscow)

defence that kept six clean sheets in ten qualifying matches; Kranjcar will have little trouble with the first part of his team-sheet. With the dependable Tomislav Butina in goal, a solid back-line will undoubtedly include the two Juventus defenders Robert Kovac as the libero and stopper Igor Tudor. Deep-lying defensive midfielder and captain Niko Kovac will patrol the middle of the park while Kranjcar has real options elsewhere and could play his son Niko up the middle or Dario Srna on the right. Up front his choices are more limited but if the sometime prolific Dado Prso can find the scoring form he had for Monaco in 2003 then the team will be doubly effective.

ONE TO WATCH
Dario Srna

Speedy right midfielder, often compared to David Beckham, Srna is currently attracting interest from a number of European clubs,

Eight goals in 32 international appearances represent a good return for midfielder Dario Srna.

Nicknamed 'Cico' as a player, Zlatko Kranjcar's unique management style seems to be working.

most notably Liverpool and Bayern Munich. He started his career with Hadjuk Split, with whom he won the Croatian cup in 2002, then moved on to top Ukrainian side Shakhtar Donetsk. Can play out wide as a winger and supply pin-point crosses for the likes of Dado Prso but also likes to get forward in the channel and can score goals, such as both strikes in the 2-2 draw in Bulgaria and, crucially, both goals in the two 1-0 wins against Sweden, one direct from a free-kick and the other from the penalty spot.

COACH
Zlatko Kranjcar
(born 15 November 1956)
Record: P16 W10 D4 L2

One of the most popular players of his era, Zlatko Kranjcar played over 500 games at centre forward for Dinamo Zagreb, scoring 98 goals and winning the league title in 1982 and the cup in 1980 and 1983. He then moved on to Rapid Vienna in Austria where he had further success before retiring in 1991 and taking his coaching exams.

The 1990s saw him coach various clubs to league and cup success, notably Dinamo Zagreb and NK Zagreb. His appointment as national coach in the wake of the disappointing appearance at Euro 2004 was a surprise. But his unique combination of tactical knowledge, gentle persuasion and steely resolve has seen the team respond positively. 'He understands that no national team can achieve results without good organisation, yet he does not make the mistake of setting us up too defensively,' says Niko Kovac, 'He encourages us to take the initiative. I feel we're much more enterprising than we once were.'

ROUTE TO THE FINALS

DATE			
04.08.04	CROATIA **3**	**0** HUNGARY	
08.09.04	SWEDEN **0**	**1** CROATIA	
09.10.04	CROATIA **2**	**2** BULGARIA	
26.03.05	CROATIA **4**	**0** ICELAND	
30.03.05	CROATIA **3**	**0** MALTA	
04.06.05	BULGARIA **1**	**3** CROATIA	
03.09.05	ICELAND **1**	**3** CROATIA	
07.09.05	MALTA **1**	**1** CROATIA	
8.10.05	CROATIA **1**	**0** SWEDEN	
12.10.05	HUNGARY **0**	**0** CROATIA	

EUROPE QUALIFYING GROUP 8 – FINAL TABLE

TEAM	P	W	D	L	F	A	Pts
CROATIA	10	7	3	0	21	5	**24**
SWEDEN	10	8	0	2	30	4	**24**
BULGARIA	10	4	3	3	17	17	**15**
HUNGARY	10	4	2	4	13	14	**14**
ICELAND	10	1	1	8	14	27	**4**
MALTA	10	0	3	7	4	32	**3**

FINALS GROUP F

		Date	Venue
	CROATIA		
	Brazil	13 June	Berlin
	Japan	18 June	Nuremberg
	Australia	22 June	Stuttgart

Dado **PRSO**

A PONY-TAILED DALMATIAN WHO ALMOST GAVE UP FOOTBALL IS NOW A HOUSEHOLD NAME IN CROATIA

Ignored by the big Croatian teams as a youngster, the lanky striker moved to France in 1994 to try and find a club. He played for various clubs in the lower leagues before being spotted by Monaco boss Jean Tigana who immediately snapped him up. He was a revelation in his first season, 1999–2000, scoring 12 goals in 20 appearances as Monaco won the French league title. Injuries plagued him for the next two seasons but he hit a superb scoring streak in 2003–04 – including four in an 8-3 win over Deportivo La Coruna – which powered Monaco to the Champions League Final.

After a season in the French second division with Rouen, Prso quit the club and got a job in a car repair shop. His evenings were spent in local bars playing pool and roulette and he was on the point of giving up football altogether. Motivation somehow kept him going until his club, San Raphael of the French fourth division, played a friendly against Monaco in 1997. A contract followed soon afterwards and Prso joined a team already featuring Thierry Henry and David

> '[Prso's] an excellent player. I'd even go as far as to say that if he'd come to us … we would have made fourth place and qualified for the Champions League by now.'
>
> Sam Allardyce,
> Bolton Wanderers manager

A series of good performances and four goals from Prso helped propel Croatia to Germany 2006.

FACT FILE | STRIKER | 25 CAPS | 8 GOALS | RANGERS

Date of birth: **15.11.1974**
Height: **190 cm**
Weight: **86 kg**
Previous clubs: **Monaco, Bastia, Rouen**
International debut: **29.03.2003 v Belgium**
Previous World Cups: **None**

Trezeguet. He spent two years on loan at Bastia and when he returned the two strikers had moved on and he took his place in the first team.

His club form soon earned him a call-up to a national team desperately in search of a goalscorer to ignite their campaign to qualify for Euro 2004. Prso obliged by scoring on his debut against Belgium in Zagreb with a magnificent header and instantly became a national hero. More goals followed as Croatia qualified beating Slovenia in a play-off. Prso then scored against France in a 2-2 draw in the group stage. However, the team's poor form saw them catch an early plane home.

In the summer of 2004 there was all sorts of talk of Prso going to Bolton Wanderers or Milan, indeed the *Gazzetta dello Sport* actually introducing him as the *Rossoneri*'s new signing. In the event he joined Scottish club Rangers, scoring 21 goals in 46 appearances in his first season and developing a formidable relationship with Nacho Novo.

Croatia are a side with a superb and solid defence, but their progress in Germany will be largely in the capable hands of Dado Prso and his strike partner.

STYLE GUIDE

⚽ Strong in the air and a nuisance anywhere in the penalty box, Prso is an ideal foil for a natural target man and can hold the ball up and release it when necessary. However, his strike rate has improved with his experience.

AUSTRALIA

NOT JUST MAKING UP THE NUMBERS

Australia have made the finals for the first time since 1974. As football continues to grow apace Down Under, the Socceroos plan to make a splash in Germany.

'We're used to picking our favourite team in the World Cup,' said Blackburn and Australian midfielder Lucas Neil, 'and now it's going to be Australia.' After three decades of dashed hopes and cruel defeats, the Socceroos finally clinched a World Cup finals place thanks to Mark Schwarzer's shoot-out heroics in the play-off with Uruguay and a team spirit galvanised by their part-time coach Guus Hiddink.

Hiddink, who has a full-time post managing PSV in Holland, took over as coach of the Socceroos after a disappointing Confederations Cup in 2005. For a team built around Premiership and European talent, he knew they should have more self-belief and sure enough the team confidently saw out the two-legged play-off with Uruguay.

Hiddink, who led the Korean Republic to the semi-finals of the last World Cup, has an impressive group of players. The hero of the play-off second leg in Sydney is the oldest of them. At 33, Mark Schwarzer has spent nine years at Middlesbrough and has been a major part of their transformation into a top ten side. Tall and athletic, he dominates his area and is a fine shot and, as he proved, penalty-stopper.

The defence is marshalled by skipper Craig Moore with Blackburn's Lucas Neill alongside him. Among his choice of full backs, Hiddink has Lazaridis and Emerton, both have served their time as wingers and love to push forward, but could find themselves struggling if pegged back.

VITAL STATISTICS

WORLD RANKING 48th **KEEPER AND DEFENCE** 5/10
MIDFIELD 6/10 **ATTACK** 6/10
STRENGTHS AND WEAKNESSES
The Australian sporting mentality and the guile of coach Guus Hiddink will give them immense confidence. But the defence could fold against a class attack.
HOW FAR WILL THEY GO?
They'll be hoping to sneak through the group stage. Anything after that would be a huge achievement.

Shoot-out hero: goalkeeper Mark Schwarzer.

Back row (left to right): Mark Schwarzer, John Aloisi, Tony Vidmar, Ljubo Milicevic, Lucas Neill. Brett Emerton. Front row: Kevin Muscat, Craig Moore, Tim Cahill, Scott Chipperfield and Josip Skoko.

The man who has been making Australia tick is central midfielder Tim Cahill. In nine months he went from the fringes of the national team to being voted both the Everton and Oceania player of the year. Next to him will be Liverpool's Harry Kewell who, despite his lack of form, has retained Hiddink's confidence.

After his winning penalty in the play-offs, striker John Aloisi won't have to buy a beer in Sydney for a while. The strapping six-footer will also be a useful foil for Mark Viduka. It seemed to take the moody but extravagantly talented forward some time to recover from Leeds riches-to-rags

Main men Harry Kewell (left) and Tim Cahill.

experience, but at Middlesbrough he has at last shown signs of discovering his old form.

Results could depend on the spirit Guus Hiddink can build in the Socceroos camp. But given a chance, they are as capable as anyone of springing a surprise.

POSSIBLE SQUAD

Goalkeepers: Ante Covic (Hammarby), **Zeljko Kalac** (AC Milan), **Mark Schwarzer** (Middlesbrough)

Defenders: Brett Emerton (Blackburn Rovers), **Stan Lazaridis** (Birmingham City), **Ljubo Milicevic** (FC Thun), **Craig Moore** (Newcastle United), **Lucas Neill** (Blackburn Rovers), **Tony Popovic** (Crystal Palace), **Tony Vidmar** (NAC Breda)

Midfielders: Marco Bresciano (Parma), **Tim Cahill** (Everton), **Ahmad Elrich** (Fulham), **Vince Grella** (Parma), **Joel Griffiths** (Neuchatel Xamax), **Harry Kewell** (Liverpool), **Josip Skoko** (Wigan Athletic), **Luke Wilkshire** (Bristol City)

Forwards: John Aloisi (Alaves), **Scott Chipperfield** (Basel), **Jason Culina** (PSV), **Archie Thompson** (Melbourne), **Mark Viduka** (Middlesbrough)

SOUTH AMERICA AND OCEANIA PLAY-OFFS			
DATE			
12.11.05	URUGUAY **1**	**0**	AUSTRALIA
16.11.05	AUSTRALIA **1** (aet)	**0**	URUGUAY

1-1 on aggregate. Australia won 4-2 on pens

FINALS GROUP F		
AUSTRALIA	Date	Venue
Japan	12 June	Kaiserslautern
Brazil	18 June	Munich
Croatia	22 June	Stuttgart

JAPAN

THEY'VE CAST OFF THEIR CHAINS, BUT WHAT PRICE FREEDOM?

The excitement of hosting the 2002 tournament behind them, Japan have been successfully guided to their third successive finals by long-time coach, Zico. Their progress has, however, not always kept a nation impatient for success happy.

Japan's adopted Brazilian hero, Zico, has tried to encourage players to rid themselves of their tactical straitjackets and express themselves. With players of the natural talent of Celtic's Shunsuke Nakamura, Bolton Wanderers' Hidetoshi Nakata, Feyenoord's Shinji Ono and Hamburg's Naohiro Takahawa, it seemed a policy that could only pay dividends.

Many applauded the coach's insistence that they stop copying the European physical style and apply their own rhythm, flair and character – but only while they were successful. With every draw or defeat, critics appeared to condemn Zico's lofty aims as masking any clear tactics or strategy. Many thought that even if Japan made it to Germany, their coach wouldn't.

In his defence, the team has taken time to adjust to Zico's demands for 'freedom football'. He is also 'cursed' by having an ever-growing number of Western-based players who miss matches or arrive exhausted after long flights. If these explanations hold water, Japan could arrive in Germany with a better chance than many are prepared to give them.

WHICH JAPAN WILL TURN UP?
Approaching the finals, Japan remain an enigma to not only the footballing world, but to their own fans. They were the first team in the world to make the finals, dropping their only points during qualification in a defeat to

Hidetoshi Nakata, now at Bolton Wanderers, is the best-known Japanese footballer in the world.

VITAL STATISTICS

WORLD RANKING 15th
KEEPER AND DEFENCE 6/10
MIDFIELD 7/10
ATTACK 6/10
STRENGTHS AND WEAKNESSES
Frustratingly inconsistent, Japan have quality players, particularly in midfield, but could ultimately struggle to either score or keep a clean sheet.
HOW FAR WILL THEY GO?
A second round exit looks on the cards unless their form improves.

Above right *Despite a disastrous spell at Portsmouth, keeper Kawaguchi remains Japan's first-team choice.*

Below *Tough and uncompromising, Takayuki Suzuki offers Zico a no-nonsense approach up front.*

Iran, but in the Kirin Cup they lost to both Peru and the United Arab Emirates. Earlier, a shock defeat against North Korea was followed a month later by a credible Confederations Cup campaign, crowned by a 2-2 draw with Brazil. Whether it is the world-beaters or the underachievers that turn up in Germany remains to be seen.

HOW THEY'LL LINE UP

Zico likes his team to play a 4-4-2 formation, but has shown he is willing to try 3-5-2. In front of keeper Yoshikatsu Kawaguchi (back on form after a dismal spell at Portsmouth), the key figure is Tsuneyasu Miyamoto, a calm and reassuring presence and skipper for the 2002 campaign. He is joined by Alex, the naturalised Brazilian wing-back, who also impressed in the last World Cup finals, and the impressive Nakazawa.

The midfield is Japan's trump suit. Feyenoord's midfield dynamo, Shinji Ono, and Takashi Fukunishi or Yasuhito Endo,

POSSIBLE SQUAD

Goalkeepers: Yoichi Doi (FC Tokyo), **Yoshikatsu Kawaguchi** (Jubilo Iwata), **Seigo Narazaki** (Nagoya Grampus Eight)

Defenders: Makoto Tanaka (Jubilo Iwata), **Yoshinobu Minowa** (Kawasaki Frontale), **Alessandro 'Alex' Santos** (Urawa Reds), **Keisuke Tsuboi** (Urawa Reds), **Yuji Nakazawa** (Yokohama Marinos), **Teruyuki Moniwa** (FC Tokyo), **Koji Nakata** (Olympique Marseille)

Midfielders: Hidetoshi Nakata (Bolton Wanderers), **Shunsuke Nakamura** (Celtic), **Masashi Motoyama** (Kashima Antlers), **Shinji Ono** (Feyenoord), **Koji Nakata** (Olympique Marseille), **Junichi Inamoto** (West Bromwich Albion), **Daisuke Matsui** (Le Mans), **Shinji Murai** (Jubilo Iwata)

Forwards: Takayuki Suzuki (Kashima Antlers), **Atsushi Yanagisawa** (Messina), **Naohiro Takahara** (Hamburg), **Yoshito Okubo** (Real Mallorca), **Masashi Oguro** (Gamba Osaka)

a real terrier with a crunching tackle, can carry out the defensive duties. For creative talent, Zico can choose from the dynamic Hidetoshi Nakata, once the golden boy of Japanese football; Junichi Inamoto, an all-action, fine passing player who has moved from Arsenal to Fulham to West Bromwich Albion without ever producing the displays he seems to reserve for the national team; and the jewel in the crown, Celtic's Shunsuke Nakamura, the emerging inspiration of the team, whose self-belief and leadership has captured the imagination of the nation.

Zico has tried a number of forwards without settling on any combination, but Atsushi Yanagisawa's running with the ball, Yoshito Okubo's pace, Takayuki Suzuki's uncompromising style and the emergence of J-League top scorer Masashi Oguro, have given him some interesting options.

ONE TO WATCH
Masashi Oguro

Back row (left to right): Takashi Fukunishi, Atsushi Yanagisawa, Alex, Takayuki Chano, Shunsuke Nakamura, Yoshikatsu Kawaguchi. Front row: Makoto Tanaka, Hidetoshi Nakata, Mitsuo Ogasawara, Akira Kaji and Tsuneyasu Miyamoto.

Gamba Osaka's 25-year-old striker has been a prolific goalscorer in the J-League, but had to wait patiently for inclusion in the national side. The diminutive forward announced his arrival with a vital injury-time winner against North Korea on his debut and then took the 2005 Confederations Cup by storm. He scored the winner against Greece and levelled the match with Brazil. If he continues to make progress, Oguro could emerge as Zico's secret weapon.

COACH
Zico
(born 3 March 1953)
Record: P55 W31 D12 L12

Above *It has been a long, hard road as the national team coach for Brazilian legend Zico, but he feels his team have at last got something to offer on the world stage.*

Left *It took striker Masashi Oguro 13 minutes to make his mark on the international scene when he scored after coming on as a substitute against North Korea.*

When he took over as coach of Japan in 2003, Zico – the star of the Brazil World Cup team of 1982 and still a hero in his homeland – had already spent a decade living in the country. He played for and later coached Kashima Antlers, transforming them from an amateur works team into one of the top clubs in the J-League. As national coach he has had total support from the Japanese FA, but an uneasy relationship with the fans. His attempts to create a Brazilian-type attitude, bring a family atmosphere to the squad and develop a winning mentality have been well received, but what he will ultimately be judged on are results.

ROUTE TO THE FINALS

DATE			
09.02.05	JAPAN **2**	**1** NORTH KOREA	
25.03.05	IRAN **2**	**1** JAPAN	
30.03.05	JAPAN **1**	**0** BAHRAIN	
30.03.05	BAHRAIN **0**	**1** JAPAN	
08.06.05	NORTH KOREA **0**	**2** JAPAN	
17.08.05	JAPAN **2**	**1** IRAN	

ASIA QUALIFYING FINAL GROUP 2 – FINAL TABLE

TEAM	P	W	D	L	F	A	Pts
JAPAN	6	5	0	1	9	4	**15**
IRAN	6	4	1	1	7	3	**13**
BAHRAIN	6	1	1	4	4	7	**4**
NORTH KOREA	6	1	0	5	5	11	**3**

FINALS GROUP F

	TEAM	Date	Venue
	JAPAN		
	Australia	12 June	Kaiserslautern
	Croatia	18 June	Nuremberg
	Brazil	22 June	Dortmund

Shunsuke NAKAMURA

LEFT OUT OF JAPAN'S 2002 SQUAD, THE TOUGHENED-UP PLAYMAKER HAS MADE SURE HE'S FIRST ON ZICO'S 2006 LIST

For a player whose supposedly shuns the physical game, Nakamura's decision to hone his craft in Scotland's hard-as-nails Premier League surprised many who had followed his career. But to the echo of Celtic fans' 'It's so Japaneasy,' Shunsuke wasted little time in posting his name to Celtic's list of cult heroes.

Playing for Yokohama Marinos, the 18-year-old scored five goals in 27 appearances in his first season in 1997. He soon made his debut for Japan and word began to spread about the mercurial left-sided midfielder. In 2000 he was instrumental in Japan's Asian Cup triumph and was voted the J-League's most valuable player.

The stage was all set for Nakamura to join Ono, Nakata and Inamoto in Japan's 2002 World Cup midfield – but coach Troussier had other ideas. Citing Nakamura's lack of physical presence, he not only left him out of his team but out of the squad altogether. Nakamura took the hint, taking the first transfer to Europe he could get – to newly promoted Reggina in Italy's Serie A.

If Japan's poor performance in the finals gave Troussier part of his answer, Nakamura's seven goals in 33 games for Reggina made it clear: here was a fully-fledged star. Zico recalled him and, quickly, Nakamura took over from Nakata as the team's fulcrum. From being playmaker and regular scorer, he progressed to become the inspiration of the

'He has got imagination and he sees passes other people can't see.'

Gordon Strachan, Celtic manager

FACT FILE

| MIDFIELDER | 57 CAPS | 15 GOALS | CELTIC |

Date of birth: **24.06.1978**
Height: **178 cm**
Weight: **69 kg**
Previous clubs: **Reggina, Yokohama F. Marinos**
International debut: **02.08.2000 v Hong Kong**
Previous World Cups: **None**

STYLE GUIDE

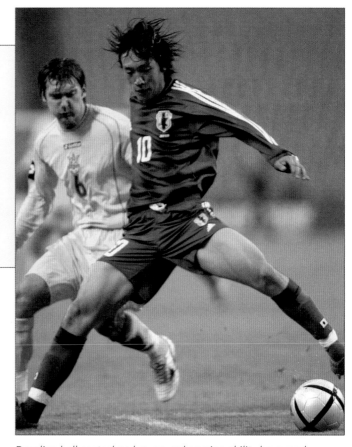

⚽ A superb, attack-minded midfielder, the elegant Nakamura is a delight to watch, his fantastic touch and immaculate long and incisive passing putting him at the centre of Japan's forward moves. Though he suffers from a lack of weight and pace, his powerful and accurate left foot presents a danger both at free-kicks and in open play.

Dazzling ball control and measured passing ability have made Nakamura a popular player with the fans wherever he's played.

team at the 2004 Asia Cup, recognised by his player of the tournament award.

This progress culminated with a remarkable series of Confederations Cup performances, when his two man-of-the-match awards were capped by a stupendous long-range strike against Brazil. The ambitious midfielder was still out to improve his game and, stifled by the defensiveness of the Italian league, he looked for a move to Spain. It was, however, Celtic who captured his signature. Scotland would not only toughen him up, but promised open football in which he could shine.

And like a rising sun, shine he did. 'That was as good a debut as I've seen in a long, long time,' said his coach, Gordon Strachan, just days after he had landed. Continuing to create goal after goal, he has encouraged many to think that similar acclaim can follow his touchdown in Germany.

FRANCE

SLEEPING GIANT READY TO STIR

Once the best team in the world, France has slid down the list lately. But with some of the finest young talent in Europe *Les Bleus* are looking to rekindle the spirit of 98.

World Cup winners on home soil in 1998, winners of the European Championships two years later in Holland and Belgium, France have struggled to find their form lately and only the return from retirement of veterans Zinedine Zidane, Claude Makelele and Lilian Thuram saw them through the qualifying campaign. Despite being drawn in an easy group, qualification was in doubt right up until the last game, only Switzerland's failure to beat Ireland in Dublin and *Les Bleus*' 4-0 drubbing of Cyprus in Paris gave them an automatic berth in Germany 2006.

EXPERIENCE VERSUS YOUTH

It seems highly likely that the returning veterans will take their places in the France squad for the finals in Germany in 2006. What seems less obvious is whether they still have the legs for it. France has such a wealth of young talent at its disposal that it would be a shame if that talent is not given its chance. But the pressure is on to repeat the glory of that day in Paris in 1998 when France beat Brazil 3-0 to win the World crown and the day when David Trezeguet's golden goal beat Italy in the European Championships Final two years later.

Coach Raymond Domenech is aware of this pressure and was mightily relieved in the summer of 2005 when Zidane announced that he had reversed his decision to quit international football and would play the remaining games of the qualifying campaign. His relief turned to delight when Makelele and Thuram agreed to do the same. At the time France were out of the qualification places and desperate measures

were needed. The old warhorses didn't disappoint and three wins in the last four matches sealed France's automatic qualification. The turning point came in the match against the Republic of Ireland in Dublin – the day that Zidane and friends returned to the international scene – when a sublime goal from Thierry Henry secured three precious points.

Whether a good or a bad thing the return of the 'three musketeers', as they have been dubbed, shows how desperate the French are for success. The press speculation about the reasons for Zidane's decision was huge but the real reason seems most likely to come from the man himself who said that, 'I realised that I don't have a lot of time left as a top professional footballer and think I should make the most of it.' However, it is essential that coach Domenech is able to

Opposite *Djibril Cisse celebrates scoring the opening goal of the game against Switzerland. The 1-1 draw left France needing to win their final game to qualify.*

Zinedine Zidane's return to the international fold ensured a World Cup berth for France but has he got the legs for another exhausting competition?

marry the experience of the old hands and the enthusiasm, speed and stamina of the youngsters or else France will disappoint again as they did in the last World Cup and at Euro 2004.

HOW THEY'LL LINE UP

With new talent emerging all the time and old talent returning to the fold Domenech is in the pleasant position of having trouble deciding his final line-up. Though the coach likes to be able to switch to 4-3-3, he normally starts with a 4-4-2 formation. Between the sticks Barthez was back in favour after a long time off the scene though for many Coupet is the better keeper. Gallas and Sangol seems a natural pairing at full-back – though both are right-footed – both

1986	BRAZIL 1-1 FRANCE (France won 4-3 on pens)	WORLD CUP QUARTER FINAL
		Estadio Jalisco, Quadalajara, Mexico

GREAT MATCH

One of the finest matches *of the 1986 World Cup was the quarter-final between favourites Brazil and the European Champions France. Brazil dominated the first half and took the lead after 18 minutes through Careca. But the French midfield, featuring Platini, Giresse and Tigana, fought back and Platini equalised just before half-time finishing at the far post from a cross by Dominique Rocheteau.*

The second half was more even and Brazil should have won it when the French keeper Joel Bats brought Zico down inside the box. However, Bats saved Zico's penalty and France were back in it. Despite chances at both ends the game stayed at 1-1. There were no goals in extra time and so the game went to penalties.

To add to the drama, Socrates missed Brazil's first kick. At 3-3 the French captain Platini stepped up … and missed. Bats then saved Brazil's last kick from Julio Cesar which left Luis Fernandez to finish the match by converting the final penalty.

Back row (left to right): Gregory Coupet, Zinedine Zidane, Anthony Reveillere, William Gallas, Lilian Thuram, Jean-Alain Boumsong, Patrick Vieira. Front row: Vikash Dhorasoo, Sylvain Wiltord, Claude Makelele and Florent Malouda.

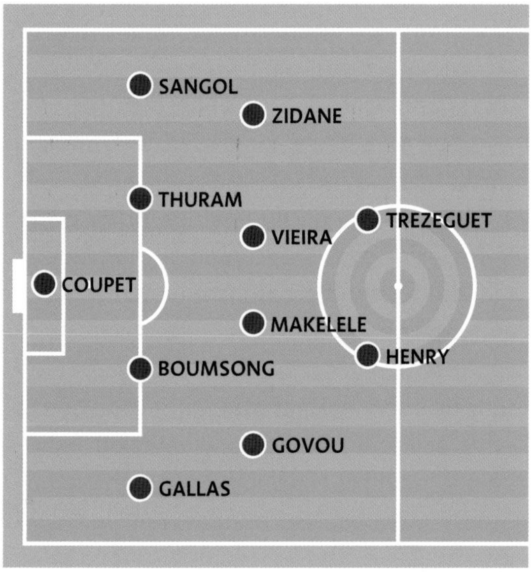

are fast and like to get the ball forward as quickly as possible. Boumsong and Thuram provide the height and muscle in the middle. Most problematic for the coach is the midfield where he has an embarrassment of riches and where someone, probably one of the youngsters Malouda or Dhorasoo, has to miss out. Up front too the coach has choices especially since the return of Nicolas Anelka. But it's hard to look beyond the mercurial Thierry Henry and David Trezeguet as the first-choice pairing, though Cisse might get the nod instead of Trezeguet.

POSSIBLE SQUAD

Goalkeepers: **Fabien Barthez** (Marseille), **Gregory Coupet** (Lyon), **Mickael Landreau** (Nantes)

Defenders: **Eric Abidal** (Lyon), **Jean-Alain Boumsong** (Newcastle United), **William Gallas** (Chelsea), **Gael Givet** (Monaco), **Anthony Reveillere** (Lyon), **Willy Sangol** (Bayern Munich), **Lilian Thuram** (Juventus)

Midfielders: **Alou Diarra** (Lens), **Zinedine Zidane** (Real Madrid), **Claude Makelele** (Chelsea), **Florent Malouda** (Lyon), **Vikash Dhorasoo** (PSG), **Jerome Rothen** (PSG), **Patrick Vieira** (Juventus)

Forwards: **Nicolas Anelka** (Fenerbahce), **Djibril Cisse** (Liverpool), **Thierry Henry** (Arsenal), **Sidney Govou** (Lyon), **David Trezeguet** (Juventus), **Sylvain Wiltord** (Lyon)

ONE TO WATCH

Vikash Dhorasoo

A stylish central midfielder, Dhorasoo joined PSG in the summer of 2005 after a frustrating season spent mostly on the bench at AC Milan. He played only 12 Serie A games for the Italian giants. Though 32 Dhorasoo's appearances for *Les Bleus* have been limited due to the fierce competition for places in midfield. He made his international debut against the Ukraine in 1999 but has only 14 caps to date. However, Domenech rates the player highly and 2006 could see him get his chance on the world stage.

Though they have an embarrasment of riches in midfield, coach Domenech will have to think hard whether to stick with old stagers like Zidane, or let in some fresh air in the shape of players like PSG's Vikash Dhorasoo.

VITAL STATISTICS

WORLD RANKING 5th=
KEEPER AND DEFENCE 8/10
MIDFIELD 7/10
ATTACK 8/10
STRENGTHS AND WEAKNESSES
Very strong defensively, however, the strikers are finding it hard to score at the other end. Drew too many matches in the qualifiers. Much depends on discipline, team spirit and whether the old stagers still have enough energy.
HOW FAR WILL THEY GO?
If Domenech gets the mix right France will be in the pot for the knockout stages, if he does not then France will be going home early.

Born in Mauritius of Indian descent, Dhorasoo has already had success at club level, particularly at Lyon with whom he won two league titles in 2003 and 2004. A forward-thinking player Domenech likes to play him in the centre of midfield behind Zidane. Clever on the ball, Dhorasoo was a regular in the World Cup qualifying campaign and seems likely to retain his place in the starting line-up.

COACH
Raymond Domenech
(born 24 January 1952)
Record: P17 W8 D9 Lo
A former defensive midfielder with Lyon and Strasbourg, among other teams, Domenech retired from playing and became a club

coach in 1984. In 1993 he joined the French national set-up as youth team coach under the tutelage of Aime Jacquet. During the next few years France rose up the world football rankings and were widely regarded as the best team in the world when they won the World Cup in 1998 under Jacquet and the European Championships in 2000 under Roger Lemerre.

Following dismal performances at the World Cup in 2002 and Euro 2004 the French Football Association turned to Jacquet's protégé Domenech in an attempt to rekindle the spirit of 98. But whether France's qualification for Germany 2006 was because of Domenech or the return of Zidane, Makelele and Thuram remains to be seen. However, Domenech remains very much a French FA man rather than the

players' favourite and there are some that say the return of the senior players has undermined his authority.

Despite all these factors, the French team will be packed with some of the brightest young talent in Europe along with some of its most seasoned professionals as well as Thierry Henry, for many the best player in the world. Domenech has the daunting task of harnessing some of the best talent in Europe with some of its most temperamental players.

ROUTE TO THE FINALS

DATE		
04.09.04	FRANCE **0**	**0** ISRAEL
08.09.04	FAROE ISLANDS **0**	**2** FRANCE
09.10.04	FRANCE **0**	**0** REP OF IRELAND
13.10.04	CYPRUS **0**	**2** FRANCE
26.03.05	FRANCE **0**	**0** SWITZERLAND
30.03.05	ISRAEL **1**	**1** FRANCE
03.09.05	FRANCE **3**	**0** FAROE ISLANDS
07.09.05	REP OF IRELAND **0**	**1** FRANCE
08.10.05	SWITZERLAND **1**	**1** FRANCE
12.10.05	FRANCE **4**	**0** CYPRUS

EUROPE QUALIFYING GROUP 4 – FINAL TABLE

TEAM	P	W	D	L	F	A	Pts
FRANCE	10	5	5	0	14	2	**20**
SWITZERLAND	10	4	6	0	18	7	**18**
ISRAEL	10	4	6	0	15	10	**18**
REP OF IRELAND	10	4	5	1	12	5	**17**
CYPRUS	10	1	1	8	8	20	**4**
FAROE ISLANDS	10	0	1	9	27	1	**1**

FINALS GROUP G

		Date	Venue
	FRANCE		
	Switzerland	13 June	Stuttgart
	South Korea	18 June	Leipzig
	Togo	23 June	Cologne

It's in your hands coach: Raymond Domenech ponders his starting line-up for Germany 2006.

LIGHTNING QUICK, ROCK HARD IN DEFENCE

An integral part of the meanest defence in the English Premiership in 2004–05, Chelsea conceding only 15 goals in 38 games on their way to the championship, William Gallas has earned himself a regular place in Jose Mourinho's starting line-up, an achievement that not many other players can claim. At his best at centre-back Gallas is used as a left back by French international coach Domenech. Though Gallas has often said he does not like playing there, his performances say otherwise. Described by Domenech as 'one of the best left-backs in the world' Gallas has little choice but to enjoy himself and get on with the job in hand.

The epitome of a modern defender, Gallas can play on the left, on the right or in the centre.

'Gallas is exceptional. He is the only player in the world who is able to play in any of the four defensive positions, and be able to be the best anywhere.'

Raymond Domenech

Born in Paris in 1977, Gallas was a product of the French national football academy, as a striker. But he turned professional in 1995 when Ligue 2 side Caen offered him a contract as a full back. Two seasons later he was signed up by Marseille where his performances during four successful years were noticed by then Chelsea manager Claudio Ranieri. A big money transfer followed in 2001 and Gallas settled in London.

FACT FILE | DEFENDER | 37 CAPS | 1 GOAL | CHELSEA

Date of birth: **17.08.1977**
Height: **183 cm**
Weight: **77 kg**
Previous clubs: **Marseille, Caen**
International debut: **10.12.2002 v Slovenia**
Previous World Cups: **None**

STYLE GUIDE

⊛ Speed, stamina and strength, William Gallas has them all in abundance. Sometimes looks a little clumsy with the ball at his feet but knows he is not a ball player and likes to pass it as soon as possible. He is also good in the air and has mastered the art of the perfectly timed tackle. Not too keen to get forward, he can often misplace passes and is sometimes weak on his crossing. However, his lightning speed allows him to get back into position with little trouble.

He made over 30 highly impressive performances for Chelsea in his first season but was left out of the French team for the 2002 World Cup. However, as his club form continued to impress he was finally called up the following season and by Euro 2004 was a regular member of the French squad.

Sometimes employed as a full back, he's naturally right-footed but can play on either flank, Gallas prefers to play at centre back. But it is this versatility that makes him so popular with his coaches. That and the fact that he is lightning quick and very strong make him the perfect defender. And he can score goals too, registering eight so far for Chelsea and also netting his first international goal against Ivory Coast in August 2005 about which he was clearly delighted, '… there was a lot to like about the goal. I jumped really high and connected perfectly with the header. The fact that it set up victory was also important, but the part I liked most was the reaction of my team-mates.'

He was ever-present for the French Blues during the World Cup qualifying campaign, putting in some tremendous personal performances, and knows that Germany 2006 will be his biggest test so far in the world's biggest football fiesta.

Thierry **HENRY**

WORLD'S GREATEST SET TO REALLY SHINE

Thierry Henry needs no introduction to English football fans. In each of six seasons at Arsenal he has scored over 20 goals, becoming the club's top goalscorer in the process with more than 185 goals in over 300 appearances. He has won the Premier League twice and the FA Cup twice, has been voted the Football Writers' Footballer of the Year and the PFA Players' Player of the Year twice and has now been made club captain. At international level he has over 70 caps, he has a World Cup winner's medal from 1998 and a European Championships winner's medal from 2000. For many, Henry is the greatest footballer in the world.

'In the end you have to say that for all we can speak about Thierry, the important thing to do is to watch him play.'

Arsène Wenger

Another pupil from the French Football academy, along with William Gallas, Henry began his professional career in 1990 aged 17 at Monaco under the tutelage of coach Arsène Wenger. Playing as a winger Henry was awarded his first cap in 1997 and was a member of Aime Jacquet's World Cup winning-team in 1998. He scored three goals in the tournament. He also scored three times during France's success in Euro 2000. By this time he had moved from Monaco to Juventus, where he spent an unhappy year out on the wing in the cold confines of the Stadio delle Alpi.

But in August 1999 his old mentor, Arsène Wenger had moved to Arsenal, and he bought him from the Italian giants for some £10 million. Wenger converted him into a striker and he has flourished there ever since. As a club player Henry has nothing more to achieve. His speed of thought is astonishing,

FACT FILE | STRIKER | 75 CAPS | 31 GOALS | ARSENAL

Date of birth: **17.08.1977**
Height: **187 cm**
Weight: **81 kg**
Previous clubs: **Juventus, Monaco**
International debut: **10.11.1997 v South Africa**
Previous World Cups: **1998, 2002**

his skills are unmatched, he can score goals from almost anywhere on the pitch and, a fact that is often overlooked in all the hype, he makes almost as many goals for others as he scores himself.

Internationally though, Henry has yet to really shine on the world stage. He is not as dominant for France as he is for Arsenal and is more prone to drift in and out of games. His form in the qualifying games for Germany 2006 mirrored those of the team as a whole: disjointed, uninspired

Thierry Henry has the skills and vision of a true match-winner.

and frustrating. Yet on a torrid night against the Republic of Ireland in Dublin Henry produced a piece of magic that secured all three points for *Les Bleus* and all but sealed their place in Germany. In a game in which he did almost nothing else, in the 68th minute Henry produced a curling shot from 25 yards that beat the Irish keeper Shay Given for the only goal of the game.

The time is now right for Henry to reproduce his club form for his country and prove that he really is one of the world's greatest players.

STYLE GUIDE

⊛ With blinding pace, superb vision, and exquisite skills on the ball there is little that Thierry Henry can't do. Though he is played as a central striker, he also plays on either flank and can drop deep to pick up the ball himself. He is unpredictable which makes it difficult for even the best defenders to second-guess him. If Domenech can get the best out of him then Thierry Henry might leave Germany 2006 with a second World Cup winner's medal.

Zinedine **ZIDANE**

RETURNING HERO SEES FRANCE THROUGH TO THE FINALS – BUT HAS HE GOT THE LEGS?

The furore surrounding Zidane's return to the international fold in the summer of 2005 should leave no one in doubt as to the regard in which the Real Madrid midfielder is held in his native France. He had announced his retirement from international football in August 2004 after *Les Bleus'* disappointing showing at the European Championships. A change of manager and a poor start to the World Cup qualifying campaign saw France slip from second to ninth in the FIFA world rankings. Cue the return of the king.

Zinedine Zidane has been regarded as one of the greatest players in the world for almost ten years. An exquisite ball player whose skills and vision are sometimes breathtaking, Zidane, born in Marseille of Algerian parents, started his career at Cannes in 1988. He moved to Bordeaux in 1992 and then Juventus in Italy in 1996 with whom he won two Italian league titles. Two years later he scored twice in the World Cup Final when France beat Brazil in 1998. The same year he was named European Footballer of the Year, the next he was named World Player of the Year and he was player of the tournament when France won the European Championships in 2000. In 2001 he became the world's most expensive player when he joined Real Madrid for over £43 million.

The ultimate midfield player, Zizou – as he is known in France – is capable of winning matches on his own, as he showed in Portugal in Euro 2004 when France beat England. With France 1-0 down and two minutes to play, Zidane scored a magnificent free-kick then kept his nerve to convert a last-minute penalty to win the match for *Les Bleus*.

But it is not just his goalscoring prowess that makes Zidane the player he is. Exquisite control, superb passing, pace, strength on the ball and the vision to play the ball into places which will hurt the opposition most directly.

France's Zinedine Zidane scores the first of his two goals that beat England in the European Championships in Portugal.

FACT FILE | MIDFIELDER | 98 CAPS | 28 GOALS | REAL MADRID

Date of birth: **23.06.1972**
Height: **185 cm**
Weight: **78 kg**
Previous clubs: **Juventus, Bordeaux, Cannes**
International debut: **17.08.1994**
Previous World Cups: **1998, 2002**

The huge price tag had no effect on Zidane when he joined Real Madrid. European Champions League winners in 2002, he scored the winner in the Final against Bayer Leverkusen, they also won the Spanish League the following year with Zidane orchestrating a series of magnificent performances during the run-in.

Whether Zidane's decision to return to the international scene was because he missed it, the sponsors demanded it or, somewhat bizarrely as some newspapers reported, he had a 'revelation', the fact is that he inspired *Les Bleus* to automatic World Cup

'When a ball drops from heaven and then it is struck by a god then there is no more to say.'

Marca, Spanish football magazine on Zidane

qualification with a series of superb personal displays. Germany 2006 will see the end of Zidane's international career – let's hope his body is up to it and that he goes out with a bang and not with a whimper.

STYLE GUIDE

Playing just behind the strikers Zidane is a playmaker extraordinaire. Flicks, feints, dummies and defence-splitting passes are all completed at speed and with extraordinary grace. Probably the most technically accomplished player of his generation Zidane was appropriately the heartbeat of the most successful team of the late 1990s and early 2000s. As if that wasn't enough, he is also a lethal goalscorer from open play, and scores regularly from free-kicks and penalties. To cap it all, Zidane even scored twice with headers in the 1998 World Cup Final against Brazil.

IRREPRESSIBLE TALENT READY TO BURST THROUGH

A late starter in the game, Sidney Govou has only ever played for one club, Lyon. He made his debut in 2000 and since 2002 has won four French league titles in a row. Famous for the engine that keeps him running for 90 minutes, Govou is often cited by coach Domenech as his utility player able to play anywhere in attack, midfield or even defence if need be. 'Explain to him what you expect and he does it. He's very disciplined, and whatever the position, he puts himself at the service of the team,' says the coach.

Currently in the form of his life at Lyon under new coach Gérard Houllier, Govou's game is based on his speed, constant running off the ball and comfort in possession. Spotted as an 18-year-old playing amateur football, he was given his first start by Lyon coach Bernard Lacombe against Auxerre. The following season he hit the headlines after scoring twice in Lyon's 3-0 demolition of Bayern Munich. Lacombe was replaced by Jacques Santini the following year, the first of Lyon's long-running title-winning sequence, and when Santini left the club at

'Some think he is less spectacular than a Henry or a Cisse but I don't think he is any less quick. Govou is just as explosive as them.'
Raymond Domenech

FORWARD | **19 CAPS** | **3 GOALS** | **LYON**

Date of birth: **27.07.1979**
Height: **175 cm**
Weight: **72 kg**
Previous clubs: **None**
International debut: **21.08.2002 v Tunisia**
Previous World Cups: **None**

the end of the season to become coach of the national team Govou was rewarded with the call-up.

A bad ankle injury in 2003–04 interrupted his progress but his return to form was rewarded with the club captaincy in 2005 and his form goes from strength to strength. Although national coach Domenech sees him as a utility player, Govou has his own opinions. 'Ideally, I like to play wide on the right, between midfield and attack. I get a lot more space there, and I don't think my finishing is good enough to justify being an out-and-out striker.' Houllier employs him in this role at Lyon.

Once hailed as the 'new' Thierry Henry, Govou no longer needs such a tag as he is forging his place in the side on his own merits. Once seen as a player with speed and little else, Govou has matured and is now more comfortable on the ball. Predominantly used as a substitute in the qualifying campaign, expect the lightning-fast striker to make the best of any chance he gets in Germany 2006.

STYLE GUIDE

⚽ Gets up and down the pitch at speed for the whole 90 minutes. Flexible utility player most at home on the right just behind the striker but can play anywhere on the pitch. A direct player, Govou likes to take defenders on and has the pace to do it. Links up well with an attacking full back. Scoring regularly this season with his club.

Sidney Govou celebrates his first international goal against Slovenia with team-mate Sylvain Wiltord.

David **TREZEGUET**

OLD-STYLE STRIKER READY TO PROVE HIS CRITICS WRONG ON THE WORLD STAGE

A prolific striker at club and international level, David Trezeguet also has a World Cup winner's medal from 1998 and scored the 'golden goal' that won France the European Championships in 2000. He also played in the World Cup in 2002 and Euro 2004, yet some people still remain unconvinced by the French player who grew up and learned his football in Argentina.

Born in Rouen in France in 1977, Trezeguet was brought up in Buenos Aires in Argentina. He signed for Platense in 1993 but was transferred to Monaco in 1995 where he teamed up with Thierry Henry and it was there he made his name. He started scoring regularly in the 1997–98 season and earned himself a big money transfer to Juventus in Italy in 2000. Since joining the Turin club he has gone from strength to strength, he was top scorer in Serie A in 2002–01 with 24 goals and has won the Italian title with the *Bianconeri* three times.

David Trezeguet scores the 'golden goal' that won the European Championships in 2000 as France beat Italy 2-1.

'Inside the area he has few rivals with his agility and finishing ability ... at the moment he is the best there is.'

Fabio Capello, Juventus coach

His international debut came in 1998 when he scored 18 goals in 21 starts for Monaco and was rewarded with a place in the squad for the World Cup in France. Though he only started one game, he scored twice during the tournament, including during the penalty shoot-out against Italy.

FACT FILE | STRIKER | 60 CAPS | 31 GOALS | JUVENTUS

Date of birth: **15.10.1977**
Height: **187 cm**
Weight: **75 kg**
Previous clubs: **Monaco, Platense**
International debut: **28.01.1998 v Spain**
Previous World Cups: **1998, 2002**

He won the French league title with Monaco in 1999– 2000, a season in which he scored another 26 goals. His reward was a place in the French squad for Euro 2000, the chance to score the only 'golden goal' to settle a major tournament and that transfer to Italy.

Trezeguet is a classic striker: tall, good in the air, able to shoot with both feet and generally on hand to score from bits and pieces in and around the box. He has scored over 100 goals for Juventus in the most defensive-minded league in Europe and has a ratio of one goal every two games over 60 matches for *Les Bleus*.

Though 'Trezegol' – as he is known – has his doubters, he is slight for a modern-day striker and has had a number of serious injuries during his career, no one can doubt his games to goals ratio, nor his ability to score goals in crucial games. Though not as fast as his strike partner Henry, Trezeguet has done enough to ensure his place in the starting line-up for Germany 2006.

STYLE GUIDE

⊗ An old-fashioned target man, Trezeguet is able to get on the end of crosses with his head or either foot. Tall and lanky, he is the sort of player who looks uninterested for 89 minutes of a game and then scores a spectacular winner. An out-and-out striker Trezeguet thinks he has a 'perfect understanding' with his partner Thierry Henry.

SWITZERLAND

THERE IS LITTLE EXPECTED OF THE SWISS AND THAT'S THE WAY THEY LIKE IT – FOR NOW

Switzerland's qualification surprised even themselves, but underestimate this collection of promising youngsters and hard-working veterans at your own risk. France did and it nearly cost them a place at the finals.

Winners of the 2002 Under-17 European championships, the Swiss have been aware they have a number of promising youngsters and already players such as Arsenal's Philippe Senderos, Leverkusen's Tranquillo Barnetta and Breda's Johan Vonlanthen have made a great impression at club level. Add the experience of Hakan Yakin and the proven striking abilities of Alexander Frei and the team has a healthy mix.

Coach Jakob 'Kobi' Kuhn, who won 63 caps as a Swiss midfielder, took over in summer 2001. A cautious approach saw him introducing his young stars gradually, taking them to Euro 2004 and then developing the best Swiss side for many years. The Swiss believe the team will reach its peak when they co-host the European Championships in 2008, but they have shown there is already enough quality in the team for them to spring a surprise or two.

A run of 14 unbeaten games since Euro 2004 saw them end the World Cup dreams of Israel and Ireland and give France the shock of their lives. Their only defeat came in the acrimonious second leg of the play-off with Turkey when two away goals were enough to earn the Swiss a place in the finals.

VITAL STATISTICS

WORLD RANKING 35th **KEEPER AND DEFENCE** 6/10
MIDFIELD 6/10 **ATTACK** 6/10
STRENGTHS AND WEAKNESSES
Throughout the team they have players with great potential, but inexperience and a lack of established class players will leave them exposed.
HOW FAR WILL THEY GO?
They could progress through the group stage, but will probably come unstuck soon after.

Tranquillo Barnetta rises to win a header in the play-off against Turkey.

Back row (left to right): Philipp Degen, Christoph Spycher, Patrick Muller, Philippe Senderos, Alexander Frei, Pascal Zuberbuhler. Front row: Johann Vogel, Daniel Gygax, Tranquillo Barnetta, Ricardo Cabanas and Raphael Wicky.

The youth-experience blend is evident right through the team. Veteran keeper Pascal Zuberbuhler has the wily Patrick Muller and the rapidly improving Senderos as his centre backs, while on the flanks the excellent free-kick taker Ludovic Magnin is often paired with the highly-rated, attack-minded Valon Behrami.

The team is marshalled by captain Johann Vogel, who consistently puts in top class performances for AC Milan in Serie A, and Hakan Yakin as the playmaker. Kuhn has a tried and trusted attacking partnership in giant target man Marco Streller and Alex Frei who rattled in seven goals in the qualifiers. Might the coach take a gamble on the Colombian-born 20-year-old Johann Vonlanthen? The lightweight forward became the youngest ever scorer in Euro 2004, but Kuhn has been reluctant to give him a steady run in the team.

Vonlanthen is perhaps the jewel in the Swiss crown of youth. The World Cup might have arrived a little early for most of them, but one or two of these stars of tomorrow might just fancy an early bathe in the limelight.

POSSIBLE SQUAD

Goalkeepers: Pascal Zuberbuhler (Basel), **Fabio Coltorti** (Grasshoppers), **Diego Benaglio** (Nacional Madeira)

Defenders: Ludovic Magnin (Stuttgart), **Christoph Spycher** (Frankfurt), **Reto Ziegler** (Tottenham Hotspur), **Valon Behrami** (Lazio), **Phillip Degen** (Dortmund), **Philippe Senderos** (Arsenal), **Stephane Grichting** (Auxerre), **Patrick Muller** (Basel), **Murat Yakin** (Basel)

Midfielders: Tranquillo Barnetta (Bayer Leverkusen), **Hakan Yakin** (Young Boys), **Ricardo Cabanas** (Grasshoppers), **Raphael Wicky** (Hamburg), **Johann Vogel** (AC Milan), **Daniel Gygax** (Lille), **Davide Chiumiento** (Le Mans)

Forwards: Alex Frei (Rennes), **Marco Streller** (Stuttgart), **Johann Vonlanthen** (Breda), **Mauro Lustrinelli** (Thun)

PLAY-OFFS

DATE			
12.11.05	SWITZERLAND	**2**	**0** TURKEY
16.11.05	TURKEY	**4**	**2** SWITZERLAND

Switzerland won on the away goals rule

FINALS GROUP G

		Date	Venue
	SWITZERLAND		
	France	13 June	Stuttgart
	Togo	19 June	Dortmund
	South Korea	23 June	Hanover

EUROPE QUALIFYING GROUP 4 – FINAL TABLE

TEAM	P	W	D	L	F	A	Pts
FRANCE	10	5	5	0	14	2	**20**
SWITZERLAND	10	4	6	0	18	7	**18**
ISRAEL	10	4	6	0	15	10	**18**
REP OF IRELAND	10	4	5	1	12	5	**17**
CYPRUS	10	1	1	8	8	20	**4**
FAROE ISLANDS	10	0	1	9	27	1	**1**

SOUTH KOREA

CAN LIGHTNING REALLY STRIKE TWICE FOR THE RED DEVILS?

After Guus Hiddink's team performed wonders in 2002, the Koreans have got themselves another experienced Dutch manager and are hoping for a repeat in Germany 2006.

How can the *Taeguk Warriors* cap the achievements, spirit and pure excitement of their 2002 World Cup campaign? Spurred on by a fanatical support, their energetic pressing game and swift counter-attacking moves brought notable victories against Portugal, Italy and Spain and eventually landed them in fourth place – the highest ever position for an Asian team in the competition.

Since then, the team has suffered by comparison with those heady days. After coach Hiddink returned to Europe, Humberto Coelho and Jo Bonfrere have both resigned after criticism from the media, fans and players. Dick Advocaat, who took over after South Korea had qualified for Germany 2006, has brought stability and good results, but more importantly has re-installed a sense of self-belief.

VITAL STATISTICS

WORLD RANKING 29th
KEEPER AND DEFENCE 6/10
MIDFIELD 7/10
ATTACK 7/10
STRENGTHS AND WEAKNESSES
They have plenty of spirit and energy, and some skill, but lack the quality to damage the fancied teams.
HOW FAR WILL THEY GO?
The second round seems a likely terminus, but they could even struggle to make it that far.

South Korea's players revelled in their success at the 2002 World Cup whey they co-hosted the tournament.

194

In a football mad country, expectations are still so high that it seems inevitable that the tournament will prove a disappointment for them. However, with players of the quality of Park Ji-sung, Lee Young-pyo and Park Chu-young, perhaps they will surprise the world again.

THE ROCKY ROAD TO GERMANY

Under coach Jo Bonfrere, South Korea took some rough roads to Germany, but eventually made it through with a game to spare. The first stage had seen embarrassments in being held by the Maldives and Lebanon and these, combined with some bad Asia Cup results, found the coach heavily criticised. A defeat by Saudi Arabia and a draw in Uzbekistan in the final qualification league piled on the pressure, but Korea were winning their home games and a 4-0 thrashing of Kuwait saw them through. What should have been a celebratory game against Iran, however, produced another defeat – and the end of the line for Bonfrere.

A veteran of 2002, it seems likely that keeper Lee Woon-jae will keep his place between the posts.

HOW THEY'LL LINE UP

The advent of Advocaat's regime means there are many places in the squad up for grabs and the starting XI is far from sorted. A hero of 2002, Lee Woon-jae, who has continued to impress, is likely to start in

Above *Kim Yong-pae scores from the spot in South Korea's 4-0 win in Kuwait.*

Right *Pacy left winger Lee Chun-soo could get a place in the starting line-up.*

POSSIBLE SQUAD

Goalkeepers: Lee Woon-jae (Suwon Bluewings), **Kim Young-kwang** (Chunnam Dragons), **Kim Byung-ji** (Pohang Steelers)

Defenders: Lee Young-pyo (Tottenham Hotspur), **Hyun Young-min** (Ulsan Tigers) **Cho Yong-hyung** (Bucheon Sk), **Choi Jin-cheul** (Chonbuk), **Lee Min-sung** (Pohang Steelers), **Kim Jin-kyu** (Jublio Iwata), **Kim Han-yoon** (Bucheon Sk), **Choi Tae-uk** (Shimizu), **Seol Ki-hyun** (Wolverhampton Wanderers)

Midfielders: Park Ji-sung (Manchester United), **Lee Eul-yong** (Travzonspor), **Lee Ho** (Ulsan Tigers), **Song Chong-gug** (Suwon Bluewings), **Lee Chun-soo** (Ulsan Tigers), **Kim Nam-il** (Suwon Bluewings), **Yoo Sang-chul** (Ulsan Tigers)

Forwards: Park Chu-young (FC Seoul), **Ahn Jung-hwan** (Metz), **Cha Ddo-ri** (Eintracht Frankfurt), **Lee Dong-gook** (Pohang Steelers)

Back row (left to right): Ahn Jung-hwan, Kim Young-chul, Kim Dong-jin, Choi Jin-cheul, Seol Ki-hyeon, Lee Woon-jae. Front row: Park Ji-sung, Park Chu-young, Cho Won-hee, Lee Ho and Lee Young-pyo.

goal, but at the back, a new generation – among them Hyun Young-min and Kim Jin-kyu – are replacing the veterans of 2002. Possible captain, 34-year-old Choi Jin-cheul, should still be holding things together and Tottenham's full back Lee Young-pyo has shown he has the energy and talent to thrive in the Premiership.

In midfield, the Red Devils have a real star in Manchester United's Park Ji-sung, here he is given a much more free-ranging role than at Old Trafford. The holding role should be performed by the hard-working Yoo Sang-chul who is another possible candidate as captain, and we could see Lee Chun-soo, a promising left winger who has twice failed in Spain but still has plenty of pace and guile.

Up front, Advocaat will have good competition for places from Ahn Jung-hwan, whose sudden-death goal knocked the Italians out of the 2002 finals, Lee Dong-gook, who has struck some brilliant and important goals in qualifying, and their very own boy wonder Park Chu-young who is just waiting to make a name for himself.

ONE TO WATCH
Park Chu-young

At only 20, Asia's Young Footballer of 2004 has already been earmarked as the future of Korean football. Top scorer and best player at 2004's Asian Youth Championship, he couldn't stop scoring for the Under-21 side, and made a sensational start to his K-League career with FC Seoul. It surprised few then, when he hit a goal on his international debut, a last-minute equaliser in Uzbekistan that was the goal that effectively sent Korea to Germany. The devout Christian has set the K-League alight but has already registered his desire to play in Europe – particularly England – and by July, the attraction could well be reciprocated.

Park Chu-young was given his international debut after only three senior appearances in the K-League. He repaid the coach's faith by scoring.

COACH
Dick Advocaat
(born 27 September 1942)

Record: P3 W2 D1 L0

The Red Devils' third Dutch manager in five years arrived with an excellent CV only slightly tarnished in the last few years. 'The Little General' famously took Holland to the World Cup quarter-finals in 1994 and went on to coach PSV and Rangers to league titles. It was with his return to Holland in 2002 that things went slightly wrong. The Dutch only qualified through the play-offs and though they reached the semi-final he was heavily criticised back home. Korea poached him from the United Arab Emirates in July 2005 – a deal possibly clinched by Advocaat bringing along his assistant Pim Verbeek – the man who had worked with Hiddink in 2002.

New coach Dick Advocaat brings a wealth of experience with him from coaching Holland, PSV and Rangers.

ROUTE TO THE FINALS

DATE		
09.02.05	SOUTH KOREA **2**	**0** KUWAIT
25.03.05	SAUDI ARABIA **2**	**0** SOUTH KOREA
30.03.05	SOUTH KOREA **2**	**1** UZBEKISTAN
03.06.05	UZBEKISTAN **1**	**1** SOUTH KOREA
08.06.05	KUWAIT **0**	**4** SOUTH KOREA
17.08.05	SOUTH KOREA **0**	**1** SAUDI ARABIA

ASIA QUALIFYING FINAL GROUP 1 – FINAL TABLE

TEAM	P	W	D	L	F	A	Pts
SAUDI ARABIA	6	4	2	0	10	1	**14**
SOUTH KOREA	6	3	1	2	9	5	**10**
UZBEKISTAN	6	1	2	3	7	11	**5**
KUWAIT	6	1	1	4	4	13	**4**

FINALS GROUP G

	SOUTH KOREA	Date	Venue
	Togo	13 June	Frankfurt
	France	18 June	Leipzig
	Switzerland	23 June	Hanover

NO LONGER A SECRET WEAPON, CAN PARK STAND OUT AS A MARKED MAN IN GERMANY?

The boy they call 'Ji' exploded onto the international scene in 2002. Goals in World Cup warm-up games against England and France set him up for a tournament in which he starred for South Korea. It launched his career and, via PSV Eindhoven, landed him at Old Trafford.

The first Korean footballer to go directly to the J-League without going through the K-League, Park joined Kyoto Purple Sanga straight from school. Making his debut in 2000, he soon became their most influential player, helping the team to their best ever position. Park made his first start for South Korea soon after and it was the national team manager Guus Hiddink who decided to play him on the wing. Park became a World Cup sensation in 2002. A stunning left-foot volley in the 1-0 group victory against Portugal made the 21-year-old a national hero and he became one of the stars of South Korea's amazing run to the semi-final. Hiddink had unearthed a gem and took Park with him when he became coach at PSV. The Korean took a while to

'The boy is coming on in terrific style. His movement off the ball and his awareness of space is exceptional for such a young man.'

Sir Alex Ferguson

FACT FILE | MIDFIELDER | 57 CAPS | 5 GOALS | MANCHESTER UNITED

Date of birth: **25.02.1981**
Height: **175 cm**
Weight: **72 kg**
Previous clubs: **PSV Eindhoven, Kyoto Purple Sanga**
International debut: **05.04.2000 v Laos**
Previous World Cups: **2002**

settle in, but in 2004–05 he inspired the Eindhoven team to a domestic double and a great Champions League run. In the semi-final against AC Milan his sparkling, incisive wing play tormented seasoned defenders and his thumping left-foot goal almost brought PSV back into the tie.

That game seemed to persuade Sir Alex Ferguson to spend £4 million on bringing the 24-year-old to Old Trafford as an eventual replacement for Ryan Giggs. Without setting the Premiership alight, he's showed enough to prove he is not just there to sell shirts in the Far East. Meanwhile, he has continued his World Cup form for South Korea and now has over 50 caps. As the team's main attacking force, Park has been responsible for creating many of their chances. National coach Jo Bonfrere called the midfielder 'irreplaceable' during the Asian Cup in 2004 and his compatriot and successor Dick Advocaat may well be making the same claim at the main event.

Rising to the occasion, Park Ji-sung's combative style of play makes him the ideal big-game player.

STYLE GUIDE

⚽ Energetic and inexhaustible, this versatile pocket battleship can play anywhere in the midfield. He is at his best going forward, making darting runs with the ball or into space and packs a powerful shot. He has been criticised for a lack of composure in front of goal, but still has a well earned reputation as a free-kick specialist.

TOGO

HIGH HOPES FOR AFRICA'S NEW BOYS

Superb form in the qualifying campaign saw Togo overcome Senegal and Mali to earn *Les Eperviers* ('The Hawks') their first-ever place in the World Cup finals.

Coached by Nigerian-born Stephen Keshi, Togo's players lost only one match during the campaign and after the 3-2 win away in the Congo that clinched their place, he thanked them for making him feel 'like the greatest coach on earth'. Seven wins from ten games kept Togo two points ahead of the more fancied Senegal with striker Emmanuel Adebayor top scoring with ten goals.

A tall and exciting striker, Adebayor plays for Monaco in France but burst on the French football scene in 2001 with FC Metz. His explosive style, surging runs and clinical finishing earned him a transfer to Monaco in 2003. His first season in Monaco colours saw him score 31 goals and has made him a firm favourite at the Stade Louis II. His national debut came at the age of 18 at the African Nations Cup, and he has been a regular since then. His greatest moment in a national shirt came in the final match of the qualification programme for Germany 2006 when he scored in the 3-2 win over Congo in Brazzaville to ensure Togo's berth in their first ever major championship.

Togo's qualification from a group that, in Senegal, contained one of the quarter-

Above *In action for French club Monaco, striker Emmanuel Adebayor is Togo's only real top-class player.*

Above right *Togo's Nigerian-born coach Stephen Keshi.*

VITAL STATISTICS

WORLD RANKING 56th
KEEPER AND DEFENCE 4/10
MIDFIELD 6/10
ATTACK 5/10
STRENGTHS AND WEAKNESSES
With little experience on the international stage Togo might be overawed by the big occasion. But their work ethic should not let them down.
HOW FAR WILL THEY GO?
Might upset one of the bigger players in their opening games but are unlikely to progress from the group stage.

Another player with European experience is attacking midfielder Adekanmi Olufade who has played for a number of clubs in France and Belgium and will add some bite in the middle of the pitch. Coach Keshi prefers to play 4-4-2 but can revert to 3-5-2 if necessary. However, it is the team's work ethic that should stand them in good stead. Solid for the most part, it is defensive frailties that might let Togo down.

POSSIBLE SQUAD

Goalkeepers: Kossi Agassa (Metz), **Safiou Salifou** (Asko), **Tchagnirou Ouro-Nimimi** (CO Bamako)

Defenders: Dare Nibombe (Mons), **Jean Paul Abalo** (Amiens), **Massamesso Tchangai** (Benevento), **Eric Akoto** (Admira Wacker Modling), **Amavi Agbobli** (Agaza), **Gafarou Mama** (Gomido)

Midfielders: Yao Senaya (YF Juventus), **Abiodan Oyawule** (Gent), **Zanzan Atte-Oudeyi** (Lokeren), **Robert Souliemane** (unattached), **Yao Aziawonou** (Young Boys Bern), **Emmanuel Mathias** (Esperance), **Maman Cherif-Toure** (Metz), **Jacques Romao** (Louhans), **Adekanmi Olufade** (Lille)

Forwards: Emmanuel Adebayor (Monaco), **Moustapha Salifou** (Rot-Weiß Oberhausen), **Kader Coubadja** (Sochaux), **Dodji Dogbe** (St Etienne), **Maman Souleymane** (Royal Antwerp)

Back row (left to right): Kossi Agassa, Jean Paul Abalo, Maman Cherif-Toure, Dodji Dogbe, Emmanuel Adebayor, Yao Aziawonou. Front row: Robert Souliemane, Dare Nibombe, Yao Senaya, Jacques Romao and Zanzan Atte-Oudeyi.

finalists from the previous World Cup is nothing short of miraculous. Coach Stephen Keshi, who played for Nigeria in the African Nations Cup in 1994, has worked wonders with a squad of players who, for the most part, ply their trade in the lower reaches of European football in France, Switzerland, Belgium and Germany. He has been able to instil some of the discipline and values he learned as a professional into players that have always had potential. 'It has been a real team effort,' he says, 'everyone has pulled together and we have managed to get the results'.

AFRICA QUALIFYING GROUP 1 – FINAL TABLE							
TEAM	P	W	D	L	F	A	Pts
TOGO	10	7	2	1	20	8	23
SENEGAL	10	6	3	1	21	8	21
ZAMBIA	10	6	1	3	16	10	19
CONGO	10	3	1	6	10	14	10
MALI	10	2	2	6	11	14	8
LIBERIA	10	1	1	8	3	27	4

FINALS GROUP G			
	TOGO	Date	Venue
	South Korea	13 June	Frankfurt
	Switzerland	19 June	Dortmund
	France	23 June	Cologne

SPAIN

THE EXTRAVAGANT TALENTS OF THE SPANISH TEAM CAN'T DISAPPOINT AGAIN – CAN THEY?

Still sore after their unlucky exit from the last World Cup, the Spanish have tempered their expectations for Germany 2006. One look at their line-up, however, with players as strong as Iker Casillas, Jose Antonio Reyes, Xavi, Raul and Fernando Torres, suggests they will once again be a team to watch.

Spain have qualified for every World Cup since 1974, but have flopped every time. In 2002, it seemed that their time had finally arrived. Sailing through the group stage, they dispensed with the Republic of Ireland in a hard-fought game decided on penalties and went on to meet joint-hosts South Korea in the quarter-final. Strong and impressive with Joaquin and Fernando Morientes playing well, they looked to have the better of the tournament's surprise package, only for some terrible refereeing decisions to thwart them. Another shoot-out ensued and Joaquin's miss saw the perennial under-achievers on the plane home again.

Luis Aragones took charge after Euro 2004 which saw another disappointing early exit. He freshened the side up with younger players like Reyes and Sergio Ramos and tightened their style of play, the coach calling for his team to control matches and play a possession and passing game. At one point he even dispensed with the running skills of Joaquin. The result has been a magnificent unbeaten run under the new manager, but has also seen the team struggle to score – surprising, especially considering the calibre of attacking players in the line-up.

Right Joaquin of Real Betis provides his sumptuous dribbling skills for the national team.

Opposite David Villa (right) scored his first international goal against Slovakia in the second leg of the play-offs.

Able to choose most of his squad from La Liga – for many the best league in the world at the moment – as well as some stars of the Premier League – such as Asier Del Horno at Chelsea, Reyes at Arsenal and Luis Garcia, Xabi Alonso and Morientes at Liverpool – Aragones has a wealth of talent at his disposal. Even on the fringes of the squad there is real quality. Many of the old guard that he has tried to dispense with are still in their prime: Real Madrid's Helguerra can still do an excellent job in defence; Mendieta seems to have found a new lease of life at Middlesbrough and Liverpool's Morientes is only 30. Also, having initially dismissed 19-year-old Cesc Fabregas at Arsenal and 22-year-old Inesta at Barcelona as too young for Germany, their club form

has forced him to reconsider. They only dare whisper it, but many Spanish fans believe this just could be their year.

FAVOURITES LEAVE IT LATE

Few thought Spain would have much difficulty topping a group of uninspiring teams in the qualifiers for Germany 2006. But, though they emerged unbeaten, five draws landed them in second place and a play-off with Slovakia. The Spanish picked their moment to come good, an inspired Luis Garcia hitting a hat-trick in a 5-1 demolition in the first leg making the second a formality, and a 1-1 draw courtesy of a goal from David Villa was enough. They had qualified, but for a long time they had made heavy work of it.

GREAT MATCH

2002	SPAIN 0-0 SOUTH KOREA (South Korea won 5-4 on pens)	WORLD CUP QUARTER-FINAL Gwangju World Cup Stadium, Korea

Spain's greatest ever position in a World Cup came in 1950 with a fourth place, but a penalty shoot-out victory over Ireland in the second round gave them hopes of bettering that in 2002.

With Joaquin and Morientes causing problems, Spain looked like ending the joint-host nation's run at any moment. On 49 minutes Ruben Baraja headed home from a free-kick, but the effort was disallowed because Morientes was ruled offside. More close shaves followed as Hierro and Morientes missed narrowly, but, eventually, Spain had a great Casillas save to thank for seeing the 90 minutes out at 0-0.

Extra time brought another remarkable decision as a Morientes strike was disallowed because Joaquin's ball had supposedly gone out of play before he crossed it. And, when in the 100th minute, Morientes turned on a long throw and crashed his shot against the left post, they might have guessed it wasn't their day. Sure enough,

penalties at 4-4 brought Joaquin to the spot and the 20-year-old saw his kick saved by the excellent Lee. Korean captain Hong Myung-bo converted his kick and, once again, Spain were heading home.

Back row (left to right): Iker Casillas, Carlos Marchena, Joaquin, Asier Del Horno, Rodriguez Vicente, Fernando Torres. Front row: Michel Salgado, Ivan De La Pena, Raul, Xavi and Carlos Puyol.

HOW THEY'LL LINE-UP

Iker Casillas, still only 25, remains the undisputed first-choice in goal with Liverpool's impressive Reina as his understudy. At the centre of defence there is youth, in Sergio Ramos who cost Real Madrid £18.5 million from Seville, and experience in Barcelona's stopper Carlos Puyol. On the flanks Chelsea's ever dependable Del Horno takes the left back place while the tireless Michel Salgado is on the right.

Michel Salgado's pace and sharp tackling have made him the number one choice at right back for many years.

If he makes it back from injury Xavi might well link up again with Xabi Alonso in midfield with Reyes providing attacking flair on the left. There is a real battle for the right berth between Luis Garcia and the mercurial Joaquin and the coach can also turn to Ruben Baraja or David Albelda if he feels the need to shore the line up further.

POSSIBLE SQUAD

Goalkeepers: Iker Casillas (Real Madrid), **Jose Reina** (Liverpool), **Victor Valdes** (Barcelona)

Defenders: Carles Puyol (Barcelona), **Pablo Ibanez** (Atletico Madrid), **Asier del Horno** (Chelsea), **Carlos Marchena** (Valencia), **Sergio Ramos** (Real Madrid), **Juanito** (Real Betis), **Michel Salgado** (Real Madrid),

Midfielders: Xavi (Barcelona), **Joaquin** (Real Betis), **Xabi Alonso** (Liverpool), **Luis Garcia** (Liverpool), **Vicente** (Valencia), **David Albelda** (Valencia), **Alberto Rivera** (Real Betis), **Ruben Baraja** (Valencia)

Forwards: Raul (Real Madrid), **David Villa** (Valencia), **Fernando Torres** (Atletico Madrid), **Jose Antonio Reyes** (Arsenal), **Fernando Morientes** (Liverpool)

At the front, Aragones has plenty of choice. Spain's captain and leading scorer Raul has also suffered a serious injury, but if fit he will be a class act. Morientes is a proven finisher, while Torres has been setting La Liga alight this season and David Villa, who has patiently waited his chance, made a good start to his international career by scoring against Slovakia.

ONE TO WATCH
Sergio Ramos

2005 was some year for the tall, slim 19-year-old; he capped a second full season for Seville

On his debut, as a substitute against China in 2005, Sergio Ramos became the youngest player to be capped by Spain since goalkeeper Juan Acuna in 1941.

by being voted best young player in La Liga, made his international debut and signed for Real Madrid for £18.5 million. Originally a right back, he is equally comfortable in the centre – his positioning, pace and anticipation marking him out as a quality defender. Some jaw-dropping long-range strikes from free-kicks also indicated there was more to come from this talented youngster.

Ramos's first season in Madrid has not been easy. Affected by the team's shaky start, he had some games to forget. His frustration was evident from the three red cards he had picked up by the end of 2005 – incredible considering Ramos had only collected five bookings in the whole of the previous season.

National team coach Aragones, having made Ramos the youngest player to be capped for 55 years, kept faith with his protégé. On his 19th birthday, Ramos made his first start for Spain in the vital World Cup qualifier against Serbia & Montenegro. With mature performances, he has kept his place ever since and, in Germany, we may just discover why Madrid paid a king's ransom for the teenager.

VITAL STATISTICS

WORLD RANKING 5th=
KEEPER AND DEFENCE 8/10
MIDFIELD 8/10
ATTACK 8/10
STRENGTHS AND WEAKNESSES
They have abundant talent in every department, but can they get it together as a team?
HOW FAR WILL THEY GO?
If they can avoid the usual disappointing performances, the quarter or even the semi-finals look a realistic ambition.

Notoriously short-tempered: coach Luis Aragones.

COACH
Luis Aragones
(born 28 July 1938)

Record: P13 W7 D6 L0

At the age of 65, Aragones was one of the oldest ever appointments as a national team coach. A former goalscoring midfielder with Atletico Madrid, he has coached Valencia, Betis and Barcelona and others but has had numerous spells as the boss at Atletico after winning them the league title back in 1977. He has concentrated on refreshing the national side, the average age of which is now 24, and he has focused almost obsessively on the necessity of ball retention. His two-year stint hasn't been a comfortable ride with accusations of racism, after comments about Thierry Henry, and criticism of his style, but Aragones is an old hand who'll see things through his way.

ROUTE TO THE FINALS

DATE			
08.09.04	BOSNIA-HERZEGOVINA	1	1 SPAIN
09.10.04	SPAIN	2	0 BELGIUM
13.10.04	LITHUANIA	0	0 SPAIN
09.02.05	SPAIN	5	0 SAN MARINO
30.03.05	SERBIA & MONTENEGRO	0	0 SPAIN
04.06.05	SPAIN	1	0 LITHUANIA
08.06.05	SPAIN	1	1 BOSNIA-HERZEGOVINA
07.09.05	SPAIN	1	1 SERBIA & MONTENEGRO
08.10.05	BELGIUM	0	2 SPAIN
12.10.05	SAN MARINO	0	6 SPAIN

EUROPE QUALIFYING GROUP 7 – FINAL TABLE

TEAM	P	W	D	L	F	A	Pts
SERBIA & MONTENEGRO	10	6	4	0	16	1	22
SPAIN	10	5	5	0	19	3	20
BOSNIA-HERZEGOVINA	10	4	4	2	12	9	16
BELGIUM	10	3	3	4	16	11	12
LITHUANIA	10	2	4	4	8	9	10
SAN MARINO	10	0	0	10	2	40	0

PLAY-OFFS

DATE			
12.11.05	SPAIN	5	1 SLOVAKIA
16.11.05	SLOVAKIA	1	1 SPAIN

Spain won 6-2 on aggregate

FINALS GROUP H

	Team	Date	Venue
	SPAIN		
	Ukraine	14 June	Leipzig
	Tunisia	19 June	Stuttgart
	Saudi Arabia	23 June	Kaiserslautern

Jose ANTONIO REYES

CAN THE GIFTED MIDFIELDER LOSE HIS TAG OF INCONSISTENCY AND DRIVE SPAIN TO GLORY IN GERMANY?

Jose Antonio Reyes might well be approaching his first major tournament with some trepidation. Left out of Spain's Euro 2004 squad, he was one of Aragones' new recruits. But, as in his career at Arsenal, though he has produced some sublime moments, we are still waiting for the great player to emerge. Germany 2006 is his chance to silence the doubters.

As a teenager at Seville there were few who had any doubts about his future greatness. He made his debut for the club at 16 and over the next few seasons stunned La Liga with his pace, vision and more than his fair share of goals. Reyes made his debut for the national side in September 2003 against Portugal and scored twice against Armenia in Spain's final match of the Euro 2004 qualification group. Then, citing his inexperience and preferring the physically-stronger Joaquin, coach Inaki Saez left him out of the squad for the finals.

'He is quite simply a superstar ... spectacular. Dribbling, magic, vision and goals wrapped in one.'

Marca, Spanish sports newspaper

By that point the 20-year-old had joined Arsenal for a record-breaking £17.5 million, coach Arsène Wenger identifying him as one of the few players who could enhance the movement, technique and pace that distinguished the champions elect. Despite an own goal on his debut, Reyes adapted to the new style pretty quickly, becoming an integral part of the

Despite early promised, Jose Antonio Reyes has struggled to find consistency to add to his naturally explosive game.

FACT FILE

| FORWARD | 14 CAPS | 2 GOALS | ARSENAL |

Date of birth: **01.09.1983**
Height: **175 cm**
Weight: **72 kg**
Previous club: **Sevilla**
International debut: **06.09.2003 v Portugal**
Previous World Cups: **None**

STYLE GUIDE

⚽ His former national team coach described his pace and technique as 'controlled slalom at tremendous speed'. Able to play wide on the left or as a central striker, Reyes' control, passing and running game are second to none. His detractors have said he hides when the going gets tough, but he's taken some rough treatment and still produced the goods.

Reyes' game. As Arsenal try to recapture their form of 2003–04, he is once again showing what a class player he can be. If all goes well in Germany, Jose Antonio could still make the impact he might have made in Euro 2004.

'Invincibles', as Arsenal underwent a record-breaking unbeaten run.

He was now a regular in Aragones' Spanish team, playing a part in most of their World Cup qualifiers. But his form began to falter. Some blamed the rough treatment he'd received by defenders in the Premiership and Champions League; while others claimed he had been disturbed by Aragones' alleged racist comments when comparing him to Henry, and upset by a hoax radio DJ who persuaded him to admit he was looking for a move to Real Madrid.

Though they might be a little rarer, those lightning turns, the fabulous flicks and the magnificent runs still illuminate

A LEGEND IN SPAIN, RAUL'S WORLD CUP PREPARATION WAS INTERRUPTED BY INJURY. CAN HE FIND HIS FORM AGAIN?

To the Spanish, even Barcelona fans, there is no one to touch Raul. He had been the spearhead of the national team for over seven years, has won Champions Leagues and league titles with Real Madrid and was FIFA World Player of the Year in 2002. If he could lead his nation to World Cup glory, he would surely gain immortality at home.

At 17 years old Raul become the youngest player ever to take the field for Real Madrid. Although originally an Atletico Madrid youth star, he crossed to the Bernabeu when their rivals abandoned their youth set-up. He was Real's top scorer with 19 goals from 40 games in his first season, 1995–96, made his debut for Spain against the Czech Republic in October 1996 and has never looked back.

At Real Madrid, he has been more than a hero. He has helped them to three Champions League victories (1998, 2000 and 2002) and three La Liga titles (1999, 2001 and 2003); he has made 100 Champions League appearances and was the all-time leading scorer in the competition, notching up his 50th goal in October 2005. It is little wonder that Michael Owen failed to threaten Raul's place in the Real line-up. Spain's leading scorer and their captain since 2002, Raul has been an inspirational figure. And yet, like the team, he has inexplicably failed to deliver at all the major tournaments. As Spain, like Real Madrid, continued to splutter through their schedule, some were beginning to wonder if it was time for the unthinkable – for Aragones to drop their former hero.

FACT FILE | STRIKER | 92 CAPS | 42 GOALS | REAL MADRID

Date of birth: **27.06.1977**
Height: **180 cm**
Weight: **68 kg**
Previous clubs: **Atletico Madrid**
International debut: **09.10.1996 v Czech Republic**
Previous World Cups: **1998, 2002**

STYLE GUIDE

Tough, lightning fast and intuitive and always likely to provide a touch of genius, Raul has been both an out-and-out striker and one of the finest 'in the hole' practitioners. His vision and passes bring others into the game and provide scoring chances. He is a great captain, leading through encouragement, by example and through sheer strength of character.

'He is incredible ... he always plays for the team, never for him. He scores many goals, gives some goals to others and he runs everywhere.'

Pavel Nedved

Still only 28, Raul fought back through sheer effort. He helped Spain negotiate the tricky qualification stage and had put in some match-winning performances for an under-par Real, which showed he was back in business. Then, in November 2005, he suffered the worst injury of his career, damaging a cruciate ligament in his left knee.

He should have regained fitness by June and as the team's skipper and talisman will be on his way to Germany. But could the injury signal the decline of a truly great player? Or might the rest prepare him well for the great tournament he has promised throughout his career? Spain, and the rest of the footballing world, await the answer.

Raul's speed of thought, his trickery and his eye for goal make him one of the most exciting players in the world.

THE X-FACTOR: XABI ALONSO (AND XAVI) COULD EMERGE AS THE DRIVING FORCE BEHIND A GREAT SPANISH TEAM

It's Luis Aragones' X-factor – the teaming up of Liverpool's Xabi Alonso with Barcelona's Xavi in the centre of Spain's midfield has given them control of the most important thing in the game, the ball. Even if his partner doesn't recover from a serious injury in time for the finals, Xabi Alonso's masterful control and passing is just what his coach has ordered.

Ever since he joined Liverpool from Real Sociedad in August 2004, the young midfielder has won plaudits in virtually every game he plays. Despite breaking his ankle on New Year's Day 2005, he recovered in time to star in Liverpool's amazing Champions League Final victory – scoring the equaliser by following up after his penalty had been saved.

'If we have good movement in attack then he can pick people out. He is one of the best passers in the world.'

Rafael Benitez,

Liverpool manager

In 2002–03, Xabi Alonso had become a key part of John Toshack's Real Sociedad team that pushed champions Real Madrid all the way in La Liga – scoring 12 goals along the way. In April 2003, after some impressive Under-21 performances, he made his debut for Spain in a friendly match against Ecuador and became a regular member of the side. When Aragones took

FACT FILE | MIDFIELDER | 22 CAPS | 0 GOALS | LIVERPOOL

Date of birth: **25.11.1981**
Height: **185 cm**
Weight: **75 kg**
Previous clubs: **Real Sociedad**
International debut: **30.04.2003 v Ecuador**
Previous World Cups: **None**

over as coach after Euro 2004, Xabi Alonso was exactly the kind of player he wanted to build the team around – he kept the ball and delivered it safely and effectively.

The £10.5 million that Liverpool paid for the midfielder now seems like a great investment. Hardly a game seems to go by without his influence in the middle of the field being lauded. It has been a similar story in his international games – with talk of him being a 'Spanish Vieira' – and with or without Xavi by his side, the X-factor could help Spain to shine in Germany.

STYLE GUIDE

⚽ The word most associated with Xabi Alonso is 'clever'. His positioning and his use of the ball shows an understanding of the game few can match. His passing is exquisite, he is comfortable on the ball and he can score goals – being especially dangerous at dead ball situations.

One of the bright young things of Spanish football, Xabi Alonso is renowned for his vision and range of passing, but he has also added defensive strength to his skills set.

Iker CASILLAS

UNCONTESTED AS THE SPAIN AND REAL MADRID NO.1 FOR OVER FIVE YEARS – AND THE BAD NEWS FOR STRIKERS IS ... HE'S ONLY 25!

Real Madrid is famously home to the Galacticos – Robinho, Ronaldo, Beckham, Zidane – yet there is a player the supporters cherish above all these – Saint Iker. The boy from the Madrid suburbs didn't cost a penny, but has saved the team over and over again. When Casillas's contract came up for renewal in 2005, the fans begged the club to keep him. Throughout all their recent crises, the keeper had been their only consistent performer. Eventually the president made him the best paid keeper in the world.

Casillas is a man who famously takes his chances. As a teenager, he was called into the first team to replace the injured Bodo Illgner and played brilliantly against Manchester United and Bayern Munich in Madrid's triumphant 1999 UEFA Champions League campaign. Two years later, having been dropped, he came on in the Champions League Final against Bayer Leverkusen and miraculously preserved Madrid's 2-1 lead with a series of fine saves. Then, in 2002, on the eve of the World Cup finals, first-choice keeper Canizares dropped a bottle of after-shave on his foot and was unable to play. Again Casillas seized his chance, making a string of saves to help Spain into the last eight including three in the penalty shoot-out against the Republic of Ireland.

'Before I came to Madrid, I already knew he was one of the best keepers in the world, but now I can say, honestly, I find him amazing. He is better than I thought.'
David Beckham

FACT FILE | GOALKEEPER | 55 CAPS | 0 GOALS | REAL MADRID

Date of birth: **20.05.1981**
Height: **185 cm**
Weight: **70 kg**
Previous clubs: **None**
International debut: **03.06.2000 v Sweden**
Previous World Cups: **2002**

Since then the Madridista has been the undisputed No.1 for Spain, playing in their entire Euro 2004 campaign, and showing excellent form conceding only 3 goals in Spain's World Cup qualifiers. In 2005 he was rated as the fourth best keeper in the world behind only Petr Cech, Gianluigi Buffon and Dida, but listen to any of his coaches and they all say he trains so well and is getting better and better. Casillas knows an opportunity when he sees one and some good performances in Germany could see him climb to the top of that tree.

STYLE GUIDE

⚽ With so much big match experience Casillas presents a composed figure. His reflex saves are renowned and – as Ireland discovered – he is a great penalty blocker but he is also magnificent in one-on-one situations. Not the biggest keeper he might not dominate his area, but he inspires confidence with his almost unerring judgement.

A superb shot-stopper, Casillas was sometimes weak on crosses – but has now improved that side of his game.

Fernando TORRES

THE TIME IS RIGHT FOR *EL NINO* ('THE BOY') FROM MADRID TO GROW INTO A MAN

Although he is yet to secure a guaranteed place in the Spanish line-up, *El Nino* is at last turning in the kind of match-winning performance he has threatened for years. Having scored Spain's winning goal in the Finals of both the 2001 UEFA Under-16 Championship and the 2002 Under-19 Championship, the nation has waited for Torres to come of age ... and waited and waited.

He marked his debut in the national team with a missed penalty and, competing with the likes of Raul, Morientes and Diego Tristan, never earned an extended run in the side. Arriving in Euro 2004 with just two caps to his name he was given 12 minutes to impress against Russia, 10 against Greece, although he did start in the defeat by Portugal, striking the post after latching on to Xabi Alonso's pass. By time the World Cup qualifiers had begun he was having to prove himself all over again under a new manager.

At his club Atletico Madrid, he never had anything to prove.

A boyhood Atletico fan, Torres made his debut at 17, scored 13 goals in his first full season in La Liga and was handed the captaincy of the team at the age of just 19. Continuing to score freely –

'Torres can play for any team in the world. He has all the qualities to go right to the very top. I would rather be playing alongside him than against him.'

Asier Del Horno

FACT FILE | STRIKER | 25 CAPS | 9 GOALS | ATLETICO MADRID

Date of birth: **20.03.1984**
Height: **184 cm**
Weight: **74 kg**
Previous clubs: **None**
International debut: **06.09.2003 v Portugal**
Previous World Cups: **None**

he has been top scorer at the Vicente Calderon for the last three seasons – it is now clear that he has often been carrying a mediocre team on his shoulders. Fast and particularly strong in the air, it is not surprising he has become a major source of attention for Europe's bigger clubs, Chelsea, Manchester United and Arsenal in particular, who are in search of a successor to Thierry Henry.

Now, all the signs are there that the boy has become a man. He seems to appreciate the Aragones style and has started scoring regularly for Spain. He hit five goals in qualification victories over Belgium and San Marino and then calmly slotted away

a penalty in the play-offs to cancel out that miss on his debut. Things had come full circle for the spirited forward. Now an experienced international, he can look forward to the finals in Germany knowing his place is a little more secure and that his skills will be on show to the world.

STYLE GUIDE

Ever since he burst on the La Liga scene, Torres has been causing defences problems with his sheer pace and strong aerial presence. He is skilful on the ball and composed and intuitive in front of goal. He likes to feed off other strikers or widemen and is not happy when playing as a lone forward.

The best of the bunch: Fernando Torres is regarded as the best of Spain's young stars, including Reyes, Joaquin and Javier Portillo.

UKRAINE

OUT TO PROVE THEY ARE NO ONE-MAN TEAM

Andrei Shevchenko may have inspired his country to a World Cup berth, but if he was their only quality player, Ukraine wouldn't have been the first European team to qualify for the finals.

Meet the 'A Team' – Andrei Vorobei, Aleksander Shovkovsky, Anatoly Tymoshchuk and Andrei Voronin. They might be playing in the shadow of the masterly AC Milan striker, but they could well be the players catching the eye in Germany this summer. For, as much as Shevchenko, they have played a vital role in the Ukraine's astonishing qualification success.

Oleg Blokhin, the former Soviet goalscoring hero and 1975 European Footballer of the Year, took over as coach after Ukraine's failure to make Euro 2004 and the team never looked back. What might have seemed a tough group – with Greece, Turkey and Denmark – was dealt with by winning four and drawing two of their first six matches. The 30-year-old Dynamo Kiev goalkeeper Aleksander

VITAL STATISTICS

WORLD RANKING 40th   KEEPER AND DEFENCE 6/10
MIDFIELD 6/10   ATTACK 8/10
STRENGTHS AND WEAKNESSES
An inexperienced defence and an ageing midfield might struggle, but they have one of the best strikers in the world.
HOW FAR WILL THEY GO?
A favourable draw has raised hopes, but the quarter-finals might be a hurdle too far.

Above right *Andrei Shevchenko: European Footballer of the Year in 2004 and one of the finest strikers in the world.*

Right *The versatile Andrei Voronin of Bayer Leverkusen.*

Back row (left to right) Andrei Gusin, Volodymyr Yezerskiy, Sergei Fedorov, Aleksander Shovkovsky, Andrei Shevchenko, Andrei Rusol. Front row: Ruslan Rotan, Sergei Shishchenko, Andrei Voronin, Anatoly Tymoshchuk and Andrei Nesmachny.

Shovkovsky was one reason they stormed the qualifiers – at one point going 636 minutes without conceding a goal. A young defence centres around one of Blokhin's prodigies, the 22-year-old Andrei Rusol.

In midfield, they play a quick passing game. Anatoly Tymoshchuk, who reads the game superbly, is partnered by the 34-year-old Andrei Gusin and Ruslan Rotan, who scored some important goals in qualifying.

In attack, Andrei Vorobei is a vastly experienced striker, while the tireless Andrei Voronin can play as a winger, a playmaker or a central striker. But Blokhin has, of course, built his team around Shevchenko, bringing him deeper when playing three up front or pushing him forward as a lone striker.

In return he struck six times in qualifying. Since then he has become the all-time leading Champions League scorer and is having a blistering 2005–06 season for Milan.

Shevchenko is perhaps the world's best striker, but if his team-mates can raise their game as they did in the qualifiers, Ukraine could easily find themselves being the surprise package of the tournament.

POSSIBLE SQUAD

Goalkeepers: Aleksander Shovkovsky (Dynamo Kiev), **Maxim Startsev** (Krivyi Rig), **Vyacheslav Kernozenko** (Dnipro Dnipropetrovsk)

Defenders: Andrei Nesmachny (Dynamo Kiev), **Vladislav Vashchuk** (Dynamo Kiev), **Sergei Fedorov** (Dynamo Kiev), **Vyacheslav Shevchuk** (Shakhtar Donetsk), **Andrei Rusol** (Dnipro), **Alexander Radchenko** (Dnipro)

Midfielders: Oleg Gusev (Dynamo Kiev), **Ruslan Rotan** (Dynamo Kiev), **Sergei Rebrov** (Dynamo Kiev), **Anatoly Tymoshchuk** (Shakhtar Donetsk), **Andrei Gusin** (Samara), **Sergei Nazarenko** (Dnipro), **Alexander Rykun** (Dnipro), **Oleg Shelayev** (Dnipro), **Sergei Shishchenko** (Metallurg Donetsk)

Forwards: Alexei Belik (Shakhtar Donetsk), **Andrei Vorobei** (Shakhtar Donetsk), **Andrei Shevchenko** (AC Milan), **Andrei Voronin** (Bayer Leverkusen), **Oleksander Aliiev** (Dynamo Kiev)

EUROPE QUALIFYING GROUP 2 – FINAL TABLE							
TEAM	P	W	D	L	F	A	Pts
UKRAINE	12	7	4	1	18	7	25
TURKEY	12	6	5	1	23	9	23
DENMARK	12	6	4	2	24	12	22
GREECE	12	6	3	3	15	9	21
ALBANIA	12	4	1	7	11	20	13
GEORGIA	12	2	4	6	14	25	10
KAZAKHSTAN	12	0	1	11	6	29	1

FINALS GROUP H			
	UKRAINE	Date	Venue
	Spain	14 June	Leipzig
	Saudi Arabia	19 June	Hamburg
	Tunisia	23 June	Berlin

TUNISIA

MUST AVOID THE PERENNIAL EARLY EXIT

As winners of the African Cup of Nations in 2004, expectations were high for the 'Eagles of Carthage'. Coach Roger Lemerre, the man who took France to glory in Euro 2000 but was sacked after *Les Bleus'* dismal World Cup performance in 2002, had built a team of defensive discipline and genuine pace.

At the end of 2004, they were lying in fourth place – having drawn in Malawi and lost to Guinea. However, a series of wins brought the African champions to the last game needing only a draw in Morocco. Even then it took a 69th-minute own goal to see them through to Germany.

Lemerre has pursued a policy of finding the best players to represent the country, however tenuous their links. Defender Jose Clayton, a naturalized Brazilian and a veteran of the 1998 and 2002 World Cups, was already in the squad and Lemerre plundered his home country for youngsters born to Tunisian parents. Among his finds were Adel Chedli, Slim Ben Achour, Chaouki Ben Saada and the French Under-21 defensive midfielder Nabil Taider.

With most of his squad playing in Europe, Lemerre has been able to transform the mentality of the North African outfit adding new tactics and aggression to their already accomplished ball-playing skills.

The real coup, however, was made on the eve of the African Cup of Nations when the Tunisian government gave another Brazilian, Francileudo dos Santos, a passport. Dos Santos (now with Toulouse) leapt at the chance of

Above *Striker Francileudo dos Santos.*

Right *At 29 defender Hatem Trabelsi is already a veteran of two World Cups.*

international football. With impressive skill and lightning pace he looks to be Tunisia's most lethal weapon in Germany.

In goal, the 40-year-old Ali Boumnijel provides a cool head and full back Hatem Trabelsi has already played in two World Cups despite being only 29. A good showing in Germany could earn him a place at a top Premiership side. Among the younger players, Guimares's playmaker Ben Achour and Rangers attacking midfielder Hamed Namouchi have made excellent progress.

Tunisia desperately want the finals win that has eluded them since 1978. Their victories over Morocco and against Australia in the 2005 Confederations Cup will give them self-confidence and Lemerre will go into the finals believing he can spring the kind of trap his own French side fell for in 2002.

Back row (left to right): Radhi Jaidi, Karim Hagui, Kaes Ghodhbane, Hatem Trabelsi, Jawhar Mnari, Ali Boumnijel. Front row: Haikel Guemamdia, Jose Clayton, Dos Santos, Slim Ben Achour and Hamed Namouchi.

AFRICA QUALIFYING GROUP 5 – FINAL TABLE

TEAM	P	W	D	L	F	A	Pts
TUNISIA	10	6	3	1	25	9	21
MOROCCO	10	5	5	0	17	7	20
GUINEA	10	5	2	3	15	10	17
KENYA	10	3	1	6	8	17	10
BOTSWANA	10	3	0	7	10	18	9
MALAWI	10	1	3	6	12	26	6

VITAL STATISTICS

WORLD RANKING 28th **KEEPER AND DEFENCE** 5/10
MIDFIELD 6/10 **ATTACK** 5/10
STRENGTHS AND WEAKNESSES
Trabelsi aside, the team lacks real class but will hope that Santos' pace can surprise.
HOW FAR WILL THEY GO?
They'll be happy with a win, any more and they'll be in dreamland.

POSSIBLE SQUAD

Goalkeepers: Ali Boumnijel (Club Africain), **Khaled Fadhel** (Erciyespor), **Hamdi Kasraoui** (Esperance)

Defenders: Wissem Abdi (CS Sfaxien), **Anis Ayari** (Samsunspor), **Jose Clayton** (El Qatari), **Amir Hadj Massaoud** (CS Sfaxien), **Radhi Jaidi** (Bolton Wanderers), **Hatem Trabelsi** (Ajax Amsterdam), **Alaeddine Yahia** (St Etienne)

Midfielders: Sofiane Militi (Vorskla), **Slim Ben Achour** (Guimares), **Adel Chedli** (Nuremberg), **Kais Ghodhbane** (Samsunspor), **Issam Jomaa** (Esperance), **Imed Mhadhebi** (Nantes), **Jawhar Mnari** (Nuremberg), **Hamed Namouchi** (Rangers)

Forwards: Chaouki Ben Saada (Bastia), **Francileudo dos Santos** (Toulouse), **Karim Essediri** (Tromso), **Haikel Guemamdia** (Strasbourg), **Zied Jaziri** (Troyes)

FINALS GROUP H

	TEAM	Date	Venue
	TUNISIA		
	Saudi Arabia	14 June	Munich
	Spain	19 June	Stuttgart
	Ukraine	23 June	Berlin

SAUDI ARABIA

THE WHIPPING BOYS OF 2002 ARE FEARFUL OF A RECURRING NIGHTMARE

The Saudis have now qualified for four World Cup finals in a row. But since reaching the second round on their first appearance in 1994, results have been getting worse – culminating in an 8-0 thrashing by Germany in Japan and Korea in 2002.

The Saudi FA is clearly nervous of a repeat of that last finals outing. With just six months to go before kick off in Germany they have recently sacked their coach Gabriel Calderon, citing a poor showing at the West Asian Cup and ill-conceived preparations for the World Cup finals.

Calderon had turned a poor team around in just two years. He built a well-organised and attacking side around stars like goalkeeper Mabrouk Zayed, Asian footballer of the Year Hamad Al Montashari and midfielder Saud Khariri, but the key was the return of veteran playmaker Sami Al Jaber.

Recalled for the opening final-round qualifier, the 32-year-old, who briefly played for Wolves, marked his comeback with a goal and six months later struck the opening two goals in a 3-0 victory over Uzbekistan that sent him to his fourth finals. The 'Sons of the Desert' had strolled through the qualifiers unbeaten and conceded only one goal in their six final group games.

Calderon, however, was replaced by Brazilian Marcos Pacqueta, the manager of Al Hilal, Saudi's top club. He will surely keep a similar squad drawing mainly from his old side and their rivals Al Ittihad and including the country's most expensive player, the $10 million Yasser Al Qahtani. Don't be fooled by the lack of big European club players – Saudi footballers earn enough to stay at home.

In front of the keeper Zayed, central defender Al Montashari organises a back line including the experienced Takar and promising young full back Al Mowalad.

Left Veteran midfielder Sami Al Jaber has over 150 international caps for Saudi Arabia.

Far left Central defender Hamad Al Montashari.

In midfield Al Jaber calls the shots, while the holding role is taken by Khariri, an influential passer. Watch out too for a third finals appearance by the injury-plagued 2000 Asian Player of the Year, Al Temyat.

Saudi Arabia's hopes of doing what they failed to do in 2002 – score a goal – rest on the shoulders of their rising star 22-year-old Al Qahtani. He could be partnered by Al Harthi, a talent yet to shine for the national team. Whether Saudi Arabia's nightmare

recurs could well depend on their opening game, an 'Arabian Derby' with Tunisia. If this well-organised side can win they could be the most successful Saudi side ever; if they lose, they'll probably be looking for a new coach.

Back row (left to right): Nawaf Al Temyat, Abdul Aziz al-Khathran, Ibrahim Al Shahrani, Mohammed Al-Daeyea, Nayef Al Qadi, Redha Takar. Front row: Khumais Al Owairan, Mohammed Al Shaloub, Hussein Sulimani, Abdullah Jumaan Al Dosari and Abdullah Zubromawi.

VITAL STATISTICS

WORLD RANKING 33rd
KEEPER AND DEFENCE 5/10
MIDFIELD 5/10
ATTACK 5/10
STRENGTHS AND WEAKNESSES
Al Montashari's well-drilled defence might frustrate teams but the Saudis rely on the ageing Al Jaber to open opponents up.
HOW FAR WILL THEY GO?
Perhaps not as humiliating an experience as 2002 but a first-round exit nonetheless.

POSSIBLE SQUAD

Goalkeepers: Hassan Al Otaibi (Al Hilal), **Mohammed Al-Daeyea** (Al Hilal), **Mabrouk Zayed** (Al Ittihad)

Defenders: Redha Takar (Al Ittihad), **Nayef Al Qadi** (Al Ahli), **Hamad Al Montashari** (Al Ittihad), **Ahmed Al Bahri** (Al Ettifaq), **Hadi Sehreifi** (Al Nassr), **Abdul Aziz al-Khathran** (Al Hilal), **Zaid Al Mowalad** (Al-Shabab)

Midfielders: Khaled Aziz (Al Hilal), **Manaf Abushgeir** (Al Ittihad), **Saheb Al Abdullah** (Al Hilal), **Saud Khariri** (Al Ittihad), **Mohammed Al Shalhoub** (Al Hilal), **Taiseer Al Jassem** (Al Ahli), **Bandar Tamim** (Al Nassr), **Nawaf Al Temyat** (Al Hilal), **Sami Al Jaber** (Al Hilal)

Forwards: Yasser Al Qahtani (Al Hilal), **Mohammed Amin Haidar** (Al Ittihad), **Saad Al Harthi** (Al Nassr), **Mohammed Al Anbar** (Al Hilal)

ASIA QUALIFYING FINAL GROUP 1 – FINAL TABLE							
TEAM	P	W	D	L	F	A	Pts
SAUDI ARABIA	6	4	2	0	10	1	14
SOUTH KOREA	6	3	1	2	9	5	10
UZBEKISTAN	6	1	2	3	7	11	5
KUWAIT	6	1	1	4	4	13	4

FINALS GROUP H			
	SAUDI ARABIA	Date	Venue
	Tunisia	14 June	Munich
	Ukraine	19 June	Hamburg
	Spain	23 June	Kaiserslautern